From the library of

SOPHENE

Published by Sophene 2025

The *Chronicle of Michael the Great* was originally written in the 12th century. Translated from the Classical Armenian into English by Robert Bedrosian in 2013.

A searchable, digital copy of the English translation can be accessed at:

https://archive.org/details/ChronicleOfMichaelTheGreatPatriarchOfTheSyrians

www.sophenebooks.com
www.sophenearmenianlibrary.com

ISBN-13: 978-1-923051-18-8

The Chronicle
of
Michael the Great

TRANSLATED BY
ROBERT BEDROSIAN

SOPHENE BOOKS
LOS ANGELES

Translator's Preface

The *Chronicle* of Michael the Great (A.D. 1126-1199) may be the longest medieval chronicle in the Western world. It begins with Creation and continues to the year 1195. Unfortunately, only one copy of the original Syriac manuscript has survived. The manuscript's close brush with extinction was due, probably, to its enormous length and the great expense required to make copies. The physical arrangement of the material, too, may have been another reason that the work was not favored by copyists. Michael presented his material in three columns of text which describe, separately, a given period's political, military, ecclesiastical, and miscellaneous developments. The *Chronicle* was written by Michael over the course of fifty years, and the various parts were assembled while he was Patriarch of the Syrian Orthodox Church.[1] The result is not a smooth narrative. Nor are the three sections discrete in terms of their contents—there is constant overlapping of ecclesiastical and miscellaneous material (such as earthquakes, famines, and unexplained phenomena) in the political and military section, as might be expected. Thus, the length and the arrangement of the material were probably negative factors from a copyist's and also a reader's perspective. As a result of these and other factors, today we have only one Syriac manuscript, which is

1   1166-1199.

TRANSLATOR'S PREFACE

missing the author's preface and has other lacunae. A Garshuni translation of it, unfortunately, has the same missing parts.

Yet if only one copy of the *Chronicle* in the original Syriac is known today, some 60 copies of medieval Armenian versions have survived. The Armenian versions are abridgements, less than half the size of the original. Moreover, the Armenian adaptors presented a single narrative, not three, and they skipped much material specific to doctrinal issues involving the Syrian Orthodox Church, as well as Michael's chronological and genealogical tables, presenting this material in prose instead. Probably these same reasons—shorter length and a more engaging and readable narrative—partly account for the popularity and abundance of the Armenian versions.

The English translation presented below is a composite text based on the two main Classical Armenian versions of Michael's *Chronicle*. Remarkably, Michael's *Chronicle* was abridged twice in the 13th century, by two separate groups. The reasons for this retranslation are unclear, but the two translations are completely different in vocabulary, syntax, inclusion or exclusion of events, ordering of events, and style. The Classical Armenian text representing manuscripts of the first translation, begun in 1216 and completed in 1229, was published in Jerusalem in 1870. The second and larger abridgement was completed in 1248. The principal translators in the second group were the well-known Armenian historian, Vardan Arewelts'i[2] and his colleague, the Syriac cleric, Ishoh. The Classical Armenian text of manuscripts representing the second translation was published in Jerusalem in 1871.

In 1868, two years before the first set of Classical Armenian texts was issued, the great orientalist, Victor Langlois, published a composite French translation based on two manuscripts at the Mkhitarist library in Venice and one in Paris. Langlois' translation is superb and is accompanied by extensive scholarly notes in which the author tries to trace the

---

2 Arewelts'i: the Easterner.

sources of the *Chronicle*'s information, line by line when he can. The manuscripts available to Langlois seem to have contained both 13th century renditions. As Langlois was a more erudite historian than Chabot, his notes also are invaluable for understanding the sources and contents of the Syriac original. In fact, Europe first became acquainted with Michael's *Chronicle* via Langlois' French translation. Until the subsequent "discovery" of the sole Syriac manuscript of the Chronicle by Europeans, it was believed that the Armenian version was all that had survived. It was also believed that the Armenian version was a full translation of the Syriac. Today we know that the Armenian versions are abridgements. But a fundamental problem exists when making assumptions from comparisons of the Armenian versions with the Syriac: we compare the Armenian with the sole extant Syriac manuscript, but do not know what the Syriac manuscript(s) that the 13th century Armenian translators used looked like. The Armenian abridgements contain some sections that do not appear in the extant Syriac manuscript—such as the riddles asked of Solomon by the Queen of Sheba, and an expanded account of the Amazons. Were these and other sections originally present in the Syriac? Again, the Armenian versions contain a small amount of material specific to Armenian history, which does not appear in the Syriac. Yet there is a significant body of material in the Syriac about Armenians which was excluded by the Armenian translators. What instructions did the Armenian translators receive regarding what to include and exclude? Eventually, such intriguing questions may receive more attention.

Comparisons of the Armenian versions with each other, and also with the Syriac original, have been made by the distinguished orientalist, Andrea Barbara Schmidt. Dr. Schmidt is currently engaged in the daunting task of preparing a critical edition of the Armenian versions of Michael's Chronicle, to be accompanied by a German translation. The renowned Armenist, Seta B. Dadoyan, published an invaluable study

TRANSLATOR'S PREFACE

comparing the Armenian Michael (Jerusalem, 1871) with Chabot's French translation of the Syriac original. Among the prominent contemporary scholars studying Michael's *Chronicle* is Dorthea Weltecke. I refer the reader to two of her excellent studies. I also refer the reader to Michael G. Morony's excellent *Michael the Syrian as a Source for Economic History* and Mark Dickens' *Medieval Syriac Historians' Perceptions of the Turks*. The contemporary scholar who has made the most thorough and systematic use of Michael's information is the distinguished historian and Syriac scholar, *Matti Moosa*. In his massive study, *Crusades: Conflict between Christendom and Islam*, Moosa introduces information from Michael on almost every page, and discusses its accuracy. In 2011, Dr. Moosa completed the first and only full English translation of Michael's Syriac *Chronicle*. Without a doubt, the publication of this important work will be a major stimulus for Western historians to incorporate Michael's sometimes invaluable data in their studies.

—

I began the present English translation in the pre-Internet era. Sometime between 1971 and 1979, my Classical Armenian teacher, Krikor Maksoudian—then an assistant professor at Columbia, and now a *vardapet* of the Armenian Apostolic Church—gave me a Xerox copy of the Jerusalem 1870 edition. Several times over the years I picked it up, worked on it a while, then put it aside again. By 2008, when I revisited the translation, I had completed some 220 pages—less than half. By this time, the Internet was not only available but full of undreamed-of treasures for completing the translation. Suddenly, works which until then had been collectors' items, became freely digitized, thanks to Google Books and others: the Jerusalem 1871 "preferred" edition of Michael's *Chronicle*; Langlois' French translation and study;

and Chabot's multi-volume French translation of the Syriac text. I downloaded this material and, full of zeal, decided to "switch" to the 1871 edition and finally complete the translation. It was at this point that I became aware that the 1871 text was a fundamentally different translation. There was no single paragraph that I could identify to "switch" over to the fuller version. Eventually I found a suitable place, based on a description of the same event (although the descriptions themselves were different). Thereafter, the translation to the end of the *Chronicle* was based on the 1871 edition, with material from the 1870 edition being incorporated into the text in italics. After completing the translation, I returned to the beginning of the 1871 edition and translated the first 200-odd pages.

It is interesting that the Seleucid or Syrian Era of dating (with the first year being 311B.C.) is followed in the 1871 edition, while the 1870 edition usually dates medieval events according to the Armenian Era (which began in 551/552 A.D.). Unfortunately, at some point, a copyist of the manuscript group represented in the Jerusalem 1871 edition decided to provide Armenian Era equivalencies for the Syrian Era dates. However, he erroneously believed the start of the Syrian Era to be ten years later than it was. As a result, these "equivalencies" are (almost) consistently ten years off. We have removed them in this edition, relying instead on the Syrian Era dates, which are usually correct, or "more correct." Michael's use of the term "Orthodox," also briefly should be noted. Orthodox to Michael means non-Chalcedonian. The damage done over eight hundred years to Armenians, Copts, and Syriacs by Greek Chalcedonians was of such a horrific nature that Michael, in his day, regarded the 11th century Saljuq invasions as God's punishment against the Byzantine Empire for its Chalcedonian intolerance.

Generally "accurate" as parts of Michael's *Chronicle* may be, we suggest that readers enjoy this work—at least in its

TRANSLATOR'S PREFACE

current edition—as a tale. It is a kaleidoscopic account of primate territoriality expressed over about two thousand years and spread across several continents. Warfare, confiscation of property, enslavement and killing are constant features. Biblical personalities rub shoulders with figures from Greek mythology; religions appear and give birth to others; and unexplained phenomena enliven the skies. Modern readers have in this *Chronicle* an unintended—though most unusual—type of literature where event follows event without interval. It is the story of humanity presented in a form which may seem cartoonish, but is, nonetheless, "accurate," and the material may be appreciated on multiple levels.

The transliteration used here is a modification of the Library of Congress system, substituting x for the LOC's kh, for the thirteenth character of the Armenian alphabet (խ). Otherwise we follow the LOC transliteration, which eliminates diacritical marks above or below a character, and substitutes single or double quotation marks to the character's right. In the LOC romanization, the seventh character of the alphabet (է) appears as e', the eighth (ը) as e", the twenty-eighth (ռ) as r', and the thirty-eighth (o), as o'.

Robert Bedrosian,
Long Branch, New Jersey 2013

BIBLIOGRAPHY

1. Chabot, J.-B. (1910). *Chronique de Michel le Syrien*. Paris.
2. Dickens, M. (2004). *Medeival Syriac Historians' Perceptions of the Turks*. University of Cambridge.
3. Langlois, V. (1868). *Chronique de Michel le Grand*. Venice.
4. Michael the Syrian (1870). *Tear'n Mixaye'li patriark'i asorwots' zhamanakagrut'iwn*. Jerusalem.
5. Michael the Syrian (1871). *Zhamanakagrut'iwn tear'n Mixaye'li asorwots' patriark'i*. Jerusalem.
6. Moosa, M. (2008). *Conflict Between Christendom and Islam*. Gorgias Press.
7. Moosa, M. (2014). The Syriac Chronicle of Michael Rabo (the Great). Gorgias Press.
8. Morony, M. G. (2000). Michael the Syrian as a Source for Economic History. *Hugoye: Journal of Syriac Studies, 3,* 141-172.
9. Weltecke, D. (1997). The World Chronicle by Patriarch Michael the Great (1126-1199): Some Reflections. *Journal of Assyrian Academic Studies, 11,* 6-29.
10. Weltecke, D. (2000). Originality and function of formal structures in the Chronicle of Michael the Great. *Hugoye: Journal of Syriac Studies, 3,* 173-202.

THE CHRONICLE OF MICHAEL THE GREAT

From Adam to the Amazons

Listen now, pious and scholarly brothers, you students and lovers of God, who seek knowledge about events and chronology. With great diligence we have gathered, examined, and summarized a multitude of important chronicles and many well-known accounts from ecclesiastical and secular documents. We have, for your sake as well as ours, selected from them only the most useful, valuable, and rational information, rejecting and removing the poisonous, inaccurate, and irrelevant material—the darkness of ignorance. Considering the reward from On High which might be accorded to our labor, we have left this as a treasure for the Church and as education for the children of Zion who come after us.

For the early authors wrote, as it were, in the dawn and noontime and, given the philosophy of those times, in an expansive, comprehensive manner. It is our misfortune, on the other hand, to live in a period when day is on the wane, and so we write in an abbreviated, contracted fashion. Seeing our era as blunted by ignorance, we wanted to dispel the darkness of that ignorance with the breath of the Holy Spirit. Thus we have resolved to pass the rays of the Sun of Justice like a torch to illuminate our hearts, and to present this book to Zion, our holy mother, to serve as education for her children who will hear about forgiveness from On High. Give us your prayers, then, so that our labors may bear fruit.

THE CHRONICLE

It is appropriate now to provide you with the names of the historians from whose works we have constructed this Chronicle.

We must begin our book with Adam, who was the progenitor of humanity, so that our building will be made on a firm foundation and be beneficial to reciters and hearers alike. But first, we must mention the names of the historians from whom we will be gathering the material for our structure.

The Jewish authors Julius Africanus, *Jesu*, Hegesippus, and Josephus wrote about the period before the coming of Christ. Anianus, the priest from Alexandria, wrote about the period from Adam until Emperor Constantine. Eusebius Pamphili made a collection of the writings of others and a work named the *Ecclesiastical History*. Sozomen and Socrates and Theodoret the Heretic began their accounts with Constantine and continued on until the time of Theodosius.[1] John of Antioch and Djebel, Theodorus, the Lecter of Constantinople, and Zachariah, bishop of Melitene wrote about the period from Theodosius until Justinian the Elder. John of Asia wrote about the period from *Emperor* Anastasius to *Emperor* Maurice. Guria *the savant* wrote about the period from Justinian to Heraclius and about the entry of the Arabs into Syria, which occurred in Heraclius' time. The blessed Jacob of Edessa made an abstract of all these events. The patriarch Dionysius wrote about the period from Maurice until Theophilus, Emperor of the Byzantines, and to Harun, Caliph of the Arabs. Ignatius, bishop of Melitene, and Saliba, the priest of Melitene, and John of Kesoun, and Dionysius *of Alexandria*, son of Saliba, wrote rich histories encompassing the period from Adam to their own times.

The aforementioned historians wrote in a rich and expansive manner, looking to delight the scholarly audience of their day. We, on the other hand, considering our twilight era and our laziness, write in an abbreviated manner, passing lightly over events.

Putting forth the same effort as these authors, we, too, with the aid of God and to the glory of God, will weave a work whose

---

1 Theodosius II, 408-450.

fabric is made up of strands drawn from these and other writers, colored with the vibrant hues of splendid flowers.

Now studious folk should not despair over chronological dates being sometimes imprecise, since the Lord's word is true, by which is meant that the precise knowledge of hours and times is reserved for the Father alone. For we found many discrepancies in the chronology of the Septuagint from what the Syrians have—the version that Abgar had translated. This version was checked by Jacob of Edessa, who pretended to be a Jew so that they not hide the Scriptural truth from him. *This translation was corrected by Jacob of Edessa, who went among the Jews because of a suspicion that they had not provided accurate exemplars of all their writings, out of loathing for the gentiles.*

Let us, remaining firm in our faith, begin examining the literature beginning with Adam, the first man. And we observe here, right at the outset, a discrepancy in the chronology provided by different historians.

For example, according to the Septuagint, Adam was 230 years of age when he fathered Seth, and then lived an additional 460 years. His entire life lasted 930 years, until the 137th year of Mahalalel. He died 60 years before the birth of Enoch. This interval is an error which the translators of the Septuagint did not realize. But according to the Syriac version, Adam was 130 when he fathered Seth and lived an additional 800 years, which correctly makes 930 years. Anianus the monk introduces evidence from the *Book of Enoch* which says that 70 years after Adam's departure from Paradise, Adam knew Eve and fathered Cain, and seven years later fathered Abel. Fifty-three years after Abel's birth, Cain slew him. Then Adam and Eve mourned 100 years for Abel and then Seth was born as a son of consolation.

The patriarch Methodius says that 30 years after the expulsion from Paradise, Adam fathered Cain and his sister, Klimia, and after 30 years he fathered Abel and his sister Beluda. After 130 years, Abel was slain, and Seth was born in the 230th years of Adam. Thus, *from this example alone,* you can see the discrepancies among historians.

From Adam until Jared, in the sixth generation, span 930 years. During this entire period, there was no king, since for Adam, God's handiwork, piety and order in counsel were enough for them. After his death, Seth ruled for 178 years. Now in the time of Seth, his sons remembered the life that had been in Paradise. They rejected marriage and went up on to Mount Hermon where they lived in chastity. And for this reason, they were called sons of God, and angels.

Seth, according to the Septuagint, lived for 205 years and fathered Enoch. According to the Syriac translation this was 150 years. The days of his life were 970 years according to both the Greek and Syriac translations.

According to Africanus and Anianus, Enoch fathered a son when he was 190 years old; according to the Syrians, he was 90 years old. He aspired to call upon the name of the Lord God and exhorted people to do good deeds. He lived for 905 years. According to the Septuagint, Cain fathered a son at 170 years of age; according to the Syriac he was 70, and he lived for 950 years.

At 165 years of age, Mahalalel fathered a son, according to the Septuagint. The Syriac version has 65 years. All the years of his life totaled 197 years.

Jared, according to both the Septuagint and the Syriac version, fathered a son at 162 years of age, while according to the Samaritan version he was 62. And his entire lifetime spanned 962 years, lasting until the 600th year of Noah.

In the 40th year of Jared, the 1,000th year *of the expulsion of Adam from Paradise* was completed. In this year, Seth's sons grew weary *of the religious lifestyle,* descended from Mount Hermon and fell into a craving for women. They were 200 men. In the same period, people established for themselves a king who was named Samarios. As Anianus relates, after descending from the mountain and abandoning their angelic conduct, Seth's descendants angered their brothers and they would not give them wives. And so these people went and chose the daughters of Cain as wives. Giants were born from their union—impious, harmful killers. And up until this period there was a fear of God and the people lived in peace. But now that ended and they fell into disorder, war, and murder. *Thus did evil increase upon the earth: prostitution, extortion, and from these, wars and murders.*

When the sons of Seth—who held the second climatic zone as their portion—learned about this, they also appointed a king over themselves, Alorus from the Chaldean country. He discovered astrology, the signs of the zodiac, and information about the planets and their revolutions. Chaldeanism was named after him. He reigned for 98 years.

He was succeeded by his son, Elp'aros, who reigned for 29 years and 255 days. He was followed by Almion the Chaldean, from the city of P'udiwilon, who ruled for 128 years and 80 days. The fourth king, Amanon the Chaldean, reigned 118 years and 130 days. The fifth king was the Chaldean Amakaros, who reigned 177 years and 197 days. The sixth king was Dinos the Chaldean shepherd, who ruled for 98 years and 230 days. The seventh king was Ewturink'os the Chaldean, who reigned 575 years and 195 days. The eighth king was Mamp'ios the Chaldean from the city of Anark'on, who reigned 195 years and 230 days. The ninth king was O'tiartos from the city of Anark'on, who ruled for 78 years and 330 days. The tenth king was the latter's son, K'sisot'ros, who reigned 177 years and 195 days. *The total of all these reigns* is 1,183 years and 205 days. And in his day the Flood occurred, according to Chaldean writings. The time of these kings was 1,183 years and the period preceding it without kings was 1,052 years, making a total of 2,242 years[2] before the Flood, according to the Bible.

Let us return to our previous narration. Now Enoch was 165 years old when he fathered a son[3] according to the Septuagint. But according to the Syriac version he was 65 years old. He

---

2 This adds up to 2,235 years.
3 Methusaleh.

discovered the letters which the Chaldeans use. Having pleased God for 200 years, he was transferred to a place which only God, who moved him, knows about. Some say that this was the Paradise from which Adam was expelled. *Some say that he was transported to Paradise; others, that Paradise was not opened but that it was a thief who kidnapped him. But it appears that Enoch was placed in the Upper Paradise by Almighty God. When it was opened by the Cross, he descended to [the Lower] Paradise. If this interpretation pleases you, it is harmless to believe it.*

When Methusaleh was 187 years of age, he fathered a son, *Lamech*, according to the Septuagint and Syriac versions. Eusebius and Anianus say that he was 165 at the time, which the Samaritans say 162. All the days of his life amounted to 962 years, which was the 98th year of Shem.

Lamech was 188 when he fathered a son according to the Septuagint, and 182 according to the Syriac version, but 53 according to the Samaritan version. His lifespan was 773 years, until the 69th year of Shem. He died 29 years before his father.

In the 1,666th year of the expulsion of Adam from Eden, Noah was born. He was a righteous man born of righteous parents and was kept for 500 years, or, according to the Syriac version, 502 years. In his 358th year, the second age was completed. *He matured to adulthood and was more pleasing to God than the other men of that period. He lived alone and did not marry until he was 500 years of age. When Noah was 58 years old, the second of the world's epochs was completed. Anianus relates about the earlier epoch that enormous, grotesque giants inhabited the earth, and that God abandoned them. Injustice had increased and the world was full of warfare. Corpses covered the summits of the mountains in heaps and were spread across the plains as well, because the spirit of the Lord's power had forsaken them. Now the blessed Noah, who had married a woman named Nemzava[4] and had fathered his three sons Shem, Ham, and Japheth, at the command of God construct-*

---

4 Or, Nemzara.

ed a large, three-storied ark as a repository for the seeds of the second growth, under the care of the Creator.

Anianus says that God forsook humanity because of the increase of its sins. They increasingly engaged in wars and battles and the world filled up with the bones of the slain, which were piled about like hills. The Lord God became angered and sent the Flood against them. *When Noah had completed his 500th year, the great Flood commenced destroying humanity on the 27th day of the second month of Iar. The waters lasted for a year, until the same day of the same month when by God's command Noah, his sons, and their wives emerged from the ark. Then, Noah offered up clean animals to God in service, and the Lord smelled the sweet fragrance. Noah revered God with sacrifices and received the blessing which had been given to the first man, as well as the prohibition not to shed the blood of rational beings and not to eat the blood of non-rational beings. And then God gave as a sign His covenant that He would not again strike at the entirety of humankind because of its sins, but would continue to punish the guilty.* Noah was the start of the third age. Josephus says that the ark landed on Mount Ewp'ime' in the Pisidia country, but, truthfully, it landed on the mountains of Ararat in Greater Armenia, which is Masis, according to other texts. *I am surprised that Josephus states that the ark came to rest on Mount Euphimes in the land of Pisidia, since Scripture accurately identifies that mountain as Mount Masis in Greater Armenia. After the Flood, Noah lived an additional 350 years. He fathered a son, Maniton, and then divided the world among his sons.*

Noah's sons were Shem, Japheth, and Ham. The flood occurred in the 98th year of Shem, and in his 100th year, he fathered a son. Then, Noah divided the world among his sons. He gave to Shem the land of Persia *and of the Syrians* and territory from Pektura *from Palestine* to India, to R'ino-Korura, which is the Nile, *and Bactria.*

THE CHRONICLE

To Ham he gave lands from the R'ino-Korura to Gadiron. To Japheth he gave territory from Madira *from Media* to the north of Gadiron.

The line of Japheth holds territory from the source of the Tigris River which divides Media and Persia. The line of Shem dwelled to the east and west of the Euphrates and Tigris. The line of Ham holds the Gihon River, which delineates their borders.

The descendants of Japheth are: the Armenians, Macedonians, Medes, Greeks, Latins, Iberians, and Aghuans. The descendants of Ham are: the Indians, Egyptians, Hittites, Jebusites, Ethiopians who are the Cushites, Girgasites, *Amorites, Arvadites,* Arut'ats'ik', *and others.* The descendants of Shem are: the At'urats'ik',[5] the Chaldeans who are the Syrians, the Hebrews, Franks, Persians, *and others.* The Shemites hold territory from east to west, through the middle latitude of the earth. The descendants of Japheth hold from the northeast to the west. The descendants of Ham hold the south.

Noah had observed the wars, murders, and deprivations prior to the flood, and thus divided up the world among them. And he placed curses so that his sons would not deprive one another of their portions.

They say that after the Flood, Noah fathered a son named Mantinos whose allotment was on the far side of the sea. Mantinos asked his father for some of the bones of Adam, *which had been kept in the ark* and Noah gave him the kneebones as a souvenir, *and then sent him to the West. It was he who developed astrology, discovered augury, and the phenomena of omens. Some say that the Madianites are descended from him. It is said that Noah also had a daughter, named "Star" who received from her father as inheritance a part of the southern regions.*

Now Noah cautioned his descendants and applied an oath with curses should they ever deprive each other. Rather, they should abide in justice in their own portions of the world living in

---

5 i.e., the Assyrians.

fear of God, lest they be killed. Noah survived until the 380ᵗʰ year of Eber, and then he died.

Shem fathered Arp'ak'sad when he was 130 years of age, according to the Septuagint. According to the Syriac version, he was 108. At 135 years, Arp'ak'sad fathered Cain. Eusebius does not mention this Cain nor his times. It was this Cain who advanced the deviation of the Chaldeans, as well as witchcraft and divination by the stars. His descendants worshipped him as a god and erected a statue to him during his lifetime. This became the beginning of idol worship. Cain built a city and named it Harran after his son. Luke mentions him in the Gospel. Moses does not mention him for some reason. *It was Cain who increased the errors of the Chaldeans, discovering magic[6] and demonstrating how to tell a person's destiny and fate based on the location of stars and the movement of the planets. His children regarded him as a god, worshipped him, and erected an idol of him during his lifetime. Thus began the great evil of idolatry. Cain constructed the city of Harran, which he named after his son. The Evangelist Luke[7] mentions Cain, since he had come to abolish idol worship, though Moses does not.*

Arp'ak'sad lived 465 years or, according to the Syriac version, 438 years. Cain was 139 years of age when he fathered Salah. Salah lived 130 years and fathered Eber, and lived for 460 years. According to the Syriac version, Salah was 30 years of age when he fathered Eber, lived 433 years and then died.

When Eber was 133 years old, he fathered Peleg and then Joktan, according to the chronicler Anianus. According to the Syriac version he was 34 and lived 343 years. There are those who say that the Hebrews were named after him. In the 120ᵗʰ year of Peleg, the world was divided up again due to the increase in population.

At that time the patriarchs of the world gathered together, took counsel, and decided to go east to search for the original place of Adam's habitation. But behold, a sea separated them from Eden.

---

6 Or, witchcraft.
7 Luke 3:36.

THE CHRONICLE

And then they recalled the great Flood and that the water had resulted from it. They were horrified, since their own deeds were the same as those which had brought on the Flood. For they had transgressed the oath they had made with Noah the righteous and brought on the curses by altering the boundaries which had been set for them. Then they said to one another: "Let us not carelessly fall prey to the same punishment. The land will be broken again and we will perish in the same waters." And so they turned back and went to the Shinar country to the wide plain of K'ghane' where they laid the foundation for a tower as they sought some means of salvation from a sudden flood.

At the beginning of the days of Reu they commenced building the Tower in the Shinar country. Now the giant Nimrod hunted game for the builders and fed them. *The principals were Lamsour*[8], *Hayk, and Nimrod.* They built for 40 years, fearing Noah's curses for they had violated the oath and were liable to his anathemas, having deprived one another of land and water. And so they conceived this plan of building the Tower to survive. But then the Lord descended and divided their languages, turning one language into 72 different languages. *Many of the builders were killed, and some claim that Nimrod, too, died in the collapse. However, we have confirmed that it was only subsequently that Nimrod was slain by Hayk, son of Torgom, son of Tiras, son of Gomer, son of Japheth. Hayk had refused to make an image of Bel and regard it as God, and so Bel came against him with a great multitude. Hayk killed him.* Now when the Tower collapsed, language became confused. God separated the one universal language into 72 languages. The line of Japheth had fifteen; the line of Ham, thirty-two; and the line of Shem, twenty-five. And each man went by his own road. Nimrod built the cities of Erech, Nisibis, and Edessa.

Now it happened that Eber, an old and devout man, had not joined the Tower builders and, they say, that the original language of Adam was preserved by him. And he named that country Babylon, which translated as "ruin" in the Chaldean language, which

---

8 i.e., Assur.

is Syriac. The blessed Jacob, Ephrem, Basil, and Gregory Nazianus attest that the language of Adam remained with Eber. The blessed Jacob of Edessa, John of Itruria, and others say that Adam's language, which remained with Eber, is the one which the Jews now use and not the Chaldean of the Asoris. But I am surprised how it was hidden from them that the first of the line of Israel was Jacob and when they crossed the sea they then were named Hebrews. The naming was not from Eber, since Ebrayets'i translates "they crossed over" and when they crossed the sea they adopted a new language as well as other gifts, according to the Psalm which says: "Jacob, leaving the land of the Egyptians, heard a language which he did not understand."[9] The original language belonged to the Chaldeans from whom the Israelites descend and they held that language in antiquity until they abandoned the old one and adopted a new one.

When Peleg was 130 years old he fathered Reu. According to the Syriac version he was 30. He lived 343 years. According to the Syriac version he lived 339 years.

From the Flood until the confusion of languages totaled 660 years according to the Septuagint and the Syrac versions.

At the age of 132, Reu fathered Serug. According to the Syriac version, he was 52. He lived 339 years, or 239 according to the Syriac version. In this period, Nimrod built three cities: Areg, Edessa, and Nisibis. Now after the dispersion from the Tower, the sons of Ham came to the country of the Phoenicians and Lebanon. Seeing the fertility and beauty of the country they liked it and settled there, not going to their own allotment to the west of Egypt. *For the descendants of Ham, on returning from the dispersal that resulted from the destruction of the Tower came to the country of Palestine by the mountains of Carmel and Lebanon. When they saw its plenty and its beauty, they forcibly took it from the line of Shem. They refused to go to their allotted lands, and settled where they were, thereby again invoking the curse of Patriarch Noah. Thus, for a second time, they inherited Noah's curse; first, they had*

---

9 Psalm 81:5.

been cursed for laughing at him, and second for changing their boundaries from those set as their portions.

In the 74th year of Reu the third era was completed, which is 3,000 years, and in his 70th year the Tower was built. After 40 years of construction, the people were dispersed throughout the world. The world was filled with wars and whoever triumphed erected a statue to the victory and worshipped it. In the 110th year of Reu, the Tower fell. After the Flood, Nimrod ruled first in Babylon and he ruled in the 40th year of Reu. When a fierce whirlwind sent by God destroyed the Tower, Nimrod was killed in the collapse. He ruled for 69 years. As Menander the Mage and Josephus in his second book relate, Nimrud's crown was woven and not made of metal.

Now when Peleg died, the sons of his brother Joktan observed that they had not received their legacy and they were angry. They set up three leaders for themselves: Saba, Ophir, and Havila. They cleverly made weapons—swords, bows, armor, helmets, shields—and began to defeat everyone and put them to flight. In order to withstand their depredations and survive, people began to construct fortresses and strongholds. This was the start and cause of weaponry. After many people were defeated by them, they beseeched the sons of Joktan to take their legacy wherever they pleased and to end the warfare against them. Saba took the incense-producing country which was called Saba after his own name. Ophir took the land of gold mines, which is India. Havila took the land of precious stone which was named after him Evilath.

Serug was 130 when he fathered Nahor according to the Septuagint and 100 years less according to the Hebrew and Syriac editions, calculating from the time of the Flood to this point. Serug lived 330 years. In his day, people learned to make *dahekan*s and money with the names of their kings on them. Serug built the city of Seruch in his name.

MICHAEL THE GREAT

The Amazons, Who were Women Kings and Other Kings of the Babylonians

In this period, there appeared the Amazons from the line of Torgom. Here is how that happened. There was a woman who was heir to Torgom's kingdom, and she did not want to marry. She arose and laid waste many lands. There was some treachery in her army which angered her to the point that she killed the male soldiers and created an army of women. Once a year, a few of them went and mingled with the men of another country. The females born from these liaisons were allowed to live, while the males were put to death. Seeing this, armies assembled from the lands of eleven kingdoms and destroyed the stronghold of that kingdom, which was the city of Ilium in the north. Thus ended the disorder and men took power as is the norm throughout the world, and male children born of those women lived and filled up the land.

Around this time there arose the Amazons, a force of women warriors. Here is how it happened. As the kingdom of Torgom lacked a male heir, the crown went to a valiant and brilliant woman who refused to take a husband. At the head of a powerful army, she triumphantly devastated and enslaved many lands, and no one was able to withstand her. But then a conspiracy arose within the army to dislodge her from the rule of the kingdom. She, however, became apprised of this and, one by one, destroyed all the men in the army, creating an entirely female force. She continued to be successful and took over many lands. She separated out the males, allowed intercourse only once a year, then separated the males again. As for the male children born, some were killed and some were given to the men to raise. It became a powerful state, and conquered a city in the northern part of Asia Minor called Ilium. Now all the kings of the country were harassed by the Amazon state and grew weary of it. And so the kings of eleven kingdoms united, went against it, and conquered the stronghold of that kingdom, thereby removing this abomination from the land. And the men took over rule of the kingdom, as was the norm in all other countries.

THE CHRONICLE

Forty years after the death of Nimrod and the destruction of the kingdom of Ham in Babylon, the Chaldean Kambiwros reigned 56 years in the time of Serug. He built the city of Shosh, which they call Isfahan. In that period the making of weapons spread, and there started the enslavement and sale of people. In the 70th year of Serug, the Chaldean King Kambiwros warred against the Kalatu people, defeated them, and they went up into the mountains. Serug taught Nahor the Chaldean doctrine of sorcery and divination by the star signs. Kambiwros ruled for 85 years. Following him, the third to rule as king in Babylon was Samiros in the 106th year of Serug. Samiros ruled for 72 years. He warred with the Greeks, the Franks, and the Canaanites and put them under taxation. He built many cities in the land of the Chaldeans and Parthians and it was he who began to designate weights and measures. It was he who put patterns and images on cloth, established the making of silk, and all sorts of dyes. This is what Samatros the mage said about him in his history, that he had three eyes and a horn. Samiros was a brave giant and removed the Nimrodians from the Chaldeans and destroyed their line.

When Nahor was 79 years of age, he fathered Tera according to the Septuagint. According to the Syriac version, he was then 29 years old. He lived 201 years according to the Septuagint, and 148 years according to the Syriac version. In the 25th year of Nahor according to the Septuagint, the trials of Job occurred.

Now let us return to our narration beginning with the series of monarchs of Babylon, where Nimrod reigned during the first 69 years. His crown was woven from cloth, as Menander the mage wrote, and not forged from metal. After his death, the Chaldean Kambiros ruled in the 56th year of Serug. It was he who built the city of Sho'sh, called Isfahan, 40 years after the death of Bel. Kambiros also began the practice of selling captives, and of mining gold and silver. He died after ruling for 85 years. Samir succeeded him in the 106th[10] year of Serug, and ruled for 72 years. Samir, of the line

---

10 Or 190th.

of Shem, warred against the Greeks and the Franks. He also warred against the descendants of Ham and the Galatians, forcibly expelling them from the mountains, and placing the line of Ham under taxation. Samir also built many cities in the land of the Chaldeans and the Parthians. It was he who began using weights and measures, dyeing, painting and decorating of temples, and money and dahekans with his name stamped on them, fabric weaving, and fabrics with patterns on them as the Mage Samandros noted. Samandros also said that Samir had three eyes and horns, was a powerful, giagantic personage, and expelled the line of Nimrod from Chaldea. In the 25th year of Nahor, the trials of Job took place, as the Caananite Arodh relates: "There was among the sons of Joktan a wealthy man named Job, who fought seven times with Satan and, by the power of God, had victory over him." Joseph the scribe says that Job's testing took place in the 90th year of Nahor. Others believe that this story concerns Yobab, son of Zareh, of the line of Isaiah[11], and took place 500 years before Moses. Now in the 7th year of Terah, Arphaxad became king in Babylon, and ruled for 18 years. After this, rule of the Chaldean kingdom was interrupted for 7 years until Belus ascended. This interregnum was due to the fact that the Chaldeans, Assyrians, and Medes were battling each other for the kingdom. Finally, the Assyrian Belus ended Assyria's submission to the Babylonians, took power, and ruled all of Asia for 62 years. Now the city of Assur is located near Mosul, and the land was called Assyria because it was originally fortified by Ashur. A certain Xarus ruled in Babylon and was slain by Terah's brother, Saheron, because, it is said, he fashioned a golden statue of Nachor, chief priest of the idols of Caanan. In this period, Damascus was built by Marigos the Hittite, 20 years before the birth of Abraham. Josephus states that "Damascus was built by Hosea, son of Aram." The historian Andronikos calculated that 1,081 years elapsed from the Flood to the time of Abraham; 3,035 years elapsed from Adam; and 431 years elapsed from the allotment of lands to the

---

11 Genesis 36:33.

time of Abraham. At this point, Greek and Syrian calculations coincide.[12]

And Abraham was 17 years of age when he willingly began to seek God. In that period, the wrath of God was visited on the Babylonians. For birds called magpies came and ate up all their fields. Everyone was so distraught by the small amount reaped from what they sowed, that they had to try to chase the birds off. Now Abraham tended his father's fields and wearied of chasing these birds, and so he sought aid from all the so-called gods. But he received no help. He appealed to the sun, moon, stars, and the sky, to no avail. Then he said: "O, unattainable God, supreme over all, creator of these birds and the fields, reveal yourself to me and chase them away." Immediately the birds departed and did not return to those fields. At that time, the grace of God's mercy dawned in the heart of Abraham, and he said: "I have found God, the creator of al." And Abraham persisted in beseeching God to appear to him.

Nahor died when Abraham was born. Apparently, the name of Abraham's mother was Milcah. After Abraham's birth, Sarah, the daughter of Terah, was born from the woman named Armut', and not from Abraham's mother as he himself told Pharaoh and Abimelich. Now when Abraham was 15 years of age, he began to seek God in this manner. The land of Chaldea was fertile and fruitful, and the population, engorged with wealth, occupied themselves with astrology, sorcery, and other vain pursuits. Now when God saw them thus wallowing in sin, He sent chastisement to them in the form of multitudes of jackdaws which ate up the ripening crops and destroyed the vineyards. And this happened for many years on end. The Chaldeans, consequently, tilled and sowed less, and retained men to ward off the birds. And they made sacrifices to their gods, and made pledges, yet their sorcerers and witches were unable to find a way out. Abraham, who was 17 years of age, guarded his father's fields and grew weary from his labors of hunting the birds. And, sighing, he implored all the false gods—the sun, moon, stars, and the graven

---

12 The editors have inserted a passage from Bar Hebraeus' *Chronography* here because of a lacuna. We omit it.

images—to give him some respite, but he was not heard. Then one night he realized that the chastisement was from God and that it was not by chance, since it lasted for such a long period. Nor was it from the false gods since they would have complied to the wishes of their worshippers once they received their due. Abraham had studied astrology under the direction of his father, who had the knowledge of his ancestors. Thus, Abraham examined this art and realized that all the celestial spheres and the stars depending on them had some other internal mover. Then, a ray of light sent by Almighty God penetrated his heart and he acknowledged that there was some unknown God moving and regulating everything, who was also the creator of everything, who had been forgotten by His own creation. It is because His will is not being done by us that his vengeance has been wrought on us. Throughout the night, Abraham confirmed the veracity of this discovery. When day broke, he went to the fields, fell on his knees, raised up his arms and exclaimed: "O, Thou unknown God, creator and motivator of all, creator and motivator of these birds, deliver us from them and reveal Yourself and Your will to us." As soon as these words were uttered, the birds disappeared from all fields in the city, and Abraham said: "Greatness and glory in the highest heaven, behold, I have found God. Besides You, there is no other God, Who quickly heeds our prayers. Goodness and power are Yours, and Your glory fills the world." Then, Abraham returned to his home and told his father what had happened. They did not believe him, but he did not cease praying to the true God so that He more openly manifest Himself.

At that time, King Belus died and his son Ninus ruled for 52 years as the second king of the Assyrians. He built Nineveh and transferred the seat of his kingdom to Nineveh from Assur. He fashioned large idols of silver and gold for his father Belus' statues, and had him worshipped. In this period were built R'about, and R'asan, and K'aghane', and then Jerusalem. *It was during his reign that the cities Arbil, Ras'ain, and Seleucia were built. And during this time Jerusalem was built by Melchisedek the Canaanite, who was said to be the son of the Canaanite king known as Melk'i. Now his father* wanted to sacrifice him to the idols. But when God saw the power that was hidden in that child—who, indeed, was worthy of being a model for His Only-Begotten—He demolished the pagan temple, burying the parents and the priests, and took the child away to a deserted spot, where he was nourished by the care of God. He became a wondrous priest of God and a king of the country and built a city named Ureshghem, which translates "Village of Peace." Abraham burned the idol house of his father which was in Edessa and his brother Haran tried to save those idols from the flames, but was himself burned to death in them.

Abraham reached the age of 60, growing more pleasing to God. And when God heard his lengthy and tireless prayers and observed his unshakable faith, He said to him: "Leave that country of yours and I will give you that part of the inheritance of your father Shem that was denied to you, and thereafter I will advise you according to your need. And I will give that country to you and to your descendants in perpetuity." Abraham heard this and told his father, who wanted to rise and go with him. They reached Harran from Ur of the Chaldeans. It was there, in Ur, that they had halted, and received dwelling places and property, and it was there that his father erected idols. Abraham set afire the temple where the idols had been installed. Now his brother, Haran, wanted to extinguish the flames, and burned to death in the presence of his father. Now some say that matters occurred differently, and that God killed Haran.

In his 60th year, Abraham, his father Terah, his brother Nahor, and Lot, the son of Haran, rose and left Edessa of the Chaldeans and dwelt in Harran for 14 years. At God's command, Abraham went and dwelt in the land of Canaan. When Abraham was 85 years of age, he went to Egypt and fathered Ishmael by his maidservant Hagar. Ishmael was 138 in the 60th year of Jacob.

Abraham was 75 years old when God again commanded him to go to the land of Canaan. He left his clan in Harran. Some say that he had a wife other than Sarah and a son named Ovreste', who did not want to accompany him. But Abraham, unswerving to the command of the Almighty, rose and departed. However, there *is a lack of certainty in this narration, since his father begat him at the age of 70 and died at 205. Step'annos says that it was after his father's death that he moved, when Abraham was 75 years old. This is a surprising assertion since Abraham was 135 years of age at the time. The Samaritan version correctly states that Terah was 70 years of age when he fathered Abraham, and that he lived for an additional 75 years. Moreover, some say that Sarah was descended from Eok'an, and a daughter of Haran. But how could Haran have been Sarah's father ten years earlier when Scripture clearly notes that Abraham was ten years older than Sarah? We believe that the way we have reckoned this chronology is correct. After Abraham had come into the land of the Caananites, he entered Egypt when he was 85 years of age. There, he fathered Ishmael from the Egyptian woman Hagar. Sarah was untouched by Pharaoh so that she could bear a son like unto Our Lord, from a chaste womb.*

King Ninus, terrified of his wife—who was much harsher than he—retreated into obscurity, some say to Cyprus, where he died.

In this period, Ninus' wife, Shamiram, ruled over the Assyrians for 41 years. She built the *tels*, hills of earth piled up to make fortresses. But we have found a different origin for the *tels*, namely, that due to the increase in idol worship everywhere, God sent a wind storm to earth which buried the idols here and there and heaped earth on them. To this day, demons inhabit them and the idols are tormented there. Also to this day, demons and witches ply their trade near the *tels* and sounds coming from the demons are audible.

Thus did Ninus' wife, Shamiram, take the crown and rule over the Assyrians. She reigned for 46 years, though other say twelve.[13] *She fashioned earthen mounds called tils as a precaution against flooding caused by rain, and for defense. However, we have discovered another explanation for these tils. It is said that when idol-worship had increased throughout the world, God became furious with the demons and caused hurricanes which shook the*

---

13 Or, 52 years.

earth to its foundations, and demolished cities and homes. Here and there the storms buried the idols and the demons under these earthen mounds. The demons dwell in them, being tormented to this day. And we hear that witches practice their arts especially near these mounds, and that the thunderous sounds of the demons arise therefrom.

Abram, now renewed with knowledge of God and endowed with a new life by revelation, was called Abraham, while his wife, Sarai, was now called Sarah. These names mean "excellent father" and "noble woman."

When Abraham was 99 years of age, he was circumcised. When he was 100, he fathered Isaac, in accordance with God's promise. The span of their servitude in Egypt was 430 years, according to the Evangelist. Then began the period of their wandering, in the 77th year of Abraham, when Abraham arose from his father's house at the Lord's command. In his 115th year, Abraham went to sacrifice Isaac. Isaac at the time was 15 years old, as we believe, though others say 30. His father Abraham was 75 years of age when Jacob was 35. In Isaac's 9th year, Abraham was informed that "your brother Nahor has fathered children." Now when Abraham was 134 and Isaac was 37, Sarah died at 127 years of age. *It is implausible that, as some say, Sarah died instantly when she heard the bad news that her son had been sacrificed. Abraham was 175 years of age and Jacob was 37 years of age when Abraham passed, full of goodness, and pleasing to God.* Then, Abraham took Kendura as a wife. Abraham at this time was 142 years old. Isaac at 38 took Rebeccah to wife and she became pregnant at age 61.

Rebeccah had gone to Melk'isedek with prayers to beseech God to tell her why there was contention between the children of her womb. God told Melk'isedek, who, taking God's command informed her so that she would know: "Two nations and two people which are in your womb shall be divided. One shall be stronger than the other, and the elder shall serve the younger."[14] Anianus says that Rebeccah gave birth in the 60th year of Isaac, while others say

---

14   Genesis 25:24.

in the 100th year. The elder was Esau, who is Edom—from whom descend the Edomites, who are the Franks. The younger child born was Jacob, from whom the Israelites descend.

During this period, Semiramis was levelling the ground in Assyria because of floods. Some claim that Abraham was involved with this labor. This was also the era of the birth of the kingdom of the Sicyonians. Similarly, a certain Kre's ruled as king over the Cretans, giving his name to that country; and Pyrrha, also called Peloponnese, ruled and gave his name to that country. Ishmael was born when Abraham was 88 years of age. The Arabs, Saracens, Ishmaelites, and Tachiks are named after him. Isaac wed Rebecca when he was 40, and she conceived when he was 60.

In this period, the Achaeans were ruled by Inachus, whom the Egyptians called Isis and Sebusis. This woman, Io, was the daughter of Hur and gave the name Inachus to the river Argos. In the 75th year of Isaac, Apis was in the 17th year of his reign in Egypt. Some called him a god, some called his name Serapis. The 180th year of Isaac was the 31st year of Levi. Abimelik the Adarite, king of the Philistines, was their friend. When Isaac was 137 years old, Jacob went to Haran, with the blessing of his father.

Abraham died when Isaac was 76 years old. When Jacob was 15 years of age Isaac was 180, this being the 31st year of Levi. At this time Abimele'k' was king of the Chaldeans. He is Gerera of the Phillistines, a friend of Abraham's house. When Jacob was 77 years old, in the 137th year of Isaac, he went to Harran with his father's blessing. Jacob was 147 years of age in the 12th year of Kahag and died 232 years after the time that God had promised to give his sons their portion of the world. He came to Egypt at 17. Now Esau took a wife from the daughters of the Canaanites and when he knew that this did not please his father, he married Ishmael's daugher Margaye't'.

In this period, Hamor, Sechem's father, built the city of Sechem, which he named after his son Sechem who had kidnapped Dinah when she was 12 years old. Then the sons of Jacob, because of jealousy, killed their maternal uncle and 3,000 people.

Esau dwelt in Se'ir. When Jacob was 80 years old, he took Leah as his wife, and at 85, she bore him Ruben. When he was 87, he fathered Simeon and, at 89, he fathered Levi. When Levi was three and Jacob was 91, he fathered Joseph. When Levi was 10, Jacob went up to his father Isaac. When Levi was 20, Joseph was sold. When Levi was 31, Isaac died at 180 years of age. Following the death of Isaac, the sons of Esau hired the sons of Ammon, Moab, and Aram and they came to Hebron and warred with Jacob and his sons. Jacob was infuriated and slew Esau with an arrow, while those who had come against him fled. When Jacob was 130 years old, he went down into Egypt, in the second year of the famine and the ninth year of Joseph's reign.

According to the Syriac version, 70 people entered Egypt; according to the Septuagint and Saint Stephen the proto-martyr, 75 people went to Egypt. The reason for this discrepancy is as follows: the Syriac version regards Joseph and his two sons as one while the Septuagint counts the son of Joseph's son, though he had not been born yet. Levi was 46 years old when he fathered Kohath. Some place Job's tribulations in this period. When Kohath was 60 years old, he fathered Amram, and he lived 133 years, until the third year of Moses. At 70 years of age, Amram fathered Moses. In the 35th year of the reign of Joseph, Aghaparos ruled as king of the Assyrians. In the 38th year of Joseph's reign, K'ebron ruled as king of the Egyptians. Amram died in Egypt 13 years before the Exodus of Israel. He lived for 135 years. Joseph was 110 years old, and died in the sixth year of Amram, 286 years after God's promise. After his death, his people entered into servitude. In this period, Amnap't'is ruled in Egypt for 43 years. It was he who began to drown the children of Israel in the Nile River.

Moses died in the 70th year of Amram, and the 350th year of God's promise. He had been thrown into the river as a child. The daughter of the king T'ermat'is—whom the Hebrews call Maria, whom K'ant'ara, king of the city of Memphis took as a wife—took Moses out of the water and, when he was 10 years of age, she gave him to Ane's and Amre's, who schooled him.

Now it happened that Moses, who had been thus thrown into the waters, was raised by Thermutis, daughter of the Pharaoh, whom the Hebrews call Mar'i, who was the wife of Kanthur, king of the city of Memphis. Moses was saved from the water in the 350th year of God's promise, and, when ten years old, he was given to study with Yanes and Yamres, sons of the Chaldean sorcerer Barkobas. They had been driven there to Egypt for stealing the boys of their country and sacrificing them to the idols which had been erected in the name of their father. They were well-versed in Chaldean, Greek, and especially Egyptian lore, and Mar'i, the queen of queens, obliged them to instruct Moses.

When Moses was 22 years old he became a ruler and constructed the city of Hermopolis, which was also called by the name of Moses' patron, Mar'ia.

In this period, the Ethiopians, who had been tributary to the Egyptians, came to themselves, rebelled, and went against the Egyptians whom they found unprepared. Among the captives whom they seized and carried off was the aforementioned mother of Moses. Then Moses became a general of Egypt, warring with the Ethiopians for ten years. He went against them over a desert full of snakes, with the help of gazelles and storks, since the snakes could not evade them. After 10 years he took Ethiopia and their queen, Thesbas, as well as retrieving his mother, Mar'i, and returned to Egypt with a reputation for valor and bravery. But Mar'i's husband was envious of him and wished to kill him, though he was wary of his wife.

When Mar'i had died, Moses buried her. Then, Mar'i's husband sent Xanthus, a persecutor of the Israelites, to kill Moses. However, Moses anticipated him, killed Xanthus, and fled into Midian. When Moses had fled, Ane's and Amre's took the children of Israel on a 15 days' journey into the desert, where they built a paradise for 17 years and very securely fortified it. Upon the completion of this work, Ane's and Amre's selected 980 innocent children from among the sons of Israel, sacrificed them to the demons, invited the leader of the demons to the sacrifice, and then established them as protectors of the paradise. Thereafter, the demons obeyed the sorcerers regarding the working of talismans and all other such artifices.

In that period lived Prometheus who, it is said, created mankind, since he vanquished ignorance with knowledge.

Moses then went among the Cushites, to Raguel, son of Dadan, son of Joktan, descendants of Kethura. Moses married his daughter Zipporah and fathered two children by her when he was 40 years of age. It is said that in this period Asclepiades the physician revealed his skill, and Atlas, brother of Prometheus, the astronomer supposedly held up the sky. Euripides says that Atlas was a mountain higher than the clouds.

And it was in this period, they say, that the Ethiopians crossed the Indus River and went and dwelled near Egypt. The Curetes and Corybantes created a Dance with weapons.

They say that, at the time of Deucalion, Thessaly experienced a flood; at the time of Phaeton, Ethiopia was burned; and that many other disasters occurred here and there, as Plato relates. Some say that in this period Cecrops ruled in Atke, which is Attica, although others say that he ruled in Egypt initially and then in Attica. The Greeks claim that he built Athens and named it after his wife. Supposedly he had two natures, some say because he was so tall, others because he spoke two languages, Egyptian and Greek. Cecrops also ruled part of Asia Minor, giving his name to the district of Cappadocia.

It was under Cecrops that the olive tree made its appearance in the Acropolis at Athens, thus giving rise to that legend. He was the one who called Aramazd Zeus, and was the first to use the ox as a sacrificial animal. In the same year, Deucalion began to rule as king in the area around Mt. Parnassus.

It was from Hellenus, one of the sons of Deucalion, that the Hellenes took their name. Similarly, the Atticans took their name from Acta.

In the 25$^{th[15]}$ year of the promise to Abraham, the city of Corinth was built. It is sometimes called Ephra. Eusebius says that

---

[15] Or, 420th.

Cronos the Athenian had a daughter named Atis, and that the land of Attica bears her name.

From the entry into Egypt until the Exodus, 215 years had elapsed. In Moses' 22nd year, the king began to harass Israel through the construction of a city. In the 28th year of Moses, they built the city of Hermopolis. The Cushites made war with the Egyptians, conquered them, took Hr'ak'usa, Moses' adoptive mother, as captive and married her. In Moses' 38th year, Yesu, son of Nawea was born, and Moses built Hermopolis. He warred with At'iubas, king of the Phillistines, for 10 years, defeated him, and retrieved his adoptive mother Hr'ak'usa from him. Now K'amp'ara, T'ermotis' husband, had a grudge against Moses and wanted to kill him. He was angry because of Moses' success, but was unable to accuse him of anything because of T'ermot'is, who was Moses' adoptive mother, and whom he had brought back from captivity. But as soon as his wife died, he sent Xanthus to kill Moses. Moses learned about this, quickly killed him, and he himself fled, going to Arabia, to Raguel of the Midianites.

Joktan was the issue of Abraham and Kendura; Dadan was fathered by Joktan; Raguel was fathered by Dadan; Yot'or was fathered by Raguel, and Yobab was fathered by Yotor. Then Moses took Yotor's daughter, Zipporah, for a wife. He was 40 years old.

In this period, the physician Asclepiades appeared, as did Cecrops, who ruled Itik in Egypt. Concerning him, some say that he ruled in the first year of Othniel. The Greeks say that he built Athens and named it after his wife, Athena. It was he who took Greek writing from the Egyptians since he knew both languages. He also brought the inhabitants of the city of Memphis and settled them in the city of Athens. Thus did knowledge germinate in the northern regions.

Now when Moses was 78 years of age, God appeared and spoke to him on Mount Sinai.

In this period in Egypt, P'sanos ruled as king. He fathered a son and named him Ramesis. It was he who caused the Israelites great harm. Also, it was he who gave Egypt its second name, since previously it had been called Aria. It was in the 430th year of God's promise, which was the 80th year of Moses, that Moses merited the visitation from God and received the command to take Israel out of Egypt. Then did the Hebrews cross through the sea on dry land, while King P'sanos and his troops drowned. Eusebius says that the drowned Pharaoh was named Kanak'aris and not P'sanos. As for those who did not follow after Pharaoh, the reason for their salvation was that they were involved in work that God had shown them.

In this period, astrology and witchcraft entered Persia, while in Athens a temple to Apollo was built called the Areopagite, which is the house of judgement. In this period, the city of Corinth was built. It previously had been called Buria. In the same period, the sages P'iwnik and Erakle's appeared. There was a land of Cyprus, which was called Aliu, before being named Cyprus, and from it Cappadocia was named. Egypt was then struck by earthquakes and for seven months people did not dare to enter their homes or cities, but lived out in the open in tents. Now after the drowning, during the Exodus, Ak'aros ruled as king in Egypt. Six years after the Exodus of Israel, Cronos ruled as king over the Athenians. His daugher's name was Atike', after whom the land of Attica was named.

Moses Crosses the Red Sea

Moses was 70 years old when he merited a visitation from God. For 10 years, he delayed going to Egypt and went at age 80, compelled by God, in the 430th year of His promise, in the 75th year of Abraham. It was the 205th year since the arrival of Jacob in Egypt. The Israelites had been in Egypt for 225 years and 400 years had passed since God's command to slay the Egyptians. The sons of Israel did not want to be saved; rather, they rejected their savior. Moses had delayed for 10 years, for this was God's decision. Going to Egypt, Moses punished them with 10 blows, in exchange for the 10 trials of Abraham and the 124 years of torment of the Israelites.

The word Egypt translates as "iron furnace." Egypt was originally built up by Mizraim, son of Kush, son of Canaan, and called Msr after his name. Subsequently it was called Aria, after Ariane. And then King Rameses named it Egypt after the Nile River, which then had that name, and is self-generating. Now the name of the monarch with whom Moses battled was P'le'sios, although others call him Kanak'aris.

When the Egyptians drank blood instead of water, they became disgusted and went to Gesem to request water. Yet as soon as the water was given, it turned into blood. Then they tried to take the water into their mouths from the lips of the Israelites, but it turned to blood as they swallowed it. Similarly, nothing could dispel the darkness that settled upon them, neither fire nor torch. And they vomited from breathing in the heavy thick air. While the firstborns of the Egyptians were thus dying, some 600,000 of the sons of Israel, from the age of 21 to 60, departed. This Exodus occurred in the year 3,842 of Adam's expulsion from Paradise, on a Wednesday, and the Jews crossed through the Red Sea on a Sunday.

When Moses cast his wand upon that sea, he said: "Aia, my God, before me." And extending his right hand, he said: "Sheraya, my God, you brought us out." And extending his left hand, he said: "Adonoi, the Lord God, is with us." Thus, having made the sign of the cross, he opened up a new path for them not only a dry route through the Red Sea, but an extremely broad and green one over which the twelve tribes of the Israelites passed with their baggage.

First went the clan of Benjamin, followed by the clan of Levi, then Judah and the others. Thenceforth they were called the Hebrews and, abandoning Egyptian, were given a new language, similar to the paternal language which they now speak. And with that, they sang "Let us bless the Lord, for He is glorified."[16]

Then Pharaoh and his troops entered the waters, pursuing them, but they were drowned instead of the children of the Israelites. The sea cast back a large portion of the slain with their weapons on the side of the Israelites, and each one recognized his former

---

16 Exodus 15.2ff.

master, buried him, taking the weapons with which they later destroyed the Amalekites. Similarly, on the other side of the Red Sea the Ethiopians, who had come from the River Ganges, took the corpses thrown back by the sea. And thus were the words of the Psalm fulfilled: "They will sustain the Ethiopians."

In this period, Heracles appeared in Phoenicia, as did the story about the discovery of the grape vine by Dionysius, which differs from that told by the Ishmaelites.

Also in this period, the court in Athens was called the Areopagite. Now after the Israelites had left Egypt, the ground shook for seven months, such that people were unable to stay in their houses. And they say that those Egyptians who were spared the drowning of Pharaoh reasoned that they had been saved by their images of gods, which were made by human hands. In this year, which was the 80th year of Moses, the Amalekites, the offspring of Esau's concubines, were defeated, and thus the Israelites avenged their ancestors. In the same year, in the second month, Moses ascended that dusky mountain to the Lord.

From the time of Adam until Moses' 80th year and the Exodus of Israel from Egypt, 3,842 years had elapsed, and in his 80th year, Moses warred against the Amelekites. In the third month of the same year, he went up onto the mountain and received the law.

Apolomos the Hebrew philosopher says that it was Moses who created letters for the Hebrews. And from this it appears that the Hebrew language is younger than that of the Syrians.

Apolimos, the Hebrew philosopher says that Moses, by the grace of God, first created an alphabet for the new language that the Israelites had received, and that, 50 days later, God gave Moses the tablets with the Ten Commandments written in it. Moses first wrote the book of Exodus about the events he had seen and was familiar with. Then he asked God: "How can I write fully of the events of your creation which I did not witness?" To accomplish this, God, unknowably and intangibly showed Moses the world for 40 days, revealed its past, and ordered that it be made in seven months, in the shape of the Tabernacle, after the seven days of creation.

Six years after the Exodus of the Israelites, Cronos ruled as king over the Athenians. That land was called Attica, after his daughter. He also ruled the land in Asia Minor called Cappadocia, named after Cecrops, which originally was called Alie. In the 20th year of Moses' rule, a king named Egyptus ruled in Egypt for 68 years, and it is said that he gave his name to that country. At the same time, they say, the temple to Apollo was built in Athens, and named the Areopagus. Now Moses died when he was was 120 years of age, and that is the beginning of the Jubilee of the Hebrews. The five books of Moses had been completed, containing, according to Eusebius, the deeds and history of 3,708 years.

Moses was 82 years of age when he erected an altar, and in the same year, spies brought grapes from the valley of Bethlehem. At the start of the next year Baghak sent Bagham the mage to curse Israel. Now Moses died when he was was 120 years of age. He wrote five books—the Pentateuch. After this, judges were established in Israel. The first of these was Joshua, son of Nun, who took the scepter of Moses and the rule for 83 years. It was he who led Israel into the Promised Land. He killed seven peoples of the Canaanites and delivered their lands as inheritance to the sons of Israel. He judged them for 27 years and died at 107 years of age. No one except Africanus puts an interval between Joshua and Othniel, who puts 30 years between them. This Othniel was judge for 40 years. But they served Chushan-rishathaim, whom Othniel killed. Those eight years are counted. The Greeks say that Othniel was a judge for 50 years.

In his day, the Bithynian cities of Malos, T'e'asos, Alkite', and Marunta were built. And in this time, cities were built in Sicily. In this period, Pelops ruled as king over the Arcadians, and this was the beginning of their kingship. From the Greeks also arose Philiste, the moralist, who wrote about animals and birds. Following Othniel, Israel served Eglon the Moabite for 18 years, years which are added to the tenure of Ehud of Ephraim, who judged for 80 years. The city of Akadmon[17] was built by Kadamos. In this

---

17   Possibly, Lacedomonia.

eighth year Ark'iat'os ruled Athens. And in his 20th year Lambaridus ruled over the Assyrians for 32 years. Balak'e' was built by the king of the Assyrians at that time. At this point, the fourth epoch was completed, which was 4,000 years.

There were 27 generations from Adam to Moses, while from Moses onward reckoning is done not by generations but solely by the names of the judges. Now after Ehud, the Israelites served Jabin for 20 years. Then Samegar grew strong and killed 600 Phillistine men with the handle of a plough. Then Sisara came with 900 iron chariots. Barak with Deborah's help defeated him. Jahel, the wife of Haber, killed him by slitting his throat. Barak's judgeship lasted 40 years. In Ehud's 13th year, the Thebans Cadmus and Phoenix came to Assyria and Sroy and Saydoy ruled. And some say that Cadmus created the Greek alphabet from Egyptian writing.

Pelops took over the kingdom of the Arcadians who previously were called Mukeats'ik'[18] prior to the descent among them of the sons of Heracles. In this period, the city of Ilium was built by Ilos and Ak'ayis was built by Ak'ioy. In this period, there appeared Sibyl, a woman who interpreted a dream seen simultaneously by 100 philosophers at Rome, in which they all saw seven suns. In this period Midos ruled over the Africans.

In the 28th year of Barak, Panawos ruled over the Assyrians for 45 years. In this time Deborah made a blessing in song. After Barak, the Midianites ruled Israel for seven years. Gideon, who had been strengthened by God, arose and destroyed them and judged Israel for 33 years. If the seven years of servitude are added to this figure, his tenure as judge is 40 years. In the third year of Gideon, Igos ruled as king of the Assyrians for 48 years. In the 33rd year of Gideon, Susramos ruled as king of the Assyrians for 19 years. In this period, in Thebes, Apollo the musician ruled. They say he was able to move rocks with the beauty of his music. In other writings, we have found that Cecrops ruled again[19] as king of Athens. At 70 years of age, Gideon became a father. After Gideon's death, Abi-

---

18 Possibly, Mycenaeans.
19 Or, the second Cecrops.

melich, the concubine's son, killed 70 of Gideon's sons and judged Israel for three years. He was succeeded by Tola for 22 years. In his eighth year, Theseus ruled the Athenians for 30 years. In Assyria, Mit'ros ruled for 27 years. In the 21st year of Tola Tarsus in Cilicia was built by Perseus, son of Danae. In this period, Carthage was built and Troy was captured. After Tola, Jair the Gileadite judged for 23 years. In his sixth year, Amukasos ruled as king in Egypt for 25 years. In his 14th year, Tutlos ruled as king in Assyria for 31 years. The Greeks call him Tautanes, and some say that it was he who captured and ruined the city of Ilium. In Jair's 16th year, Ment'os ruled over the Athenians for 22 years.

After Jair, Israel served foreigners for 19 years and Jephthah judged for six years, though others reckon 24 years. They say that the musician Philon, who introduced choirs, lived in this period. He also made statues with the feet separated, as though walking. In this period, the cities of Kiwrine'[20] and Sur were built, 440 years before the construction of the Temple.

In the fourth year of Jephthah, Dimap'os ruled over the Athenians for 33 years. Over the Egyptians there ruled Giusbululite' and others like him, in order, for 188 years.

In this period, the Latins, called Romans, began to rule. Their first king was Aenas who ruled for three years. Following Jephthah some say that Elon became judge. The Septuagint places Abdon here, who judged for eight years. After Abdon, the Philistines ruled for 40 years. After Elon and Abdon, Samson from the line of Dan judged Israel for 20 years. In the third year of his tenure, he warred against the Philistines. In his fifth year, the affair regarding Ruth took place. In his second year, Tute'os ruled the Assyrians for 40 years. In Samson's 19th year, Zeus died and was buried in Crete after living for 880 years. Because of his longevity, he was called after the name of the star, even though his parents had named him Dios.

Now following Samson, the children of Israel passed 12 years without a judge. John the Historian writes that Samegar judged after Samson for 40 years, while Africanus says that they

---

20 Possibly, Corinth.

had no judge then. There was peace at the time and no one experienced harassment from anyone. Eli, according to the Septuagint, judged Israel for 20 years, while the Syriac version says 40 years. According to the Septuagint, Eli lived for a total of 78 years. Eli became a prince at age 38 and in the 17th year of his authority, Samuel was born. Samuel was presented at the altar at age 20. After Eli's death, the Ark of the Tabernacle was in the House of Aminadab for 20 years. In the 42nd year of Samuel's life and in the 20th year of his authority, the children of Israel requested a king. With this, the era of the judges ended and their kingship recommenced with Saul.

Saul, the first king, at age 40—which was the third year of his reign as king—defeated the Amalekites. In his 10th year, David was born, and in the 22nd year of Saul's reign as king, David was anointed king by Samuel. And Samuel then was 65 years old and David was twelve. In his 28th year, David killed Goliath. In the 31st year of his reign there was a festival to Nawad in Ramah and Saul prophesied among the prophesiers that David would be king. He prophesied as to the wickedness of his House. Samuel the prophet died when David was 30. Five years after the death of Samuel, Saul and his son Jonathan were killed, having reigned for 40 years.

David ruled in Hebron for seven years. It was he who built Zion, then ruled in Jerusalem for 33 years. In the 10th year of his reign, he removed the ark and put it in a tent. Now while he was bringing the ark, the grace of God inside pitied Adam, and he threw himself on Adam's grave. Hosea died since he wanted to restrict the grace to Adam. This is what Jacob of Edessa relates.

The prophet Nathan, who protected David, was in Gabawon. He was the first to know when David was about to fall into sin in with Bathsheba. He came to save David, but while traveling, he encountered a dead person and by the time they had buried him and Nathan had reached David, the adultery had already occurred. And so Nathan turned back in sorrow. When Uriah was slain, Nathan came and reprimanded David for these two evil deeds. Nathan gave him a sign—the death of Bathsheba's first-born son—

and David feared God and repented. In the 39th year of his reign, David selected 188 men from the Levites, organizing them into 23 choirs of 12 men each, to serve the ark and to sing Psalms. He also made war with the surrounding peoples and defeated all of them. He lived for 70 years, reigning for 40 years.

Then Solomon, who was 12 years old, reigned for 40 years. He removed the priest Abiat'ar from the priesthood and killed Adonia and Yovab. In the fourth year of his reign, Solomon began building the Temple and completed it in eight years. This stood on the mountains of the Amorites, which is now Jerusalem. It is written in the Biblical book of Kings, that 480 years after the exodus from Egypt, the Temple would be built. Paul says the same, that "God gave them judges for 450 years until the prophet Samuel," leaving out the 30 years of their servitude to foreigners. In their 34th year, Solomon built an idol house for the Moabite Camos and the Ammonite Moloch where there was also a home for the Greek goddess Aphrodite. The Moabite temple was built in seven years and the Ammonite temple in thirteen years. Their height was 30 cubits and their width, 50 cubits. And Solomon made many golden ornaments for them and a representation of a bronze sea with bulls. Solomon pulled down Antioch and built T'etmur near Hems, as well as Malu, Hesur, Makdur, Gazare', Be'dur, upper and lower, and Beghe'ovt', seven cities. In the first year of his kingship, a son, Rehoboam, was born from his marriage to Naamah the Ammonite. In Damascus, Solomon's enemy Hadad was ruling. Solomon's life span was 52 years. Epiphanes says that Ahijah prophesied to Solomon that he would anger God sometime in the future. He similarly upbraided Rehoboam that he went treacherously before God. It was Ahijah who saw the vision in which yoked oxen were trampling Israel and the priesthood. Ahijah said to Solomon: "your women distance you from God." He also reprimanded Jeroboam, son of Nabat, because of his wives and he died and was buried at Shiloh in front of an oak tree.

The Queen of Sheba Visits Solomon

To King Solomon came Nessa, the queen of a southern realm, who was said to be descended from the line of Noah's daughter, Aster. She came from a place in the south where, to this day, women descended from the patriarch Noah rule. Solomon's reputation for wisdom attracted her and she tested him with enigmatic questions, some of which we have provided here.

The first question concerns the nature of God. "What is your God, and who does He resemble?"

Solomon replied: "My God Is, and is above all beings. He has no fixed image. Every being has its opposite. However, my God, since He is not created, has no opposite.

"How does the celestial globe turn, right to left, fully or partly?"

"This turning is done in two ways. The heavenly circumference turns to the right and to the east, then through the south and west, and the north, returning to its point of departure. By the same order, it goes around in a day and a night with all the fixed stars. As for the planets, which some call wandering stars, they move left from West to East, each according to the low or high position of its zone, according to the narrowness or breadth of that zone, achieving a revolution in 30 years as well as 30 days. For Cronos is Saturn, while Sahra is the Moon."

"Before there was being, where was the creator of all, and after the dissolution of everything, where will He be?"

"Before the creation of all was the Lord Himself and His being was full of its essence. He enjoyed endless goodness. Since the creation of the world, it is in Him that created beings exist. After the dissolution of the world, He also will continue to exist in Himself and in the souls of saints, and they reside in Him. He adds to their glory and He will be further glorified by them."

"Why is it that an Indian woman who eats pomegranate ceases to conceive?"

"The nature of the pomegranate is cold and wet and the country of India is hot and dry. The Indian woman is cool and moist. Consequently, when elements of the pomegranate and the woman merge, contrary to the nature of the country, then women no longer can become pregnant."

"Why does an Indian man become sterile after drinking wine?"

"The nature of the wine is dry and hot, and it induces sleep. The same may be said for the nature of mankind. Thus when a man drinks often, he become impotent."

"Is wisdom general or specific? Does it come from nature, from study, or as a blessing?"

"Wisdom is general in genre, partial in type, natural as regards animate beings, trees, and plants. The situation with humankind is mixed. It may be attained through study, as one labors to understand something; or it may be a blessing of grace from God. This latter type is not given to all but only to those selected as worthy of it."

Question: "What was the plant which was crowned not by nature but surrounded by a halo of rays and nurtured by flames which were woven into garlands for undeserving sons?"

Answer: "Surely you have heard that God appeared to Moses as a burning blackberry bush, and that that visitation stimulated questions and answers."

Question: "Identify the foreign mother, the sons born in prostitution, and nourished in impiety, revealed as thieves, and kings living in plenty."

Answer: "You insult my fathers and myself. Tamar was considered a murderer who nourished my ancestors after they had been stolen from Judah."

Question: "Name the thing which is repulsive and nauseating, which is transformed by the clouds and nourishes kings."

Answer: "You refer to menstruating women who nourish kings and paupers when babies, through the milk of their breasts."

Riddle: "What is the diner who, seeking different tastes, increases the number of cooks, yet receives only the same flavor?"

Answer: "If you have an excellent cook, let us add him to the thousands we have; however, as you say, there is but one excellent taste. But should there be one wicked chef, opposed to Our Lord, then the bitter taste will remain until Judgement Day."

Riddle: "The bridegroom is invisible, and the nuptial is unchangeable. The bedchamber is pure; but the spouse full of rage brings a great shame to the matter."

Answer: "Do not insult our people which is forever wedded to God with unspoken words. Nor do we bear the shame of prostituting ourselves to foreign gods. It is fitting that you worship a bird called T'riane, the phoenix. But now, answer a riddle from me."

"There is a formidable tower, with lethal weapons, and a three-sided temple, whose rocks are joy, whose foundation is love, whose construction is water, the start of whose deliverance is caresses, whose ceilings are dance, whose columns are enjoyment, whose discovery is strange, whose residents are not persons. Pursuit of it is in vain, its turrets spring from within itself, its windows are isolated, the instruments are contrary to its construction, and its guards are invisible."

And the Queen replied: "We heard that you were wise, but did not believe that you were prescient. Now we know that your God is the sole God of the visible and the invisible". The Queen then praised the construction of the Temple and its attendants who were divided into 12 classes to serve before the Lord each month. Each class had 24,000 people in it, with 6,000 judges and 4,000 harpists, and 4,000 porters arranged by Solomon's father, David. The dimensions of the Temple were 60 cubits long by 20 cubits wide and 120 cubits high. It had 10 gold tables[21] and 10 gold towers. Outside, to the right and left, were two columns of 37 cubits height, which were named Boas and Yak'um, meaning "Strength" and "Righteousness." The Holy of Holies was 20 cubits wide and 20 cubits high, which greatly astonished the Queen. And she departed from him greatly edified.

---

21 Or, altars.

MICHAEL THE GREAT

Solomon subsequently repented for his sins. Recalling his father's command, he entered a room and expiated. Solomon died at the age of 52, having ruled for 40 years.

After Solomon's death, the twelve tribes divided and were under Jeroboam, son of Nabath, who ruled for 22 years. Under Rehoboam there remained two peoples, and they were called Judah and Israel. Rehoboam ruled as king in Jerusalem for 17 years and lived to age 58. In this period lived the prophet Samea who reprimanded Rehoboam a second time on the altar and said to Judah: "Do not fight with Israel since your division was from the Lord." He tore his garment into twelve parts, giving ten pieces to Jeroboam the Nabatian and two pieces to Rehoboam, Solomon's son. Epiphanes says that the prophet's name was Iud, who hailed from the country of the Samarians and that he was killed by a lion as he strayed from the word of the Lord. After Rehoboam, his son Abiah ruled for two years. Jeroboam arose against him with 40,000 troops and 50,000 men of Israel were killed. Abiah had 14 wives who bore him 24 sons and 60 daughters.

After Abiah, his son Asa ruled for 41 years, living for 60 years. He dug a well near Masep'a to the awe of the king of Israel. Asa in the 15th year of his reign burned the idols he found and eliminated prostitution from the country. He also removed his mother from the queenship because she worshipped Astarte, and he burned the idols of his mother. In the 29th year of Asa Elah ruled over Israel for two years. His servant, Zimri killed him and ruled for seven days. Israel was divided, some following Amri and some, Tibni. Amri was victorious and ruled for 12 years. He purchased the mountain Samaria from the Samarians' lord, built a city there, and named it Samaria. It was later called Sebastia, and today is called Nablus. When Tibni saw that Amri had triumphed, he set fire to the court and burned to death in it.

In the 41st year of Asa, P'ark'iris ruled in Egypt for four years. After Asa, Jehoshapat his son ruled, for 29 years. In Jehoshapat's second year, Ahab, Amri's son, was king of Israel, for 23 years. He took for a wife Jezebel, daughter of Ethbaal, king of

Tyre and Sidon. He built Jericho which was cursed by Joshua, son of Non. He started it under his first born Abhiram and finished it under his younger son, Zertsel. Under Abhiram he laid the foundation and under Zertsel he hanged the gates, according to Jesu. But there are diverse accounts about this, such as that it was built by the order of Ahab and his sons, Abhiram and Zertsel.

In the second year of Jehoshapat, Carpantus ruled over the Latins for 13 years. In Jehoshapat's fourth year, Ubrantios ruled over the Assyrians for 50 years. In his 13th year there ruled Iskok'oros in Egypt, for six years. In his fourth year Amkalos ruled over the Assyrians for 30 years. In his 19th year in Egypt, Basanik'os ruled for nine years. In his 23rd year, Agripa ruled over the Latins for 41 years. In his 29th year, Ochochias ruled over Israel for one year. After him, his brother, Joram, ruled for 12 years. In the same year Joram ruled over Judah for 8 years. After him Ochochias ruled for one year. Joram, king of Judah, son of Jehoshapat, took for his wife Athaliah who was Ahab's sister and killed his brothers. The Lord struck him in anger and he died and Ochochias ruled the kingdom. He sent Elisha to anoint Jehu, son of Amghi over Israel.

He killed Joram, son of Ahab and Ochochias, king of Judah, and Jezebel, 15 years after killing her husband, Ahab.

After the death of Ochochias, king of Judah, his mother Godoghia lost all her sons. But one baby was preserved by Jehoiada the priest. Then Godoghia herself ruled for 6 years. Jehu ruled over Israel for 28 years. He burned the temple to Baal called "bull" together with its worshippers. The chief priest Yovidea killed Godoghia and enthroned Joas, a boy of six, over Judah. He reigned for 40 years.

In the second year of Joas, Diogenes ruled as king over the Athenians for 28 years. In Joas' 10th year, Akraganis ruled the Athenians for 22 years. In the 22nd year of Joas, Esnuk'os ruled over the Egyptians for 21 years. In Joas' 23rd year, Romulus ruled as king over the Latins for 19 years. This Romulus was extremely proud in his ways and was burned together with his court in fire sent from heaven. In the 37th year of Joas' reign, Elisha died, 50 years after the assumption of Elijah. In the 27th year of Joas, there ruled over Israel Yovak'az for 17 years. In the 31st year of Joas the judge over the Athenians was Baraklis, for 19 years. Joas, after the death of Yovidea, deviated from the Lord. He killed Zak'aria, son of Yovidea in the Temple, then he himself was slain by one of his servants.

Then his son Amasia ruled for 29 years. He was conquered by the Edomites and brought their gods to worship them. He lived for 54 years. In his 10th year, Yovas ruled over Israel for 16 years. Antoninus ruled over the Latins for 37 years. In the second year of Amasia, Est'ron ruled over Egypt for 17 years. During this period Arip'an was judge over the Athenians for 20 years. In the 17th year of Amasia, T'onos Konkogheros, called Sardanapalos, ruled over the Assyrians for 20 years. In his day, Jonan went to preach in Nineveh. Sardanapalos regretted his deeds and turned to the Lord in repentance. After this repentance, there was warfare between him and Varbak the Mede, the Medes who are the Mark'. When Sardanapalos saw that he had been defeated by the Mark', he burned himself to death.

The entire duration of the Assyrian kingdom was 1,196 years, which was after the overthrow of the Babylonian kingdom. Counting from the first year of Belus, father of Ninus, there were 1,300 years. Varbak the Mede, with the assistance of the Armenians, eliminated the kingdom of the Assyrians, turning it into the kingdom of the Medes.

After his death, the king was the Chaldean P'ul, called E'p'ua, from the line of Ninus. From him descended the kings Tiglathpilesar, Shalmaneser, and Senek'erim, who are mentioned in the books of the Bible. These kings ruled over the Cilicians and P'ilip'ians. From them descended Nak'onos, Nak'ubolos, Nabupalasar and Nabugoghonosor. Their total regnal years, from P'ul until Alexander of Macedon, is 424 years. Now after the death of Alexander there ruled Seleucus, Antiochus, Kilikos Seleucus Callinichus who built Cilicia; Soros who built Soria after which the

Asorik' are named. Until Soros, they were called Chaldeans; and Seleucus, who built Seleucia. Antiochus rebuilt Antioch after it had been ruined by Solomon. Similarly, Seleucus at Alexander's order rebuilt Edessa—which had been built by Nimrod and demolished by Senek'erim. This same Seleucus established a multitude of people to dwell in Tarsus in Cilicia. Because of the unhealthy nature of the place, they had not lived there previously.

In the 18th year of Amaziah, king of Judah, Jeroboam ruled over Israel for 40 years; while in Egypt, Tulo't'is ruled for 13 years. Amaziah fought with Joas, king of Israel, was wounded and died. Then the Israelites came to Jerusalem, demolished 400 fathoms of the wall, took the gold and silver from the House of the Lord and the House of the king, and returned to Samaria. Amaziah was brought to Jerusalem and buried. Then his son Azariah succeeded him for 52 years. Reaching the age of 68, he died.

In the first year of Azariah, who is Uzziah, T'aspinos was judge of the Athenians for 27 years. In the second year of Uzziah, Statis ruled as king in Egypt, for 25 years. In the 10th year of Uzziah, P'rikos ruled over the Latins for 23 years. In the 27th year of Uzziah, Usrat'on reigned in Egypt for 9 years. The Egyptians called him Erakle's. In the 28th year of Uzziah, the judge of the Athenians was Agmistor for 20 years. In the 29th year of King Uzziah of Judah, Zak'aria reigned over Israel for 6 years and 4 months.

After Zak'aria, Sellom ruled over Israel for one year. He was followed by Menahem for 10 years. In his 24th regnal year Uzziah dared to cast incense in the Temple, and became covered all over his body with leprosy. and Isaiah was prevented from prophesying for 24 years. He remained silent for 28 years, until Uzziah died, and thereafter prophesied for 61 years. In the 33rd year of Uzziah, Romulus ruled the Latins for 43 years. In the 34th year of Uzziah, P'ua, king of the Babylonians arose and went against Samaria, took 1,000 talents of gold from Menahem and turned back. In the 36th year of Uzziah, Basmos reigned over the Egyptians for 10 years. In the 40th year of Uzziah king of Judah, P'ake'e' ruled over Israel for 10 years. In the 41st year of Uzziah, Ko'nos the second king ruled over the Macedonians for 12 years. Over the Assyrians there reigned Tiglathpilesar for 35 years. In the 46th year of Uzziah, Kuk'ros reigned over Egypt for 44 years. In the 48th year of Uzziah, the first king reigned over the Lydians.

Tiglathpilesar, king of the Assyrians, arose and enslaved Judah and a large part of Israel. This was the beginning of the captivity of Israel. Grandee princes were taken captive: Inabe'l, Be't'mek'a, Enok', Kants, Esur, Geghad, Gawdi, and the country of the Nephilim. After the death of Uzziah, the glory of the Lord appeared in the Temple. After the death of Uzziah, his son Jotham ruled for 16 years. He conquered the Ammonites and put them under taxation. In the third year of Jotham, the third king of the Macedonians, Tunios ruled for 38 years. They are related to the Armenians. After Jotham his son, Ahaz ruled for 16 years. He worked evil before the Lord.

Pekah, king of Israel, took Hr'ason, king of Damascus, went against Judah, and killed 120,000. Then Ahaz sent mercenaries from Tiglathpilesar and he came and killed Hr'ason, enslaved the Edomites, and departed. In the second year of Ahaz, Hosea revolted from Pekah, killed him, then ruled over Israel himself for 9 years. In the 7th year of Ahaz's reign, Shalmaneser ruled over the Assyrians for 14 years. He came against Israel and placed it under taxation. After a while Hosea rebelled and sent to Abimelech the Kushite, which is Ethiopia, who then was in Egypt, to come to aid him. In the 7th year of Hosea and the 8th year of Ahaz, Shalmaneser arose and came against Samaria, besieging it for 3 years. Then he captured Samaria and took the 10 tribes captive to Babylon. The total years of the kings of Israel was 250, and then they were eliminated. Dating from Adam there were 4,330 years.

Ahaz took down the model of 12 bulls on the sea which King Solomon had made. After the death of Ahaz, Hezekiah ruled in Jerusalem for 29 years, living 54 years. Samaria remained under Assyrian control. In the 8th year of Hezekiah, Shalmaneser sent guards to the Samarian areas. Up to this point, those called Latins had 15 kings. In the 7th year of Ahaz, Romulus ruled. He built the city of Rome in his name, though some say it was named after his daughter, who was named Hr'ome'. Thereafter they were called Romans.

In this period, the island of Rhodes was built up. It has the fruit of juniper trees. In this period the city of Salinos was constructed in Sicily, and the city of Trabizond was built in Pontos. In Bithynia, Kizikon was built, in Italy, Colonea and Lukania were built. It was at this time that the Lacedemonians Spartans set up their first kings. The first was Abios, and others ruled for 340 years. In this period in Rome they built 24 temples, two areopagi, and 324 streets, 80 golden idols, and 64 statues made from ivory, and 46,603 mansions. There were 1,795 princely houses, and 1,352 acquaducts to bring water to the city. There were 2,074 bakers, and 3,785 bronze talismans. After a long period of time, Titus and Vespasian brought to Rome the gates of Jerusalem, the columns of the Temple and other things, and they added to the adornments of Rome.

The circumference of the city is 40 miles and each of the four sides has 12 miles inside. A mile corresponds to 12 acres, the length of a path drawn by oxen. The number of inhabitants were 120,000, and the second time they were counted there were 160,000 inhabitants. The third census found 270,000; the fourth, 460,000; the fifth, 4,600,000. During the reign of Claudius the population of Rome was 6,940,000.

During the reign of Augustus and Archelaeus, son of Herod, there was a great famine in

Rome when a *mod* of grain cost 27 and a half *dahekan*s. During the reign of Titus a plague occurred there in which 10,000 folk died in a single day.

In this period lions devoured the Samaritans. Shalmaneser sent from captivity a priest named Ezra, who taught them the faith and who wrote for them in Syriac the five books of Moses. It is for this reason that the Samaritans do not accept other books or prophecies excepting Genesis.

In the 6th year of Hezekiah, Senek'erim ruled as king of the Assyrians. His troops went to Jerusalem and killed 185,000 people. Senek'erim, after ruling for nine years, was slain by his sons who went to Armenia. Then his son Esarhaddon ruled for three years. In Egypt, Sawik'on the Indian ruled for 12 years while P'ritikos ruled over the Macedonians for 51 years. In the 18th year of Hezekiah, Beldan who is Baghtan, ruled over the Assyrians. He sent an offering to Hezekiah in Jerusalem for the return from eclipse of the sun, since he knew that the god of Israel was a sign of life for Hezekiah. And he preached the name of the Lord God throughout the country of the Babylonians and Assyrians. He also fashioned an image of the true God and had it worshipped. And he turned his entire land from worshipping the sun.

In the 20th year of Hezekiah, Kurtakos ruled the Medes for 13 years. In the 29th year of Hezekiah, Archos the Indian ruled in Egypt for 20 years. Following Hezekiah, Manasseh ruled for 55 years. He lived for 67 years. In the second year of his reign, he killed the prophet Isaiah and shed much innocent blood. And he was dropped by the hand of God and fell into the hands of the Assyrian troops. They took him captive to Assyria and placed him in a well, in fetters. He recited solemn prayers of repentance to the all-powerful Lord. God accepted his entreaties and released him in his 37th year. The prophet Isaiah was buried in Siloam which received the grace of healing. Selov was called "sent" and for two reasons. One was because of Isaiah who is called the one who is sent[22] in the Biblical passage which says "Here I am, Lord, send me."[23] The other reason was that when foreigners came to cut off the water supply and when Isaiah went among the people, he was sent by God to Jerusalem to resist the besiegement by the Assyrians.

In the 4th year of Manasseh, Diuk'layos ruled over the Medes for 54 years. In the 21st year of Manasseh, Martis ruled Egypt for two years. In the 29th year of Manasseh, Arge'os ruled the Mace-

---

22 Առաքեալ — Apostle.
23 Isaiah 6:8.

donians for 38 years. In the 33rd year of Manasseh, Step'ant'os ruled in Egypt for five years. In the 25th year of Manasseh, Sennacherib the Younger ruled over the Assyrians for 35 years. In the 40th year of Manasseh, Taklios ruled as king over the Romans for 32 years. It was he who introduced royal purple clothing and a golden scepter. We call him Tullos. At this time in Egypt there ruled Nek'on for 18 years. In the 44th year of Manasseh, P'somitikos ruled in Egypt for 44 years. In this period, the first construction of Byzantium took place by Prince Biwzos; and after 970 years, it was expanded and renovated by Constantine and renamed Constantinople. In this period, the institution of judges in Athens came to an end.

After Manasseh, Amon ruled Judah for 12 years. In his third year, Phraortes ruled as king over the Medes for 14 years. In the 12th year of Amon's reign, Nabupalasar ruled over the Assyrians for 32 years. He was a mage. In the same year, Philip ruled over the Macedonians for 38 years. In the third year of Amon's reign, Josiah was born. Amon worshipped idols. His servants attacked him and he died. He lived for 24 years.

His son Josiah ruled as king in Jerusalem for 31 years, and lived for 39 years. He had four sons: Yovhanne's, Yovakim, Yovak'az, and Zedekiah. In these days Sop'onia from the line of Shmawon was prophesying. In the 10th year of Josiah, Markos Anikos ruled as king over the Romans for 24 years. In the 13th year of Josiah, Jeremiah began to prophesy. In the 14th year of Josiah, Kostandos ruled as king over the Macedonians for 32 years. He went and conquered Nineveh and the Assyrians. In Josiah's 30th year, Neco who is Nep'sos, ruled as king in Egypt for 6 years. He arose and went to the Euphratean areas, warring against the Assyrians at Mnbe'ch. Then Josiah arose and went against him, without God's command, and was killed by him and buried in Jerusalem. His son, Yovak'az ruled after him. After three months, Neco the Lame turned and took Yovak'az to Egypt, establishing the latter's brother, Yovakim, as king. Neco also imposed a tax of 10 talents of gold and 100 of silver. He ruled for 12 years.

In the third year of Jehoiakim's reign, Tarkinos Ubrikos ruled as king over the Romans for 38 years. In the same year, Nebuchadnezzar the Chaldean, son of Nabupalasar, ruled the Assyrians for 44 years. He came to Jerusalem and took into captivity the vessels from the House of the Lord. He also laid a tribute on Jehoiakim and took Daniel and his companions into captivity. And he rebuilt in the name of the Assyrians the city of Manbij, which had been pulled down by Neco. He placed there the idol of Cainan, and called the city Hieropolis, which translates "city of priests" after the sorcerer priests, whose sect was later studied by Bardesan.

Once again, Neco came to the Euphratean areas and was killed by Nebuchadnezzar. Then P'sant'os ruled in Egypt for 17 years. In the 8th year of Yovakim and the 5th year of Nebuchadnezzar, the latter came to Jerusalem, took the tribute, and departed. In the 8th year of Nebuchadnezzar, Yovakim died and his son Jehoiachin, who is Yek'onia, reigned for three years. He departed from the ways of the Lord. Then Nebuchadnezzar came to Jerusalem, captured Yek'onia, his mother, and princes and took them to Babylon where they were kept in fetters for 35 years. Then Nebuchadnezzar made Zedekiah king in Jerusalem. Earlier, Nebuchadnezzar's father, Nabopolassar, had sent him to Jerusalem and when he returned, he found that his father had died, and he took over the kingdom. In the 19th year of Nebuchadnezzar, Nabuzardan came and burned Jerusalem and the Temple after the captivity and death of Zedekiah, who had ruled for 11 years. In the fourth year of Zedekiah, there ruled over the Medes Astyages for 38 years. In the 11th year of Zedekiah, Vaphres reigned over Egypt for 27 years. In the same year Zedekiah was taken captive with all the Jews excepting a few poor folk who worked for the court. However, before the destruction of the Temple, the prophet Jeremiah had taken and was keeping the Tabernacle of the Lord.

THE CHRONICLE
Jerusalem's Time of Troubles

In the fourth year of Yovakim, which was the first year of Nebuchadnezzar, before the 11th year of Zedekiah, which was the last destruction of Jerusalem, and after the destruction of Jerusalem, Nebuchadnezzar arose and went against Tyre *which is Sur*, demolished it, and threw the stones into the sea. The Tyrians took their belongings, also threw them into the sea, and then fled by boat, *while they took what they could carry with them aboard ships and fled to Carthage.* The Assyrians killed Hiram, king of Tyre. Tyre had been ruled by the kings of Judah throughout its entire history. Nebuchadnezzar gave Egypt over to the troops for looting in return for their work at Tyre.

In the 27th year of the captivity of Jerusalem, Nebuchadnezzar died after a reign of 20 years. His son Amel-Marduk succeeded him for three years. It was he who removed Yovakim from prison and had him eat at the royal table.

After him came Belshazzar for two years. In the first year of Belshazzar's reign, Daniel saw the vision of the four beasts, on the example of the four kingdoms of the world. Darius the Mede slew Belshazzar and turned the kingdom to the Chaldeans. In the time of Darius the Mede, Daniel was put back into prison but subsequently Darius appointed him as superior to all the princes. Then Cyrus the Persian killed Darius and did away with the kingdom of the Medes and Assyrians. Cyrus put the seat of his kingdom in Babylon and made Daniel faithful to him.

Daniel, inspired by zeal for God, destroyed the idol of Bel which was erected in the name of Vilos, and he slew the dragon. Furious at him, the king again threw him into a den with seven lions. Then Habakkuk was sent by God to bring food to Daniel, and Daniel was saved from the cubs of his enemies. In this year, Habakkuk died and Daniel saw a vision by which he learned that the 70 years of chastisement had ended, that chastisement which God had revealed by means of the prophet Jeremiah. Daniel fasted for 21 days. He saw by the Tigris River a man dressed in white, who told him: "For 21 days I have fought with the prince of the Persians in order that the sons of your people be returned." And indeed, in the first year of Cyrus, 50,000 of the Jewish captives returned and they began to rebuild the Temple.

In the 60th year of the captivity of the Jews, Cyrus was killed by his wife, *Tomyris, queen of the Massagetae,* and Cambyses took over his realm. The Jews say that he was styled Nebuchadnezzar, who slew Arp'ak'sat' the Mede. During Cambyses' day the affair of the woman Judith occurred, she who slew Holophernes who was of the line of Magog, who are the Turks.

After Cambyses had ruled for eight years, his two brothers, who were mages, took the kingdom, for seven years. After them ruled Darius the Mede, *son of Hystaspes,* for 36 years. In his third year was completed the second 70 year captivity of the Jews after the burning of the Temple. The first 70 year captivity was determined by Jeremiah and testified to by Zak'aria and Ange'as who said: "How long will you have no mercy on Jerusalem and the cities of Judah against which you have had indignation these 70 years?"[24] From Solomon's construction to the sixth year of Darius totals 508 years. In the 15th year of Darius, the fifth century was concluded; and in the 16th year of Darius, the sixth century began.

In this period, Haggai, Zechariah, and Malachi prophesied. Zerubbabel, son of Shealtiel, son of Jeconias, led the captives back. The High Priest was Jeshua, son of Jehozadak. Some say that Zedekiah's son, Shealtiel, was born in Babylon after his blinding. In this period, Chilon, one of the Seven Sages, was ephor in Lacaedamon. Similarly, Tarquin is said to have invented instruments of torture, prisons, and the use of racks and chains for torture and commanding convicts to work in the copper mines. In these times, Theognis was recognized as a poet.

After Darius his son, Xerxes, ruled for 21 years. In the second year of his reign, he took Egypt, and in the 21st year he took and burned Athens, and captured many cities. In his day, the affair

---

24 Jeremiah 1:12.

of Esther took place involving Mordecai and Haman who was of the Amalekites. But the historian, John of Asia, does not believe that the events involving Esther occurred at this point, for if they had why did Ezra not write about them? And some say that the return of the Jews occurred then, while others put it under Darius.

After Xerxes, Artawanos ruled for five months, and after him Artaxerxes Longimanus ruled for 41 years. In his seventh year, the scribe Ezra went to reconstruct the walls of Jerusalem. Through God's grace, he wrote down the Old Testament. Through God's care, old exemplars had been preserved in various places which later were found to agree with one another.

In the 20th year of Artaxerxes, his cupbearer, Nehemiah, went to assist Ezra. He remained there in Jerusalem, building, for 12 years. This foundation of Jerusalem was laid during the priesthood of Yovidia, son of Elisha. Nemiah also had the burnt ashes of sacred writings retrieved from a well where they had been forgotten for 70 years. When he placed them on the altar, the sacred flame lit, as before.

Following Longimanus, another Artaxerxes reigned for two months. After him, Sogdianos ruled for seven months. He was followed by Darius Nothus, the bastard, for 19 years. In the 15th year of his reign Egypt revolted from the Persians and set up Dionysius as their king, after an interregnum of 124 years.

After Alexander, Pertikos ruled over the Macedonians for 28 years. In the 19th year of Darius, Orestes ruled the Macedonians for three years. Meanwhile in Rome, Calorion reigned. He warred against the Gauls and Galatians. After 100 years the Romans were conquered. They took Rome and demolished it to its foundations, leaving only the royal palace. In the same period, there was a severe earthquake and the earth swallowed many cities. The Persians were ruled by Artaxerxes Mnemon for 40 years. The Hebrews say that it was under him that the events of Esther occurred. In the 15th year of Artaxerxes, the Autocrat of Rome named Africanus destroyed Carthage and rebuilt it in his own name, calling it Africa. In Egypt, Ephirites ruled for six years, while Archelaus ruled over the Macedonians for four years. Then Dalamutos ruled again for one year. And then Pusinos for one year, followed by Amundis for six years. In the 16th year of Artaxerxes, Archelaus ruled the Maceonians for 18 years. In the 20th year of Artaxerxes, P'sunt'os ruled in Egypt for one year and after him, Maris for one year, followed by Niktapis for 18 years. In the 35th year of Artaxerxes, Alexander ruled over the Macedonians for one year, followed by Ptolemy for three years. In the 40th year of Artaxerxes, Dios ruled the Egyptians for two years.

He was followed by Nectanebo for 12 years. After Artaxerxes, another Artaxerxes called Ochus ruled over the Persians. He subdued Egypt and eliminated their kingdom. Nectanebo, king of Egypt, fled to Ethiopia, knowing through magic about the impending disaster. They say that he, Nectanebo, was the father of Alexander. The kingship of Egypt was empty for 42 years until the advent of Punt'imos called Ptolemy, one of Alexander's friend.

Artaxerxes Ochus, king of Persia, made the Jews submit and took and settled them by the Caspian Sea in the city of Hyrcania. In this period Philip, Alexander's father, ruled as king over the Macedonians for 28 years. Philip's wife's name was Olympias. It was in this period that the philosophers Aristotle and Epicurus appeared. In the 13th year of the Persian king Ochus, Alexander was born in the eighth year of his father's reign. After Ochus, his son Arisbole's ruled as king over the Persians. He was followed by Darius, son of Artaxerxes, for six years.

In the first year of Darius' rule Philip's son Alexander ruled over the Macedonians for 20 years. At first he ruled over Hellas. Although he was just three cubits in height, he was very intelligent and brave. He eliminated 35 kings of the world. He possessed 120,000 troops. In the sixth year of his reign, which was also the sixth year of Darius, Greeks and Persians warred at Sis in Cilicia, and Darius died. With him ended the kingdom of the Persians which had lasted 231 years.

Alexander built 12 cities named after himself. He established the Gate of the Huns so that they would not pollute his land.

That Gate was made of iron and stood 12 cubits high and eight cubits wide. He came to Jerusalem and offered prayers to God and the Jews allowed it. He honored the High Priest Antromak'os, and when the Samaritans killed the High Priest Antromak'os for allowing a pagan to worship God, Alexander heard about this. He came to Jerusalem, destroyed Samaria, and exterminated the people. Then he brought Macedonians and settled them in Samaria. After a reign of 12 years and seven months, he died from poisoning in Babylon. He was the first king of the Greeks. After him, Ptolemy ruled in Egypt. It was Ptolemy who brought Alexander's body to Egypt and buried it. Thus was fulfilled the prophecy that the he-goat would conquer Darius the ram. And thus, too, was one horn removed, leaving four horns, Alexander's comrades.[25] There were 10 horns after that; the horns divided into 10 kings.

Ptolemy ruled for 40 years. In his first year he took Jerusalem through treachery. Then he took captives under the High Priest Onias to Egypt. Other kings were called Ptolemids after Ptolemy's name. In the fourth year of Ptolemy's reign, Antigonus ruled over all Asia for 18 years. He rebuilt Antioch after the name of his son, Antiochus. In the 13th year of Ptolemy, Seleucus ruled for 33 years over the Assyrians and Babylonians as far as the Indians. He finished the construction of Antioch and also built Seleucia, Laodicea, Apamea, Beria which is Aleppo, Balue, and Marash and settled Jews in them. And he honored them and allowed them to go and come to him as his dear ones. It was in this period that the great Tower of Alexandria was built in the sea of Nephros, and named Prutos. It was built by Sostratos of Kandi in a place across from Alexandria between land and the sea. Seleucus seized Demetrius in Cilicia and killed him. Demetrius had been ruling in rebellion; and then Seleucus himself ruled all of Asia. The start of his reign, which was 12 years following the death of Alexander, also marks the inception of dating according to the Syrian Era.

After the first Ptolemy ruled as king in Egypt, Ptolemy Philadelphius reigned for 38 years. In his first year, Ptolemy Ceraunus

---

25 Daniel 8.7-8.

ruled over the Macedonians for one year. He was followed by Meleager for two months and Antipater for 26 days. After Antipater, Sosthenes ruled for two years. In the fifth year of Ptolemy, Antiochus Soter reigned for 19 years, after Seleucus. In the sixth year of Ptolemy, Antigonus ruled over the Macedonians for 36 years.

Concerning the Translation of the Old Testament on the Island of Cyprus

In this same year, the 34th year of the Syrian Era,[26] 72 translators translated the Old Testament books on the island of Cyprus, *though others say that it was done in Alexandria, Egypt.* The group of translators comprised six men for each of the 12 tribes of the children of Israel. They were, from the line of Ruben: Yovsepos, Ezekiel, Eghise'e', Zak'aria, Yovhanne's, Ezekiel; from the line of Shmawon: Juda, Shmawon, Ade', Samuel', Mat'e', Saghamia; from the line of Levi: Noam, Yovse'p', T'e'odos, Bosos, Urania, Tukisos; from the line of Juda: Jonathan, Abari, Elise', Anania, Zak'aria, Ezekia; from the line of Issachar: Isaac, Jacob, Jesu, Shmbat, Shmawon, Levi; from the line of Zebulon: Juda, Yovse'p', Shmawon, Zak'aria, Shmawon, Saghamia; from the line of Gad: Smbatia, Sedekia, Yakovb, Isahak, Esayi, Matt'e'os; from the line of Asher: T'e'odos, Yason, Jesu, T'e'odotos, Yovhanne's, Jonathan; from the line of Dan: T'e'op'ile', Abraham, Idasmos, Isan, Eremia, Daniel; from the line of Naphthali: Jeremiah, Lazaru, Zachariah, Bania, Eghishe', Tat'an; from the line of Benjamin: Yovhanne's, Ilawos, Edki, T'e'odos, Nersam, Ezekiel; from the line of Joseph: Caleb, Samuel, Joseph, Juda, Jonathan, T'osdi.

They translated the Bible into Greek on the island of Cyprus, took their work to Egypt, and deposited it in the Palace. Others say that the translation was made on the island of Pharos. However, the truth is as we have described it.

---

26 B.C. 277.

In 62 of the Syrian Era,[27] and after 72 years of submission to the Greeks, the eastern areas of the Persians and the East reasoned that "the Macedonians have split apart and have grown weak. Moreover, they are distant from us and keep us in disorder with torments. What is there between them and us? Come, let us have a king closer to us." And they enthroned over themselves Arshak the brave, one of the descendants of Abraham from Kendura, in the city of Bahl,. This bordered the country of the Medes.

Moreover, the people of the land of the Hyrcanians who lived in the northern parts of the land of the Persians, when they saw that the House of the Persians had enthroned their own king, also enthroned a king of their own, sometimes obeying the Parthians and other times, not.

Similarly, the Armenians established their own king after the brave, triumphant and frightening kings from the line of Hayk who had done away with the kingdom of the Medes and had subdued all the kingdoms of the North and all the surrounding peoples. *We have not seen this described in their books and chronologies, and so we will write about it here.* Such Haykazean kings ruled until Alexander, who killed King Vahe' the Haykid and did away with the kingdom of the Armenians. The Armenians had remained without a king until this period, when again they established their kingdom from Palestine to the T'etalik', and to the other side of the Caspian Sea and Mount Caucasus. This new line began with Arshak's brother, Vagharshak, and endured until the last Arshak. We leave a description of them to other learned and trustworthy writers.

Following Philadelphius, Ptolemy Eugertes ruled Egypt. And in the same year there ruled over the Syrians Seleucus Callinicus, and over the Macedonians Demetrius Phillipus. In this period the High Priest was Onias, son of Simon the Just. This Onias did not want to pay taxes to Ptolemy and wanted to come to Jerusalem. They sent Josephus to make peace and he found favor before Ptolemy and received from him rule of the military over all Judah.

---

27 B.C. 249.

In 87,[28] Seleucus Ceraunus ruled over the Syrians for three years. He was succeeded by Antiochus the Great for 36 years. It was in this period that the Maccabeans were martyred.

In 93,[29] Ptolemy Philapator ruled over the Egyptians for 17 years. He greatly harassed the Jews. Antiochus fought with and defeated him, and then put Egypt under his rule. Leaving Egypt, he took Jerusalem. The first Book of Maccabees describes this.

In 110,[30] Ptolemy Epiphanes ruled over Egypt for 21 years. He sent the general Scopas who subdued Judah and Palestine. Then Antiochus arose against him, defeated him, and took the cities for himself. This Antiochus paved the roads of the cities and placed markers called parasangs to measure distance along the roads. He built stone bridges over rivers and streams and made the roads level to ease travelling. In the 11th year of his reign, he made war against the Romans and was defeated. He sent his son to Rome as a hostage and provided a yearly tax of 1,000 talents of gold. This was the beginning of Syria's payment of taxes to Rome.

In the third year of Antiochus, Philip ruled over the Macedonians for 24 years. And it was in this time that the prophecy of Daniel was fulfilled, which said that the king of the North would war against the king of the South—that is, Antiochus with Ptolemy. Some say that Ptolemy had given his daughter to him, but later took her back.

This Antiochus died in the land of the Elamites, stoned to death in the temple of their goddess Nena. Antiochus had earlier become possessed by a demon. Shmona and her sons were killed by him. Antiochus then took the advice of the wise men who told him to have fetched the remains of the people he had killed, to fall on his face in front of them, and to repent. And Antiochus commanded that the relics be brought to him. They placed the remains in baskets and brought them by donkey until they approached the city of Hadax, where some folk encountered them and informed

---

28   Of the Syrian Era, B.C. 224.
29   Of the Syrian Era, B.C. 218.
30   Of the Syrian Era, B.C. 201.

them of the king's death. They hid the remains at the place where they heard these tidings.

Afterwards, the relics were revealed through miracles. And they built a monastery there which exists to this day. After the death of Antiochus, Seleucus ruled and his loyal Diodorus greatly harassed the Jews and was punished by God.

In 131 of the Syrian Era,[31] there ruled in Antioch Antiochus Epiphanes, son of Antiochus who had been a hostage in Rome for 11 years. He went against Ptolemy in Egypt and the Romans stopped him. And so he turned and went against Judah. He gave the dignity of High Priest to Onias' brother, Jason, which caused disturbance between the two brothers. Matthias, son of John, son of Shmawon the priest who was of the sons of Jonathan sat in Modin. He had five sons: John, Shmawon, Judah Maccabee, Eliezer Awaran, and Jonathan. He killed those who had transgressed God's commands and then arose with his sons onto the mountain and rebelled from Antiochus.

In the year 149,[32] Antiochus Epiphanes died in Persia, suffering the same blows as his father, through the anger of God. For it had been Antiochus the Great who had defiled the Temple by erecting in it the image of Zeus, and on Mount Gerizim he built a temple to Zeus Xanthus as the Samaritans had requested. In the 18th year of Ptolemy, Epiphanes Eupator ruled for two years. He greatly harassed the Jews. He sent his military commander, Xo'r'gho'ra, with 120,000 troops against Jerusalem. Eliezer died under an elephant and a great multitude of Jews were destroyed. When they buried them, they found underneath their clothes images of the idols.

In this period Onias, without God's command, built a temple at Elispontos in Egypt similar to the Temple of Jerusalem. Priestly activity was conducted there according to the religious laws. Judah Maccabee rennovated the Temple in Jerusalem which continued to flourish until the era of Titus and Vespasian. After

---

31 B.C. 180.
32 Of the Syrian Era, B.C. 162.

Judah came Jonathan who was slain along with Alexander by Tryphon. Simon then occupied his position. He sent to Rome a golden shield and had brought a bronze tablet as a sign of the oath of allegiance. And he sent his son John and destroyed the troops of Antiochus and was freed from their taxes. It was in this period that the second Book of Maccabees concluded.

In 174,[33] Simon was slain by Ptolemy and his place was taken by John. In these times, a Jew became head of Edessa and remained in power until the ancestors of King Abgar came there. In this period John, the High Priest of the Jews, went to Hyrcania to war with them and for that reason was called Hyrcanus. In this period, Antiochus Agrippa reigned. He came to Jerusalem and harassed them. John Hyrcanus opened the tomb of King David and removed gold and the ornaments of all the kings, and took 3,000 talents of gold. Of this he gave 300 talents to Antiochus who then departed. In this period Hyrcanus ruined Samaria.

In the year 196,[34] Antiochus Soter reigned *in Egypt* for 17 years. In the same year, Antiochus and Hyrcanus with him went and killed the king of the Parthians, Sistis.

In the fourth year of Ptolemy, Antiochus Cyzikus ruled in Asorestan for 18 years. In the 11th year of Ptolemy, John Hyrcanus died and his position was taken by Aristobulus, son of Jonathan, for one year. Earlier he had been crowned king and now became High Priest. His two brothers, Alexander and Antiochus, treacherously killed each other according to the prophesy of their father with whom God spoke. Following Aristobulus his other brother, John, called Yanne', took his position for 17 years. He tormented his own people, the Jews.

In this period, Ptolemy was chased away by his mother, Cleopatra, and Ptolemy Alexander ruled for 10 years. In his sixth year, the kings of the Asians and Syrians were eliminated and Antioch submitted to the Romans. The books of the Old Testament and their narrations end at this point. From Adam to this point,

---

33 Of the Syrian Era, B.C. 137.
34 Of the Syrian Era, B.C. 115.

THE CHRONICLE

5,072 years had elapsed, and from here until the birth of Our Lord is an interval of 124 years. The duration of the kings of Asia, from Seleucus who ruled after Alexander until the Romans ruled, was 216 years.

In 222,[35] the persecuted Ptolemy returned to his throne and ruled for eight years. In 237,[36] Ptolemy Dionysius ruled for 30 years. He was the son of Soter and the brother of Cleopatra. In the fifth year of Ptolemy there died John Onias also called Alexander, and his wife, Alexandra, also called Salome who kept the religious laws, ruled the kingdom for nine years. She had three sons: Hyrcanus, Aristobulus, and Antiochus. Hyrcanus became the high priest but his brother disputed with him until he took the kingdom. Then Pompey, the military commander of the Romans, came and carried off Aristobulus in chains and established Hyrcanus as high priest for 34 years. He rebuilt the wall of Jerusalem which had been demolished by Pompey. It was at this time that the Jews became tax payers to the Romans. Pompey took much territory from the Armenians, Syrians, and Arabs, and grew so great that he was styled *Autocrator*.

In this period, Ptolemy died and Cleopatra ruled for 22 years. In her second year Pompey was slain by Gaius Julius Caesar.

Herod lived in these times. Here is his genealogy. Herod's father, a man named Antipater, son of Herod, was from Ascalon and was chief priest of the idol of Apollo. He was enslaved by the Edomites and his father, Herod, was unable to save him. He was nourished and raised among the Edomites and took as a wife Cypridis, the daughter of Aretas, king of the Arabs. He became friendly with Hyrcanus the high priest and helped him in his battle with his brother. For this he went to Pompey and became acquainted with the Romans. They designated him prince of the Jews. Now Antipater had four sons and a daughter named Salome. The sons Joseph and Phessalus were princes of the Jews with their father. One of the Jews poisoned Antipater and two of his sons, and then

---

35 Of the Syrian Era, B.C. 89.
36 Of the Syrian Era, B.C. 74.

Herod became prince of the Jews in his father's place. In his hour of need Herod went to Rome and informed them about the goings on.

In this period Barzaphran, the general of Armenia, came and enslaved Judah and took captive Hyrcanus, Herod's brother Pheroras, while Herod fled to Rome. *For it happened that when Barzaphran, military commander of the Armenians, had come to Jerusalem and captured it, he deposed Hyrcanus and replaced him with Antigonus. Then Barzaphran took Hyrcanus and Pheroras to Armenia, bound in chains.* Then he took over the kingdom of the Jews. Herod came back and killed Antigonus whom the Armenians had installed, and he himself sat on the throne. Then when Hyrcanus returned from the Bagratids after their attack on Jerusalem, Herod also killed him and his son, Jonathan. With this the prophecy was fulfilled which says: "Ruler and chief shall not depart from Judah until the one appears to whom the kingdom belongs."[37] It was at this point that leaders departed from the Jews.

And then it was that the Lord was born like a king's son in Bethlehem, in fulfillment of the prophecy of Daniel about the sevens, that "there shall be seven weeks and then sixty-two weeks,"[38] beginning in the sixth year of Darius and lasting for all eternity. In Abgar's translation of the Bible, it says that Daniel had grown ill and was dying by the Tigris River and he fell on his face and cried out to the Lord: "God, show me Your Christ before I die." And Gabriel came to him and said: "Rest in peace, oh fortunate man, for the time has not yet come. First, your prophecy about the sevens, then Christ will come and be crucified and He will come to you in hell and free you. So comfort yourself with the hope of His coming."[39]

Before Daniel's vision, they used the word *Bombios* to style the designation of kings. But at this point they called them *Autocrator*. In this period, the idols which were on Mt. Olympus were

---

37 Genesis 49:10.
38 Daniel 9.22-24; Jeremiah 29:20.
39 Daniel 9.21.

burned by lightning as Caesar Augustus reigned. This same emperor demolished the island of Lusitania and then began to wreck the islands one by one, since he found disturbances on them. But prior to this, there ruled Gaius called Julius. He was called "Caesar" which means in Latin "from the stomach" since this is how he was born, after his mother had died. It was his good fortune to rule as king, for kingship among the Romans had been disrupted for 462 years, from Tarquinius until Gaius Julius. From the founding of Rome until the second kingship, 702 years had elapsed. Now this Julius Caesar went to Egypt and strengthened the kingdom of the woman Cleopatra. The word "Gaius" translates *kaynan*. Andronicus says that Caesar ruled for five years before being slain secretly. Then Augustus reigned for 56 years and six months.

In the eighth year of Augustus, Herod ruled over the Jews and obstructed their kingship and priesthood. He took the ephod and bestowed it for bribes. He ruled for 35 years.

They did not accept him in Jerusalem at first, until he started to fight, pulling down the two walls and killing many of the Jews. Then he ruled over them. It was he who arranged that the high priest would change each year. Herod sent to Babylon and had Ananias brought back. He made Ananias High Priest for a year, even though he was not a Levite. After him, he made Aristobulus high priest. Aristobulus was son of the high priest Hyrcanus and his brother's wife. Then Herod killed him and reinstated Ananias. He transgressed the limits of the law and changed them each year for bribes. As a result, there were many high priests. However, when the time came for entering the Holy of Holies, none of them dared to do it. Only Zachariah and Abia were designated to enter, for they were not like the others, being pious and just.

In the third year of Augustus, Samosata fell under Roman control. The Armenian troops who had been near the Euphrates were defeated and gave taxes to Mesopotamia. In this period, Augustus' general, Antony, rebelled from Augustus. He went to Egypt, attracted by the fame of Cleopatra, with whom he fell in love. And he ruled with her. Then Augustus came against him and seized him. But at the entreaties of senators, he let them live and things calmed down. Augustus sent a great number of captives to Rome from there. Cleopatra had a grudge against the Jews, and the Arabs and requested from Antony rule over them, which he gave to her. On this account a second disturbance arose between Augustus and Antony. Again, Antony was defeated together with Cleopatra who also resisted Augustus. When Antony and Cleopatra saw themselves defeated, both committed suicide. Then Augustus killed Cleopatra's children named the Sun and the Moon. With this ended the Egyptians' monarchy, which dynasty the Greeks called Ptolemid, and which lasted for 296 years, and thereafter they were controlled by the Romans. Some say that after Augustus killed Antony, Cleopatra, and her children, he started to be called *Sebastos*, which means "victorious."

In this period, Judas the Galilean appeared in the city of Gamagha. He and the Pharisee Sadovk arose and said: "It is improper for us to pay taxes to the Romans." In the 19th year of Augustus, Augustus sent his military commander, Tiberius, to Armenia, and made peace with them. Returning from the Armenians he went to the land of Cyrenaica and subdued those folk who lived beyond Egypt. In this period, Herod built up Samaria and called it Sebastia after Augustus' name. He built P'anion in P'ania, and enlarged the palace in Jerusalem. He built the tower called Strato's Tower in the city and named that city Caesarea, after the emperor. He rennovated Gabas in Galilee. Herod frequently shed blood: he killed his wife named Mari and killed all those wise men among the Jews who knew the law.

In this time glad tidings came to the Blessed Virgin, and after nine months and five days she bore the life-giving Word of God, our Lord Jesus Christ. This was in the 43rd year of Herod, which is 315 of the Syrian Era.[40] From Adam's expulsion from Eden until the birth of Christ, 5,284 years had elapsed, according to Eusebius. But according to the Septuagint, it was 5,198 years. According to Ananius, it was 5,091, and according to others, 5,503

---

40 A.D. 4.

years. According to the Syrians, it was 5,026 years. Jesus' birth took place at the end of the year in the 12th month, on a Monday. *Accordingly, that time arrived and Jesus Christ, the anointed of God, was born in Bethlehem of Judah in the 44th year of the reign of Augustus. And the fire that descended from Heaven burned the homage paid to those idols, which supposedly housed deities, on Mount Olympus.*

This transpired in the first year of the reign of Abgar, and the 32nd year of Herod. Thus, in the temporal sense, our King Abgar was reigning at the same time as our Lord. According to the Septuagint, this occurred in the 5,108th year from Adam. According to Eusebius, the birth of Jesus took place in the 5,284th year; according to Anianus, 5,091 years; according to others, 5,503 years. Now according to the Syrians it was 5,026 years from Adam. The birth occurred on the first of the month of Nisan, on a Monday in a year of 12 months. It was at the time when Cyrenius was sent by the Senate to Syria and Palestine to take a census and levy taxes. For Rome had heard about the rebellious Theudas and Judas who were saying that the Jews should not pay taxes to a mortal king, and it was furious. This unprecedented measure was a result of the rebels.

In the 43rd year of Augustus, the Senate of Rome sent Prince Kiwrianos to make a census of the Jews and impose a tax. This was the cause of Judas the Galilean and many others saying: "It is not right that we should pay taxes to a mortal man." This was heard in Rome and the Romans were angry and conducted a census which had not been done until then.

In this same period, our Lord was born. Lucianus the Roman, who was in this area, described it. He wrote to the emperor telling him what had happened and saying: "Persians have come and entered your realm. They have brought gifts for a child born in Judah. But who he is or who his parents are, we still have not heard." Then the emperor wrote back: "We have established Herod as king over the Jews. He will write to us." The Magi arrived in the 35th year of Herod. Eusebius and the Nysian say that the Magi were descendants of Baghaam, while Jacob of Edessa says that they were descendants of Shem from the line of Ilam. Others say that they were descendants of the kings of Arab and Saba according to the words of David. They were three kings as three people offered gifts. Some say, with Micah, that they were eight kings, eight rulers of men. Saint James says they were 12 princes. It was found in books that they came with 3,000 cavalry and 500 infantry. When they reached the Euphrates River, at the place called Callinicus, which is Ragha, and learned that there was famine in Judah, they left their multitude there and 12 princes with 1,000 cavalry went on and saw Jesus. When they had seen him, they returned to their troops.

Their names were: Dahandur, son of Artawaz, Shat'e'p', son of Gudbar, Arshak, son of Mahdug, Zrewant, son of Variguid, Arihu, son of Xostrov, Artashe's, son of Uliat', Esht'ank'uza, son of Ishron, Mehduk', son of Hum, Ark'shirish, son of Sahapan, Saltana, son of Beltan, and Marudok', son of Bel.

The name of the king who sent them was P'ir-Shapuh. Some say that it was two years after the birth that the Magi arrived, but others say that they were advised by the stars two years in advance and then they arose and came. The Lord was born at night, and the Magi arrived in the morning. Mary, the Mother of God, remained in Bethlehem for 40 days and then went to the Temple. The old man Simon took the Anointed One in his arms. By the command of the Holy Spirit, Simon, who was one of the translators of the Septuagint, was kept alive from the time of Ptolemy. Now when Simon had been translating the book of the prophet Isaiah, he came to the passage which says: "Behold a virgin will get pregnant and give birth".[41] When he had written this translation, he regretted it and said: "How will the pagans believe this? Rather, they will laugh at us." He erased what he had just written and again was saddened and said: "But my colleagues will translate this passage and I will be ridiculed because of the discrepancy of having omitted it." In sorrow, he and his colleagues fell asleep and when they awoke they saw that passage written, as it were, in wondrous gold letters.

---

41 Isaiah 7:14.

Overjoyed, Simon wept and envied the era of the one born from a virgin, the eyes which would see Him and the lips which would kiss Emmanuel. Then the Spirit said to him: "You will not see death until you have seen the Anointed One." And the word of the Lord was fulfilled. At that time, when the promise was made, Simon was 60 years old, and he lived an additional 344 years until his wish came true. Now Joseph and Mary took the child and went to Nazareth after presenting Him in the Temple. At the angel's order they went to Egypt 62 years after the birth of the Lord. Others say that they went there two years after.

Herod destroyed the children, having been fooled by the Magi. He furiously burned the writings of the Jews and wiped out recollection of the kingdom and the priesthood so that he and his own sons should inherit the kingdom. However, by the providence of God, these writings were preserved in Egypt and in other lands. And God struck Herod with wicked pains from head to foot. All his limbs festered and the doctors were unable to help him. They put him into warm olive oil as a treatment and his pains increased. He seized the principal folk of the Jews and put them into prison. And then he ordered his son-in-law, Alexius, and his sister, Salome, that when he died, they should kill the people he had imprisoned. That way, the Jews, unwillingly, would weep on the day of his death. And they actually did this. Herod, tormented by wicked pains, killed himself—dying wickedly in the 35th year of his reign. Augustus designated Herod's son Archelaus as king. He ruled for nine years. After nine years, he was exiled to the city of Vienna because of his wickedness. Rule was taken by the tetrarch named Herod. In the same year, Augustus died and Tiberius reigned for 23 years.

The first Herod had nine wives and eight sons. From Dosios, he fathered Antipater, the son who killed his two brothers and was slain by his father. From Mari, who was Hyrcanus' daughter, he fathered Alexander and Aristobulus. Aristobulus was killed by Antipater as was the Herod called Antipater, the one who married Herodiade and killed John the Baptist. From the Samaritan

Melkos, King Herod fathered Archelaus who ruled after him. From Cleopatra of Jerusalem Herod fathered Herod and Philip. The latter took Herodiade from his brother as a wife. Later he, Philip, was slain by her. From Pallas, King Herod fathered Phazael.

King Herod's grandsons were as follows: Aristobulus, Alexander's brother, fathered Herod who ruled as king in Chalcis; Agrippa, called Herod, was the one who killed James, brother of John the Baptist and died, worm-eaten. He expelled his father-in-law and took over the kingdom. He had a son named Agrippa, who ruled after him, as well as the daughters Berenice and Drusilla who became the wife of Prince Felix. In the 14th year of Tiberius, which is 337,[42] Pilate was sent as prince to Judah, and one year later—5,537 years after Adam—the Lord was baptized in the Jordan by John. This was on January 6th, which is the 21st of the month of Tebeth, on a Sunday.

That same year Germanicus Caesar became more powerful against the Parthians, and Tiberius made Drusus part of his realm. He himself was poisoned to death. In the same year, the palace of Pompey burned down. In Tiberius' time, Herod built the cities of Tiberius and Bayis. Pilate put the image of Zeus in the Temple and the Temple's treasures were squandered on building an aqueduct in the water.

Concerning the Selection and Martyrdom of the Apostles

In this year the Apostles were chosen:

Simon Peter, from the clan of Nepthali. It was he who built the first altar in Antioch. In the time of Emperor Claudius, Peter went to Rome, remaining there for 25 years. In the 13th year he was martyred by Nero. Andrew, his brother, who preached in Nicaea and Nicomedia, in Scythia and Achaea. The first episcopal throne at Ephesus was his. James, son of Zebedee, from the clan of Zabulon, who was slain by Herod Agrippa. His body was buried

---

42 Of the Syrian Era, A.D. 16.

at Marmarike'. John, his brother, who preached in Asia. He lived until the seventh year of Trajan and died a glorious death. Philip, from the clan of Azer, in Beth Said. He preached in Africa and was buried in Pisidia. Bartholomew, from the clan of Issachar, from the village of Adawir, who preached among the Armenians and died a wondrous martyr's death in the city of Ubianos, which is now called Haghbat. He was martyed by the wicked and pagan Sanatruk. Thomas, from the clan of Judah preached among the Parthians, Medes, and Indians, and was martyred there. Matthew, from the clan of Issachar, from Nazareth. He died in Gabala, was burried at Antioch and later his remains were transported overseas. Simon the Canaanite, from the clan of Ephrem, reposed in Hama, though in another place we found it given as Cyrrus. Judas, called Thaddeus, who, because of his wisdom was called *Lebeos*, which means heart and soul, preached in Armenia and Asorestan and was martyred by Sanatruk in Armenia, at the place where he struck a rock and 13 streams gushed forth. The names of the Twelve Apostles and the other, our Savior Jesus Christ, remain till this day as a cure for all diseases and sicknesses. Judas' venerable body and the relics of his bones and of the blessed Sanduxt, were buried at the sites of their martyrdom. James, son of Alphe from the line of Manasseh, who died in Seruj. Judas the betrayer from the line of Dan from the village of Iscariot. Matthew, his replacement, from the line of Ruben, who was martyred in the country of the cannibals.

Josephus wrote about our Lord as follows: "In our day, there appeared a man named Jesus who worked many miracles. It was clear that he was the Anointed. Out of envy, they betrayed him to the judge Pilate. They killed him on the cross. But after three days, they saw him alive and those who believed in him did not quit him. And it was confirmed that he himself was the son of the living God."

Now according to Josephus' testimony, the Twelve Apostles, whom we named above, were the first to believe in Him. Then they chose 72 disciples, named as follows: Ade', Axe', Lazarus, Anania, Yakovb, Eghia, Barnabas, Sosthenes, Cyriaque, Yovse'p', Nicodemus, Nathaniel, Judas, Justus, Sylla, Barnabas, Yovhanne's, who is Mark, Amius, Nigh, Yason, Manil, Kiwrine', Alexandrus, Shmawon, Kiwrine', Lukios, Cleophas, Sime'on, Yovsa, Budisos, Diwstros, Zabidon, Titus, Patroba, Ermi, Ason Kritos, Priscus, Luke, Aristobulus, Demas, Timothy, Levi, Ephrem, Herovde's, Silubanos, Nicetas, Yovhanne's, T'e'odos, Nikos, Martulos, Lasion, Zak'aria, son of a widow who died in Nayin, Simon the leper, Stephen, Eustace, Apeghe's, Iston, Shmawon, Yovse'p', who is Barnabas, Erasos, Aminas, Yulios, Philipos, Prok'oron, Nikanovr, Timon, Parmena, Agabos, Kep'as, about whom Paul said that he would turn against him.

And Paul himself, a vessel of selection, who—although he considered himself unworthy to write the Gospel—was a great figure for everyone. In this period, Philo the philosopher, an Alexandrian Jew, appeared. He wrote about events of the Jews, about Gaius who deified himself, about the ascetics of Egypt, an interpretation of Genesis, about the products of the earth, and about the mentality of the just, who pray upon rising. Philo wrote about the decay of language, on the work of teaching, on the diverse names of writings, and on two Testaments, five homilies about seeing things in dreams, five homilies about the spirit leaving the body, four homilies on the laws of the faith, and many other things. In the days of Emperor Claudius, his writings were placed in the royal treasury in Rome.

In this period, there were seven sects among the Jews, as Josephus tells us. First were the Scribes, called the Lawkeepers; second were the Levites, who held the ancient traditions; third were the Pharisees, who believed in resurrection as did the Scribes, and also in angels and the soul. They fasted twice a week, baptized frequently, believed in astrology and fortunes. The fourth sect was the Saducees, who did not accept resurrection, angels, and the soul, and were named after a certain priest called Sadovk. The fifth sect was the Baptists, who said that a man could not live unless he was baptized every day. Sixth were the Abstainers, who did not eat anything animate and did not accept Moses and the prophets and they had other sacred writings instead of what the others had. Seventh were those who keep the faith, accept the prophets, and God in one person, and they do not comprehend the power of Scripture.

Concerning Abgar, who sent an aritist to Jerusalem to make a portrait of Christ

In the 19th year of Emperor Tiberias, Abgar, king of the Armenians, wrote a letter of entreaty to Jesus and sent it via his loyal envoy, Anania, begging Him to come to him and be his co-ruler. Abgar believed in Him and revered Him before His torments. And Jesus wrote an answer felicitating Abgar. He promised that after His resurrection He would send to him through one of His disciples a preacher and cause of life. Abgar, because of the warmth of his love for our Lord, again sent the artist Yovhanne's to make His picture and bring it back so that he might enjoy it. Yovhanne's went but was unable to duplicate His beauty because it was transformed from glory to glory. The artist was amazed. Then this source of pity and mercy requested a cloth, put it over His face, and impressed His features on it. This occurred 24 days before His torments. The cloth was brought back and given to Abgar, and very great miracles and wonders resulted from it prior to the arrival of the Apostle Thaddeus. In the same year, the Lord died, was buried, resurrected, and appeared to His disciples. He blessed them, confessing the Holy Spirit. And then He ascended to Heaven. Now in that same year on the day of Pentecost, Pilate introduced the image of Caesar into the Temple, as Josephus informs, and a voice was heard from the Divine Grace there, saying: "I depart from this place and will never return." Philo recalls this in his second book.

In the 19th year of Emperor Tiberias, Abgar, king of the Armenians and Syrians, heard the news about Our Lord, worshipped and believed in Him. He sent Him a letter via his loyal envoy, Anania, beseeching Him to come and heal his own ailments. These were ailments he had acquired some seven years previously in Persia. And Abgar asked Jesus to rule along with him.

Now the Lord promised that after His crucifixion and resurrection He would send a physician from among His disciples to heal him, and He also made him worthy of a reply and greetings.

The fortunate king, to satisfy his longing sent his painter John to make a portrait of Him in place of His presence. John came and saw Jesus and tried to capture His beauty on the fabric Abgar had provided. But he was unable to do this, because Jesus' face was transformed from glory to glory and rejoiced in the faith He would bring to the heathens. And so, the Source of Kindness asked him for the cloth, placed it over His face, and impressed His features upon it. Then He returned it to the painter.

This occurred seven days before the Passion of Christ. The icon was brought and presented to the king and it worked many miracles before the coming of the Apostle Thaddeus to Edessa. That same year the Lord voluntarily died on the Cross, was buried, resurrected, destroyed Hell, freed creation, and after 40 days rose to the Father.

Here is what Josephus wrote:

In our day a man appeared who was named Jesus. By the number of miracles he wrought, it appeared that he was the Christ. But because of jealousy, the impious betrayed him to the judge Pilate, and they crucified him. After three days, he was seen alive. Those who believed in him did not abandon their faith in him. And to the present, the belief in him grows. And it was confirmed that He was the Christ, son of the Living God.

Josephus adds that during the same year at the time of the feast of Pentecost, Pilate placed an image of the emperor in the Temple. And a voice was heard saying: "I will leave this place and never return." Philo recalls the same thing in his second book.

Now concerning the seamless robe of the Lord, Saint Ephrem records that the soldiers cast lots for it rather than dividing it. It fell to a soldier under the command of the centurion Longinus, who subsequently took it and brought it to the land of the Galatians, to his own city of Mok'son, where it is revered to this day. Another centurion, a Laz, delivered his portion of the clothing to his own

THE CHRONICLE

city of P'ud,[43] *the capital of the Egerians, where it was placed in a glass vessel and suspended in the Church where it remains, untouched by anyone and visible to everyone. This was the seamless robe woven by Abgar's sister and presented to Our Lord by the messenger Anania.*

Agrippa went to Rome where he accused his father-in-law, Herod. And Herod was arrested by Tiberius. Abgar, king of the Armenians, wrote to him three times about Christ's divinity, and complained about the Jews. Abgar also wrote to Nerseh in Babylon and to the Persian king. This was done through God's providence so that there would not be conflict about the new faith and so at first the spread of the blessed Gospel would proceed without resistance. Christianity quickly spread during the reigns of these kings who did not reject Christ's divinity. This was influenced by King Abgar, the first blessed king who extended his hand to Christ, just as David had said. Tiberius, died after living 78 years, and having reigned for 23 years.

Herod reigned for 23 years. It was he who killed John the Baptist, and Herod and his wife were punished by the Lord. They were put in prison in fetters in Pawania in Spain, and then both of them were killed. After Tiberius, Gaius reigned. He removed Agrippa from prison and made him king of the Jews. At the same time, he sent the judge Felix to Egypt where he greatly harassed the Jews for five years and polluted their place of worship with unclean sacrifices. For this reason, the Jews sent envoys to beseech Gaius. The delegation included the Hebrew philosopher Philo of Alexandria.

But Gaius did not listen to them. Instead, he sent the prince of the Syrians to Patrania to put his image in all the sanctuaries and temples to be worshipped as a god. And thus was fulfilled what was said in Daniel[44] about reaching the depths of abomination.

In this period, there appeared Simon, Kerindos, and Menander. And Philo and the Apostle Peter met one another in

---

43   *Poti in Mingrelia.*
44   Daniel 9:27.

MICHAEL THE GREAT

Rome and conversed with each other in the presence of Gaius. Philo asked John, who was a student of Christ: "What is God?" and John replied: "God is love." When Philo accepted this, John took him to his home, became friends with him, and Philo believed and was baptized. Gaius was slain by one of the eunuchs because of his extreme severity. He had reigned for four years. Then Claudius reigned for 14 years. Agrippa ruled for seven years after being tetrarch for three years. He attacked Herod and later the angel of God struck and killed him.

During Claudius' reign, one time on the feast of Passover, suddenly there was a mob in Jerusalem at the Temple. Thirty thousand people trampled each other to death. Claudius set up Agrippa's son, Agrippa, as king of the Jews and sent Felix as judge for the Galileans and Samarians. Claudius, after reigning for 13 years, died in his own home. Then Nero ruled the kingdom for 13 years. Nero sent Festus and removed Felix, before whom Paul had appeared. Once again, Nero removed Festus and put Lambius in his place. Then he removed Lambius and put Belurus in his position. It was during his tenure that the Jews revolted from Caesar. In this period, in Rome, fire fell from the sky and burned many structures with mobs of people in them. Nero, in the 13th year of his reign, started a persecution against the Church and killed the Apostles. He sent Vespasian and his son Titus to Jerusalem because of the rebellion of the Jews.

Now the general and historian Josephus was fortified in the city of Yodfat. Vespasian went there, took the city of Yodfat and destroyed it. General Josephus went before him and said: "I bring glad tidings to you, Vespasian, for soon Nero will die and you will rule in his place." For this reason, Vespasian did not kill him. Meanwhile, Nero, who was loathed by everyone, killed himself. Then Galba ruled for seven months and was killed in Rome. Suratolos ruled in Germany and Otho ruled in Rome. The latter killed himself after three months. Then Vitellius ruled for eight months, but a mob went against him and killed him. When news of this reached Vespasian's troops who were with him, they declared him emperor and Dictator. When this happened, Vespasian left his son Titus over Jerusalem and went to Egypt, subduing those areas for himself. From those parts he went by sea to Rome and ruled over them for nine years and nine months.

Titus took Jerusalem on the Feast of Passover and 1,260,000 Jews died. Jerusalem was pulled apart completely and the Temple was burned in the month of Ahek.[45]

From the time of Adam's expulsion from Eden 5,437 years had elapsed, and from the resurrection of our Lord, 40 years. From the initial construction until this destruction, 2,192 years had elapsed. Jerusalem was taken in the third year of Vespasian. Prior to this there were 3,000,000 people in Jerusalem. On that Passover when they assembled, there were sacrificed for Passover 250,000 lambs and each lamb fed ten pure people, while the impure were unable to eat. Those who ate totaled 2,100,000. Sixty thousand people died from the sword, 1,100,000 died of hunger, and 100,000 were taken captive. Those over the age of 15 were sent to Egypt to work at making bricks, while those under 15 were divided up among the troops. This was the 40 year period that God gave as time for the Jews to repent, and when they did not repent, God exacted vengeance for the blood of the son of God. With this, the kingdom of the Jews ended.

There remained only the kingdom of the Romans throughout the whole world, with the exception of the Armenians who also had their own kings. After Vespasian, his son Titus reigned. In his second year, he was deified by the troops and, in his impious mind, he himself believed this. An angel of the Lord struck him and he died. Then his brother Domitian reigned for 15 years and five months. He expelled from Rome all the astrologers and witches and also commanded that vineyards not be planted. In this period, Christianity grew. Patrophilus asked his teacher Ursinus: "What does it mean that such a multitude believe in a man who was crucified? Even the philosophers Theodorus of Athens, Africanus of Alexandria, and Martinus the *hypatos* believe in him, abandoning the

---

45 August.

pleasures of this world." Ursinus replied: "Do not be surprised by this, for I believe that the very gods have submitted to him. And Patrophilus asked: "How is that?" Ursinus said: "It is because his doctrine, which is about purity, innocence, and unselfishness, makes it clear that it is above all those other doctrines."

Domitian stopped the induction of eunuchs into the army. During his reign two months had their names changed: September became Germanus, and October became Parthenicus. Domitian also ordered that the race of David be exterminated, so that there would be no heir to the kingdom of the Jews. He also persecuted many Christians, among whom was the evangelist John.

In this period, Apollonius of Tyana made many talismans with much diabolical power and said: "Alas, the son of Mary preceded me. Otherwise, I would have subdued the entire world through my art." Now Domitian was killed because of the severity of his ways and the line of Vespasian was eliminated. Then Nerva, who ruled for one year, and was declared a god by the Senate, sickened with disease and died. He was followed by Trajan for 19 years. He persecuted Christians and Simon, son of Cleophas, bishop of Jerusalem and Ignatius, bishop of Antioch, were martyred. At the emperor's order, Plinius Secundus killed many Christians. However, he repented and wrote to Trajan, saying: "The Christians are good in everything, except that they do not sacrifice to the idols and they worship Christ in the morning." Trajan responded: "Kill them."

In this period, the Jews in Egypt rebelled and made a man named Lysias their king. He took the Jews and went to Jerusalem. Then Trajan sent Lucius who destroyed myriads of them. In these times, the Jews of Cyprus fought against the city of Salamis. Having taken the city, they killed the Greeks in it. Similarly, the Jews in Libya fought and warred with the Greeks. The Greeks in Alexandria and in Cyrene started a war and were destroyed by them. In this period, the philosopher Secundus the Silent appeared. After Trajan, Hadrian reigned for 21 years.

In the fourth year of his reign, the line of Armenian kings at Edessa came to an end. Princes remained there while the kingship remained in Greater Armenia. *After Trajan, Hadrian ruled for 21 years. In the fourth year of his reign the kings came to an end in Edessa. In Greater Armenia a king remained.* In the 18th year of Hadrian, the Jews of Jerusalem rebelled, deceived by a man named Star.[46] Hadrian sent troops and crushed them and expelled the Jews from Jerusalem, such that they did not dare even to look toward Jerusalem. He demolished Jerusalem and built nearby a city, Ilius Hadrianus, settling Christians and pagans in it. He ordered that the ears of the Jews be cut off so that they would be noticeable wherever they were. He also stipulated that Christians should not be persecuted without cause. In the 21st year of his reign the first council was held at Nicaea with 23 bishops, and they anathematized Sabellius the Libyan who said that the Holy Trinity was contained in one person. They also anathematized Valentinian, who claimed that Christ's body had been brought from heaven. The translator Aquillus lived in these days.

Following Hadrian, Antoninus Pius—called Sebastus and Abgar—and his sons ruled for 22 years. The name Antoninus translates as "father of the land." In his day Justin of Nicopolis, which is near Jerusalem, went to Rome and gave a letter of petition to the emperor and the persecutions of Christians ceased. In his day, Polycarpus, the bishop of Smyrna, was martyred.[47] At this time, Cerdon, who is Marcion, and Mark came to Rome, saying that there had been no resurrection, and that the religious laws were wicked. Nor would they say that Jesus the son was the one about whom the faith and the prophets had prophesied, but rather the son of the invisible benefactor. And they were witches. When baptizing they would speak "in the name of the invisible father, the true mother, and in the name of the son which descended on Jesus." And they added other things to this.

---

46   Bar Kochba.
47   A.D. 155.

MICHAEL THE GREAT

In 475 of the Syrian Era,[48] there reigned Marcus Aurelius along with the son of Antoninus and Lucius, for 19 years. In the first year of their reign, Vagharsh, who was ruling over the Persians, came to the land of the Romans and laid to waste many districts. Antoninus, Lucius, and brothers went against them and subdued Parthia and Persia. Lucius Verus, who had grown strong, was designated *Caesar* among his brothers. There were also wars among the Romans and Germans, the Karuts, Sarmatians, and Galileans. Again, Lucius grew powerful and was called *Autocrator*. Lucius ruled for nine years and died. Antoninus took his son, Commodus, as a co-ruler in the kingdom, since he was harassed by those around him. Antoninus sickened and died. Then Commodus ruled for 13 years and was strangled in his stable. After him Pertinax ruled for six months and was slain. Then Severus ruled for 18 years. In his first year there was a great war between the Jews and the Samarians. In Severus' ninth year he stirred up persecution of Christians and many were martyred. In his day, there arose a barbarian people in the northwest. Severus went against them and was killed. Then his son, Caracalla, ruled for seven years. He returned those who had been exiled because of their faith. One such was Alexander, bishop of Jerusalem. Caracalla was killed in Mesopotamia, between Edessa and Harran. Then Macrinus ruled for one year[49] and was killed. Then Antoninus Elagabalus reigned for four years. In his time, Nicopolis was built in the land of the Philistines and called Emmaus. After him ruled Alexander, son of the pious and believing woman Mame, who effected many good things for Christians. In the third year of his reign, in the year 542 of the Syrian Era[50] there ruled in Persia Artashir, son of Babak. With him begins the Persian kingdom which lasted for 418 years and is called the kingdom of the Sasanians. Twenty-seven kings of that line ruled one after the other, until the Arab kingdom of Muhammad arose and eliminated it.

48   A.D. 163.
49   A.D. 217-218.
50   A.D. 231.

THE CHRONICLE

After Alexander, Philip ruled for seven years, and the Christians were in peace. In his first year Shapur, son of Artashir, ruled for 31 years. In this period the thousandth anniversary of the building of Rome was completed. Decius killed Philip and his son and ruled for one year, to be slain by Burdos Herenius. Then for a year there ruled Burinos[51] and Damurinos, and Gaghos, and Balos. Then there ruled Valerian and Gallienus[52] for 15 years. And they stirred up persecution against the Church. Shapuh, king of the Persians, laid waste to Syria and Cilicia and Cappadocia with slave taking. Goths crossed the Danube River, enslaved the land and took their captives back with them. And then Gallienus stopped persecuting the church of God and, by the grace of God, the faith grew through miracles performed by the hands of holy men, and so that God would exact vengeance from the persecuting kings, those enemies of truth.

In the year 588,[53] Claudius ruled for one year. After him, Aurelian ruled for six years and six months. He built another wall for Rome, renewed persecutions, was struck by lightning and died. And the persecution ceased. Then Tacitus ruled for six months, until he was slain in Pontus. Then Florian ruled until he was killed in Cilician Tarsus. Meanwhile Hurmazd ruled in Persia.

In 593 of the Syrian Era,[54] Constantine was born. Following Florian, Probus reigned for seven years. In the same year, Vahram reigned in Persia for three years. After Vahram his son reigned for 15 years. Now when the senator wanted to rebel against Rome, he fortified himself in Antioch, but he was slain. Following Probus, Carus and his sons Carinus and Numerianus ruled for two years. Carus died in Mesopotamia while Numerianus was killed in Africa and Carinus died fighting in Cappadocia. Then Diocletian ruled and here began dating according to Diocletian's era, which began in 594 of the Syrian Era.[55] After Diocletian, there ruled

51 Hostilian.
52 253-268.
53 Of the Syrian Era, A.D. 277.
54 A.D. 282.
55 A.D. 283.

Maximianus, whose sister was Diocletian's wife and Maxindes, who was Maximian's son ruled in Rome while Constantine ruled in Gaul. Both reigned at the same time.[56]

Diocletian and Maximian ruled jointly in the East. In these times Egypt rebelled. The Romans went to subdue it and many were slain. In the 11th year of Diocletian, Narseh ruled in Persia for seven years. He was followed by his son Hurmazd[57] for five years.

Concerning the Severe Famine that Occurred in Diocletian's time

Now in the 19th year of Diocletian, churches were demolished, persecutions increased, and with this came a severe famine to the point that one *modi* of grain cost 2,5000 *dram*s. And then, because of Diocletian's wickedness, God struck him. He gave up the kingdom to Maximian who was no less evil. As for Diocletian himself, he was troubled by various pains and he festered. Diocletian knew that this blow was from God and wrote a letter of peace for the Church and permitted the building of churches.

Maximian did not want this and was unable to cancel the order. Rather, he temporarily stopped the persecution. But again, he claimed that "the gods command that we continue the persecution," and he started to persecute and to remove Christians from the city. And then the land was punished by plague and so much premature death, to the point that ten corpses were buried in one grave. He intensified warfare with the Armenians and the wrath of God came upon him and he died in bitter pain.

After this Constantine's father, Constant, ruled. He had two wives, Helena and Theodora, Maximian's daughter. In the eighth year of his reign, he associated with himself as ruler his son Constantine, Helene's son, who was co-ruler with his father for three years. Then the father died, and Constantine ruled in 623 of the

---

56 In the West.
57 Hormizd II, 302-309.

THE CHRONICLE

Syrian Era.[58] John of Asia says that the father had turned to worshipping the Christian God and that Sylvester cured the father of leprosy. Peter and Paul had appeared to Constant, advising him to summon Sylvester to baptize him. Socrates the Roman testifies to this. Ignatius of Melitene says that when Constantine ruled, others were ruling: Maximian, the other Maximian, Maxence, and Severus, all four of whom were persecutors and that when Severus died, his princes gave the kingdom to Constantine and declared as *Caesar* his son-in-law, Licinus. After ruling for seven years, Constantine made Licinus his co-ruler. Licinus secretly persecuted Christians and subsequently rebelled and was killed by him.

In the third year of Constantine, Shapur reigned as king of the Persians for 70 years. Constantine went to battle against Maximian who was in Rome. Constantine reasoned with himself, saying: "The idols in no way helped former kings." And he declared: "If God helps me in this war, I shall worship Him." In the middle of the day, he saw a radiant cross with writing on it that said: "With this shall you conquer." Others with him also saw it. That night, Christ appeared and said to him: "Make a model of the cross which appeared to you and you shall triumph." Arising at dawn, he did this. And so it became a law of Christian emperors to put a cross at the head of the army. When the battle took place, the cross that had appeared did conquer the impious one who was drowned in the Tiber River. Now Constantine's wife, Diocleta, was Diocletian's daughter. The two of them were baptized together since Constantine still had not been baptized.

In this period, the great Gregory, who was glorifying Armenia with very great miracles, converted all the Armenians to the faith. Gregory was to them a preacher and chief priest with venerable grace like the blessed Apostles of Christ. *In these times appeared the sun of the East, the wonderful Grigorios Part'ew.*[59] *With very great and unusual miracles he illuminated all the Armenians*

---

58 A.D. 312.
59 *Gregory the Illuminator.*

in the diocese of the Apostles Thaddeus and Bartholemew, resembling them in every way. It was he who baptized his relative, King Trdat, and, taking him, went joyfully to Constantine, witnessing many miracles along the way.

Constantine greeted them and held festivals to celebrate their arrival, with all the grandeur of his kingdom.

They consulted together about the regulation of the Church, and about the good of the land, and they made an unbreakable vow with each other. Then the Armenians returned to their own land filled with honors and gifts.

In the third year of his reign, Constantine enlarged Byzatium, making it grow by four *mils*. He adorned it with ornaments and transferred the seat of the empire to it from Rome. He called it Constantinople after his own name. He made its inhabitants free, built a church to the great Irene and another church named after the blessed Apostles. He appeared as the sole *Autocrator*, placing all his cares in the hands of God. He ordered that churches should be built throughout the country and that the pagan temples be demolished. Constantine also made it a law that no one should be a soldier or horseman who had not experienced rebirth in the blessed baptismal font. T'ĕodos says that artists adorned boards and masonry with images to delight the viewers. And chroniclers have adorned this period with words.

The Heretic Arian

Now it was in this period that the presbyter, Arius of Alexandria, appeared among seven priests whom Satan used as a weapon, attempting to repeat the worship of created beings. For Satan had him say that the Son of God was a created being. Arius had six other like-minded priests as is demonstrated in the letter written to Eusebius of Nicomedia. Their names are Eusebius of Caesarea, T'ĕodos of Laocidea, Julian, bishop of Tyre, Athanasius of Anazarb, Grigor of Taruth, and Athis of Lydia. When their wickedness was revealed, Bishop Peter anathematized them. And Arius began to take many adherents including Maris of Chalcedon, Eusebius of Nicomedia, and Melitos, bishop of the Egyptians—who, during the period of persecutions, had made sacrifices to pagan gods and was removed from his position—Aithales, and many others.

In this same period, there occurred a severe earthquake in Egypt which damaged many buildings and their inhabitants, and presaged the Arian heresy. There was a similar rent in the Church over the feast of Pascha, since the Eastern areas[60] along with the Jews commemorated Zatik on the 14th day of the lunar month, while the Western areas always celebrated it on Sunday. First, Alexander held a meeting of a multitude of bishops in Alexandria and anathematized Arius and those who shared his views. He also wrote imprecations condemning Arianism and had them taken to all the churches in the country. However, the corrupting flames were not quenched until the matter came to Emperor Constantine's attention. The latter was deeply saddened and wrote letters to Bishop Alexander and to Arius so that they reconcile with each other and in order to remove the evil idea from Arius' mind. But this did not quell the conflict in the Church and the heresy began to spread. Then, Constantine the Great promulgated an order throughout the country that an assembly be convened at Nicaea in Bithynia. Three hundred and eighteen bishops assembled.

The principals were: Osius from Cordoba, Vitus and Vincent, priests from Rome representing the Pope, Alexander of Alexandria, Aristake's of Greater and Lesser Armenia, Julius of Sebastia, Eustace of Antioch, and Jacob of Nisibis.

The emperor had built a large and expansive palace where the assembly was seated. He himself, standing, personally served them. And they observed the grace of God on the emperor's face, and they placed a chair for him in their midst and begged him to be seated. The emperor, however, ignored this and continued standing and serving their needs and listening to their discourse. There were, among the bishops, thousands and tens of thousands of priests and deacons. The emperor saw to all their needs at his own

---

60 Of the Byzantine empire.

expense, from the 20th day of the month of Iar until the 18th day of the month of Haziran.

Initially, they began to discuss matters using the rhetorical style of philosophers, and many of them followed this practice. Then, a certain young prince arose and said: "Christ and the Apostles did not address us using artful words, but rather with a firm faith preserved through virtuous deeds." And so they were silent and left matters to the churchmen, who established the profession of faith of the Apostles. There were many who were opposed to this. The emperor removed the dissidents from the ranks of the assembly and the count of participants was incremented with true believers. There were some who presented to the emperor letters of opposition and jealousy regarding each other and Constantine reconciled them and burned the disputatious letters. The emperor implored them to commemorate together the Feast of the Resurrection of Christ, and also urged that Sunday should be glorified with assembly and occupation with religious matters.

And thus did they designate Sunday to celebrate the Resurrection of Christ our God following the old Jewish festival of Pesach. They also designated that Sunday should be revered by rest from activities, with readings from the canons of the Apostles and other theological writings, rather than with pleasurable activities, and that Saturday should be devoted to commemorating the martyrs. The emperor himself stipulated that those dishonoring the priests and bishops should be executed with an evil death. *For the emperor had heard about this from Sylvester and from Gregory the Parthian[61], and thus did they canonize this by order of the Holy Spirit. With his own hand the emperor issued an edict ordering death by evil and bitter torture for those who dishonored the clerics.* This meeting took place in the 20th year of Constantine, which was the 5,833rd year from Adam. The emperor dismissed the assembly with honor and gifts. And they anathematized Arius, Eusebius, bishop of Nicomedia, Theognis, bishop of Nicaea, Maris of Chalcedon, and Theonas of Marmarica—the principal men.

---

61 *Gregory the Illuminator.*

Now it happened that Empress Helena, *the emperor's mother,* had a vision while dreaming. She arose and went to Jerusalem with Sylvester, the patriarch of Rome, and discovered the statue of Astghik which is Aphrodite, on the tomb of Christ, as well as the blessed Cross of Christ which had been buried for a long time. After torturing Jews she found the Cross which had been buried by Judas. At this time the bishop of Jerusalem was named Macarius. After building churches, the empress entrusted them to Macarius. She established a class of virgins and clerics in Jerusalem and cared for them at her own expense.

But Arius, by means of some other cheats, tricked the emperor into seeing him and hearing his doctrine from him. The emperor so ordered granting an interview. Arius wrote a lengthy document reflecting the faith of Nicaea, and a short one reflecting his own false doctrine, which he concealed in his sleeve. He presented the long bull to the emperor and said: "I profess nothing more than this." When he received the longer document back from the emperor, Arius put his hand on the shorter document containing his own blasphemies and said: "May there be severe curses on anyone who claims that I glorify God in any way differing from what is written here." And the emperor believed him to the point that God disgraced him with creating a division. The emperor was even more confirmed in the faith and with great care took pity on the churches, allowing them freedom throughout the country and making their property and earnings free from taxation. And he said: "All churches should have the complete Old and New Testaments available, and orphans and widows should be maintained at Church expense, and clerics should be knowledgeable in Biblical writings. Moreover, the Church should maintain some astronomers skilled in the science of calendars, to keep the accurate observance of feasts and heavenly bodies, though the Church should not entertain the other nonsense of astrology." *He also ordered that portable canvas churches be constructed to take along when he was traveling during battles, so that the mass and communion could be properly celebrated in his presence.*

Constantine had three sons. The senior son was named after his father, the middle son was named Constans, and the youngest, whom he made *Caesar*, was named Costas. The eldest son adhered to Orthodoxy until death, as did the youngest. Emperor Constantine had his eldest son reside in Constantinople, the middle son, in the Eastern parts, and the youngest in Rome. This period saw the beginnings of Christian faith among the Indians and the Iberians. Constantine created a tent church to circulate around with him. He built a large octagonal church in Antioch. And he built a bridge over the Danube River, by which he led the troops to the Scythians, who are the Russians. Some of the Russians he killed while others he converted to Christianity.

In this period, Shapuh, king of the Persians, came to Nisibis and turned back in disgrace. Jacob of Edessa says that "Constantine wanted to go against the Persians and, going to Nicomedia, became ill, asked for baptism, and was baptized. For until then he had not been baptized, hoping to be baptized in the Jordan River. He made a will concerning his three sons and entrusted it to an Arian priest named Eusebius. Constantine, who had reached the age of 65 and reigned for 32 years, died peacefully on the great Sunday of Pentecost, which was the 22nd day of the month of Iyar. His body was taken to Constantinople and placed in the Church of the Holy Apostles.

According to the will, the eldest son received the throne of Constantinople, the middle son, Antioch and the Eastern areas, and the youngest, Rome. On the day of Constantine's death, the middle son was close by in Nicomedia and took the will from that priest Eusebius. Constantine's senior son went to Rome, to the land of his younger brother. *Constantine the Great also had a brother named Dalmatius who had two sons, Gallienus and Julian.* Constantine's youngest son, Costas, designated Dalmatius as *Caesar* in Rome. He was the brother of Constantine the Great. Dalmatius killed Constantine, the eldest son of Emperor Constantine, against the will of the younger brother. Then Costas killed Dalmatius in return for the slaying of his brother the king.

Now Dalmatius had two sons, Gallienus and Julianus, and they wanted to kill them too but did not, for Gallienus was sick and Julianus was a boy, and so they thereby escaped. Later, Costas was reconciled with them and put them into school in a village named Makali, close to Armenian Caesarea. When they had advanced in their studies, they became lovers of martyrs and began building a martyrium to Saint Mamas. The part built by Gallienus stood fast, while the part built by Julian crumbled—which presaged what was to come.

The middle brother, Costas, established Gallienus as *Caesar* in Antioch. He rebelled against the emperor. When the emperor heard about this, he sent and had him killed, and put Julian in prison. However, through the intercession of Empress Eusebia with the emperor, Julian was removed from prison and sent to Athens to study philosophy. Gregory the Theologian, Basil, and his brother Gregory Nazianus were there in Athens and they prophesied what was to happen regarding Julian.

In this period, Constans, son of Constantine the Great, built a city in the Seleucia and named it Constantinople. In the sixth year of Constans, Magnentius rebelled and seized Italy and Africa from Constans, and ruled in Sirmium. Through treachery the troops killed Costos and his brother's son, Constantine, who had ruled with him for three years. Now when Constans heard about this, he became filled with rage and killed Magnentius and along with him Ophilus who ruled with Magnentius and was of the line of the emperors. On the day of their slaying there appeared the sign of the Cross in the eastern part of the sky. The emperor entered Rome in great splendor. Returning to Constantinople, he made Julian *caesar* and gave him for a wife his sister Helene, who was called Costia.

In this period, the Jews who were in Palestine rebelled and killed Roman troops. The emperor sent and destroyed them. Julian went to Gaul against the barbarians, triumphed, and, waxing proud, was hailed as emperor by the troops. When Emperor Constantius heard about this he was terrified and was baptized by the bishop of Antioch, Euzoius, who was an Arian. Then he arose against Julian and died in the area between Cilicia and Cappadocia, having lived for 48 years and having reigned for 25 years.

Although he had been deceived by the Arian bishop Sebios and liked the Arians, still he did not claim that the Son of God was a created being but rather that He was born from the Father, though lesser. It was Emperor Constantine who legislated that unbaptized troops should not fight in wars, without this spiritual shield. At the hour of death he repented Arianism and accepted Orthodoxy and then died. *But before he gave up the ghost, he repented and professed Orthodoxy, saying: "Although I never regarded the Son of God as a created being, they gave me to state that he was inferior to the Father. And so did I sin before Him. Now I profess that the Son, the Holy Spirit, and the Father are consubstantial."*

Julian the Apostate

Julian took over the empire after being *Caesar* for five years. He reigned for two years. I have also found it claimed that Julian was Constantine the Great's brother's son. For they say that Constantine the Great had two brothers from the same father, Lamtius and Kostius. Lamtius had a son bearing his own name; while Kostius had two sons, Gallus and Julian. Gallus rebelled and was killed. Julian became *caesar*. After he had conquered the barbarians, he was passing along a street when a crown made of cloth fell and landed on his head. This became a cause for some to say that it was a sign of victory and for others to claim that it was a sign of approaching destruction. I have confirmed the first narrative rather than the second. However, since Julian was practiced in sorcery and in serving demons, he attributed his victory and the emperor's death to the demons. He was steeped in sorcery, wore the garb of philosophers, the dyed leather known as *atim*, ridiculing the imperial purple. *He abandoned his wife, and donned the garb of philophers.* It was he who began secretly to pollute waters with the blood of sacrifices and have this sprinkled on all foods so that eaters and drinkers would receive and do his will. When Julian entered Constantinople, he was declared *Autocrator*.

Julian was the son of Asklepius. When his brother Gallianus was slain for fomenting rebellion, Julian took refuge at the holy altar and was spared through the intercession of the patriarch Athanasius. Licinius had a daughter named Eluthra who had inherited her father's property after his killing. She remained a Christian virgin. Desirous of visiting Jerusalem for prayer, she entrusted her property to Julian as he appeared to be a selfless philosopher garbed in skins. Her property consisted of 13 gold crowns decorated with precious stones, 155 kendinars of gold women's ornaments, 97 kendinars of precious gold, plus invaluable and innumerable garments.

Julian schemed with his teacher, the pagan Melenus, not to return Eluthra's valuables, and he hid them in his home. Thus when the woman returned home, he deceived her and swore on the Gospel that he did not have the property. Thus, Eluthra was returning home in sadness. Now on the way she chanced upon a sundial which contained the image of an idol. This demon spoke to her, saying: "Worship me and be good to me the way your father was, and I will return your property to you." But Eluthra did not heed these words.

Now it happened that Julian was traveling on that same road and the same demon addressed him, saying: "I will expose you before the entire country, since you took the belongings of Eluthra, which I had given to her father who was dear to me, and you swore a false oath." Then Julian was terrified. He related this to Melenus who advised him: "Worship him, so he will not deliver upon his threats." Then he took him and they sacrificed to the demons. It happened that Melenus had a daughter who was pregnant. They sacrificed her, removed the baby and made a burnt offering of it. Then Melenus took Julian into a deep cavern, the dwelling place of demons, where he was promised a lifetime of 100 years and rule over the entire world. Julian mutilated himself and accepted the demons. When he became caesar and afterwards acceded to the throne, his faith was further strengthened and he began engaging in witchcraft and sorcery, to sacrifice to the demons, and to mix the blood of the victims with the water and food, so that everyone who ate and drank shared their spirit. When he learned that there was a bronze statue of Christ that performed many healings in the home of a woman at Caesarea who was troubled with bloody flux, he ordered that it be demolished and that the image of an idol be erected there. However, the idol was burned by fire hurled down by the Lord.

Julian then went to Antioch. When he entered the city, he was informed about what had happened and he became vexed. At that very moment, he espied a Christian doctor of the Church. He said to the philosopher Libanius: "Ask the priest where the carpenter's son is." The reply given back was: "He is plying his father's trade. He is making a coffin for your king who will die in Persia." Though deeply wounded by this, neither of them made any response at the time. When Julian had entered the city, he increased the stipends for the troops he was mustering to take to Persia, which made the currency more dear.

When Julian came to Antioch, he caused the currency to increase in value while making bread and wine more abundant. The rabble insulted him, asking: "Why do you let your beard grow so long? Cut it and make a rope out of it and put it on the horns of your sacrificial animals and, using it, lead them as offerings to your false gods." Julian was enraged and wanted to put the city to the sword. However, the philosopher Libanius calmed him down, saying: "Death is not the fitting response. Rather, give insults in place of their insults to you." And so Julian assembled them, insulted them, and let them go. Now on the mountain of Antioch there was a monastery named after Paul and the grave of Bishop Babelas was also located there. Julian wanted to erect a statue of Apollo there and to cast lots about his going to Persia, but the demons made him no reply. Julian realized that it was because of the presence of Babelas, and he ordered that Babelas' body be removed to the city. The Christians joyously took it singing psalms and carrying lanterns. Then the demons began to speak to him nicely. Julian, delighted, had two tables placed before the altar, one piled with incense, the other, with gold. He put fire before them and declared: "Let whoever casts a handful of incense on the fire take a handful of gold." Many simple-minded folk were thus fooled and took the gold. Afterwards, they sat down to eat and drink. Then, in accordance with custom, they made the sign of the cross over the wine. Then someone said: "What is this? You make the sign of the cross after apostatizing?" Terrified, they asked: "When did we apostatize?" And the man replied: "When you took gold after the incense." They put down the wine, ran outside and threw the gold in the emperor's face saying that they were Christians. Julian let them be tormented rather than killed, so that they not acquire the names of martyrs.

Julian changed the names of cities: he renamed Caesarea to Mazaka, and Constantinople to Biwzandia. He deceitfully built hostels, poor houses, and places where orphans and widows could be cared for. He commanded that pagan legends be read and that the children of Christians not be excluded from secular learning. He left Antioch with threats about what would happen when he returned peacefully from Persia. He sent to Edessa to prepare for receiving him, but they refused. He then went to Harran, sacrificed to the demons, and honored the Jews there, commanding that they go to Jerusalem, rebuild the Temple, and make sacrifices according to their faith. The Jews took 3,000 measures of lime, gathered up those who had been dispersed, went and began to rebuild. A fierce wind scattered the lime and cement they wanted to build with, and fire descended and burned the structure and their tools. The Jews in Edessa rose against the Christians, and were killed by them.

Julian delayed in Harran and again sacrificed to the demons in front of idols he had erected in Harran. And while sacrificing, the crown fell from his head and the horse nearby trampled him and tore his clothes. Julian's friends said to him: "This is because of the Christians whom you are taking with you." Julian therefore turned back 22,000 of the Christian troops. However, he did not retire the standard of the Cross, which by custom they kept at the front, saying: "Who knows, if the Persians defeat us, it will be a defeat for the Cross." He took along with him 395,000 fighters, not including attendants and laborers. Wherever he went he erected idols and made sacrifices and queries, and the demons said: "We, a multitude of gods, are coming along with you in a brigade and will bestow on you the fate and good fortune of Alexander, and the star Ares is at the head of your troops." Julian arrived at Ctesiphon, and ruined it. King Shapuh fled and sent to him, saying that he would give him a great amount of treasure if he would turn back. Shapuh then assembled the Persians and came and encamped by the Tigris River.

Messengers went back and forth between them, but they were unable to make peace. Then suddenly an arrow came and pierced Julian's entrails, making his blood gush forth. Taking some of the blood in the palm of his hand, he hurled it skyward, saying: "Oh, Galilean, you have triumphed. Take and add my kingdom to your divinity." But Julian would not don either armor or helmet, priding himself on the promise of the gods for protection. Perhaps the arrow which hit him was shot not by a man but from the power of God. Thus was fulfilled the prophesy made about him in Antioch. There Julian had pulled down an image of Christ in the home of a woman suffering from bloody flux where many healings took place, and erected idols in its place. Fire descended and burned the idols. They came and told him about this before he had entered Antioch. At this time he noticed a Christian *vardapet* and said to the philosopher Libanius: "Ask him, where is your son of a carpenter?" And the priest replied: "His work is present here where he makes a coffin for the death of your king." And they were silent. This indeed came to pass, for they made a coffin through the will and power of the carpenter's son, and they put Julian's body in it.

They chose a military commander named Jovian and said: "Rule over us as emperor in place of Julian." And Jovian replied: "I will not rule over devil worshippers." They responded in unison: "All of us are Christians." Then Jovian had the crown

THE CHRONICLE

placed on the Cross and said: "Come and worship." And everyone worshipped. Then Jovian took the crown and put it on his head. Now because of hunger and high prices, they made peace with the Persians. The Byzantines gave up Nisibis, depopulated, since they removed the multitude of Christians dwelling there. Then the Byzantine army turned back, bearing with it to Cilicia the corpse of the impious Julian; and they kept it, disrespectfully, in the confines of Tarsus. Julian left behind forty discourses.

Now Jovian was a good and pious man and delighted the Christians. And many wounds were healed. However, we were not worthy to enjoy this, for he did not live long. Between Galatia and Bithynia he experienced a pain in his intestines and died, after reigning for only seven months. He did not even reach Constantinople. When the troops reached Nicaea, they enthroned Valentinian,[62] a wise man who was from the city of Cibali in Pannonia. They wanted to select his co-ruler also, but Valens said: "That is at my discretion, not yours. You selected me and I shall select my own colleague." They accepted this and Valens chose his own brother, Vaghes, who had been baptized by the Arian bishop, Eudoxus, and held his doctrine. Valens designated him as ruler in the East, and he greatly supported the Arians.

Valens took Rome and adhered to the faith of Nicaea. He declared as Augustus his son Gratianus. Then he went to Marcianopolis in Egypt. When he arrived there an earthquake occurred, the likes of which had never happened, and had never been heard of. For when the sea shook, it hurled ships over the city wall and then retreated to a lower level than before. A multitude of folk gathered to loot the ships. But then the sea returned and drowned all of them and then spread out over the land, engulfing many cities and districts. This was a sign of the corruption of Vaghes. Valentinian reproached his brother for his evil ways. When he would not heed him, he got angry and did not aid him in his war with the Goths, saying: "I will not help a man who wars against God."

---

62 Valens, 364-378.

Then Valentinian himself went to fight in Sarmatia. The Sarmatians were terrified and, through emissaries, requested peace from him. Valentinian was astounded by their coarseness and ignorance. He asked them and learned that those emissaries who had come to him were the most select of the Sarmatians. He grew angry and said: "Woe to the Romans who have left kingship and reign over animals to me." Then, with a great shout, Valentinian encouraged the troops not to make peace with them, but instead to exterminate them. From the strength of his shout, veins in his throat burst and he died at the age of 84, after ruling for 11 years. Valentinian had two wives, contrary to law: the first was Severa and the second, Justina, daughter of Justin. Now Justin previously had seen a vision in which some purple material was coming forth from him and became a prince, and he told people about this. When Valentinian heard about this, he killed him so that, he said, no king would descend from him. Later, he took Justin's daughter as a wife. She bore him a son who was named Valentinian after him and three daughters: one of whom was Gallia, who became the wife of Theodosius the Great and bore him Arcadius and Honorius. Upon Valentinian's death, the eldest son, who was born from the first wife, was not nearby. And so others among the troops put the crown on the head of Valentinian's youngest son, who was a four-year-old boy.

Vaghes made Gratianus military chief and sent him to war against the Goths, where he was defeated. Vaghes insulted him and Gratianus retorted: "The defeat is not mine but yours, for you fight against Christ."

In this period Mawie', queen of the Tachiks,[63] caused much harm to the Romans. She promised peace if they would ordain as bishop of their district the hermit Moses. When Vaghes heard this, he sent to the desert seeking out the cleric named Moses. Finding someone they brought him to Vaghes, however Moses did not want to be ordained by the Arians. Instead, he wanted ordination

---

63 Arabs.

from exiled Orthodox clerics. The emperor so ordered. Receiving the episcopate from the persecuted Orthodox, Moses departed. When he went back, many Tachiks became Christians.

For Queen Mawie' was Roman by nationality. She had been captured by the Tachiks. Because of her beauty, she became wife to the Tachik king, and when he died, she ruled over the kingdom. Due to her, many converted to Christianity.

In this period, Vaghes constructed the *dimison* in Antioch, a prison for the Orthodox. Then suddenly there appeared an army moving through the sky, physically visible. In this period a child was born in Antioch having one eye, four feet, four hands, and a beard.

In these times the Goths arose and enslaved many districts: Scythia, Thrace, Mysia, Macedonia, Achaea, and all Hellas. Vaghes fled to Constantinople and the rabble insulted him, saying: "Give us weapons and we will go and fight." Vaghes went, infuriated, threatening them that should he return in peace he would demolish the city. He went but was defeated by them. And he fled to a village. The fighting barbarians surrounded the village while Vaghes hid in a silo full of hay. Searching for him unsuccessfully, they burned down the village and he perished in the hay, in an anticipation of the eternal fire. Vaghes lived 50 years and reigned for 17 years.

Then ruled Gratianus, who, in the days of his father Valentinian, had been *Autokrator* in Rome. He reestablished Orthodoxy and took as his co-ruler Theodosius the Spaniard—the man who had been the first to declare Gratianus emperor. Gratianus swapped with him, giving Theodosius Constantinople and all the eastern areas. In this period, at their order, Ras al-Ayn was constructed. Now when the barbarians learned about the demise of Vaghes, they came as far as the walls of Constantinople. Theodosius rose and destroyed them, then went on to their land and made them tributary. And there was peace in the Church and the land after 40 years of Arian evil.

In this period, Artashir,[64] king of the Persians, died and his son Shapuh[65] took the rule.

The Priest Melitos, Who Ruled that Ignorant Folk Not be Ordained

In the third year of Theodosius, Gratianus was killed by the dictator Maximius in Rome. Then, Valentinian the Lesser ruled in Rome. Theodosius and Valentinian warred with Maximium the dictator, killed him, and entered Rome in splendid glory. Then Theodosius came to Constantinople. He sent an official, the *Strategos*, to the East. When he arrived at Antioch, he observed conflict in the Church. He made peace and established Melitus on the patriarchal throne. Now in the fourth year of Theodosius, he wanted to cleanse the Church of Arians. He convened a large assembly of 150 bishops. The principals among them were: Melitus of Antioch, Timothy of Alexandria, Cyril of Jerusalem, the blessed Nerse's of Greater Armenia who had returned from exile, Gregory the Theologian from Constantinople, and Gregory of Nyssa. And they anathematized first the heresy of Arian, then the heresy of Macedonius who dared to claim that the Holy Spirit was a creation. They established the faith of Nicaea and added to the Creed mention of the Holy Spirit, for this question arose subsequently.

After ten years of heading the episcopate, Gregory the Theologian quit Constantinople and Nectarius took over that See. When Theodosius saw Melitus, he said: "I saw him in a dream, blessing me as emperor." Melitus died at that council. Gregory of Nyssa delivered a funeral homily about him, and his body was brought to Antioch. Melitus stopped unqualified priests from administering communion, and stipulated that only the most perfected people, acknowledged by all, should be selected as clerics. For a certain priest at Antioch had ordained as deacon a person who was

---

64 Artashir III, 379-383.
65 Shapuh III, 383-388.

committing adultery with a wealthy woman and, as a result, there was much killing. Melitus commented that "It is better to ordain a thornbush than an ignorant and unprepared person."

At this time, Theodosius was in Thessalonica and became ill. He encountered and was baptized by Ascolius and was healed. Then Theodosius came to Constantinople and built a large church to Anastasius. In this time, he fathered a son from his wife Flacilla and he was named Honorius. After giving birth, Flacilla died. There was a statue of her in Antioch, but when they learned of her death, they dragged it and dumped it in the marketplace. Emperor Theodosius was enraged by this. He removed from Antioch the honor of being called a capital and gave this instead to Laodicia, making it an Evangelical See. Judges wrought many killings over that affair. Now when a hermit named Apollo heard about it, he came and reprimanded the princes and wrote a letter to Theodosius, saying: "It is unnecessary to get so angry over one image. People, who are the image of God, are being polluted. You can make many bronze statues, but you cannot fashion an image of God. Do you not know this? How many more of our souls dishonored by sins will be required with no one caring that it is the image of God which is being insulted?" And when the emperor heard this, his rage quieted and he reconciled with the city.

In this period, Thessalonica, the main city of Illyria, rebelled from the emperor, slaying by lapidation the emperor's prince, who was in the city. Enraged, the emperor commanded that the city be destroyed. Seven thousand people died, the innocent along with the guilty. Then Bishop Ambrosius came to the city of Milan and encountered the emperor at the door of the church, as he was trying to enter. The bishop stopped him and asked: "Are you not ashamed, you who are covered with blood, to enter the house of God? Turn back, and receive this ban which God has sent to you by my hands." And the emperor turned back *with tears in his eyes.* Eight months later, when the feast of the Nativity came, the emperor sat *in his chamber* and wept bitterly. The magistrate Rufinus *made bold to approach him* and asked: "What is wrong, O

King, why do you weep?" He replied: "How could I not cry, for servants and beggars may enter the church while I am banned both from the church and from Heaven. *They may enjoy the heavenly blessing of this feast while I am deprived of it.*" Rufinus said: "I will hasten and beseech the bishop." The emperor responded: "I do not believe that he will listen to you or see me, a man who has scorned the laws of God."

Nonetheless Rufinus went, while the emperor piously followed behind him. Now when the bishop saw Rufinus, he cried out: "Foul one, *advisor of impiety and encourager of evil*, all this happened because of your advice." Rufinus fell at his feet, pleading and saying: "Lo, the emperor is coming behind me *in all humility and relying on the intervention of the holy feast.*" The bishop said: "I will not allow him in church and, should he desire it, I will accept murder from him as he has murdered others." Rufinus then went before the emperor and related what the blessed man had said, and the emperor responded: "Let me go and I will gladly bear the insults I deserve." He went and stood outside in tears, pleading. The bishop called to him, saying: "Brazen heathen, why have you come here?" The emperor replied: "Holy Father, I will gladly accept your insults and anathemas and will do nothing without your approval. Only do not close the door in my face, so that I can see inside the Church of God from outside, and hear your voice." The bishop remained in the church and said: "What penance have you done that you should see the door of the church and me?" And the emperor replied: "Only show me the medicine for my wounds and I will do as you say." The bishop said: "You are severe against wrongdoers. Write a law that wrongdoers must be held for three days before punishment, and should there still be doubts, let it be for 40 days and have inquiries made with witnesses and examination so that the matter be clear and can be discerned when your anger subsides, and then punish accordingly. *You are cruel and hateful towards the guilty, and too easily believe the slanderous insinuations of informers and intriguers. I want you to write in your own hand a law requiring that three days pass before acting on the betrayals you hear about, and that 40 days pass before executing those condemned, during which time inquiries must be made as to the facts, during which time your heart will become tranquil and your anger will lessen. And furthermore, see that all the judges and princes under your sway comport with this."* This edict was written at once, and the emperor sent to all the judges and princes in the land for them to act accordingly. Then the bishop commanded the emperor to enter the church. He entered and threw himself on the ground, saying: "I grovel on the ground. Lord sustain me with mercy." Then, in tears, the king stood up and went near the altar and wanted to go to his own seat, but the bishop stopped him, saying: "Until you complete your penance it is fitting that you remain behind and beneath everyone else." The emperor accepted this in all humility and went to stand with the other penitents. Such was the emperor's piety and faith.

In this period, through the bishop's efforts, they discovered the relics of the prophet Habakkuk and Michah in Eleutheropolis in Palestine. In Jerusalem they found relics of St. Stephen and those with him, due to Bishop Yovhanne's of Jerusalem, *a very virtuous man who preached orthodox sermons.* In the 13th year of Theodosius, the emperor had his son Arcadius proclaimed in in the East and at the same time the princes Eugene and Arbogast treacherously killed Valentinian in Rome. Theodosius enthroned Honorius in Rome. Theodosius arose with a small number of troops against the many rebels. The latter said to the emperor: "Let us wait until reinforcement troops arrive." And Theodosius entered a cave alone and cried out to the Lord. The Evangelist John *and Philip, one of Christ's Apostles,* and the Apostle Peter appeared and said to him: "Fear not and do not await assistance, for we have come from Christ to help you." And that is what happened, for at dawn the two tyrants were destroyed. However, when the emperor left off his labors and came to Milan, he was seized by a pain in the intestines and died. He had lived 60 years, reigning as emperor for 16 years and eight months. In this period, in Persia, Vahram Kermanshah, son of Shapuh and brother of Artashir, reigned for 11 years.

Now Theodosius, during his lifetime, had been urged by bishop Jamblichos to persecute Arians, but he had not listened. One day, the emperor was seated with his son, Arcadius, when Jamblichos entered. He greeted Theodosius, but did not even look at the son. It appeared to the emperor that he had not seen the son, and so he said: "Father, bless my son." Jamblichos replied: "You, emperor, are enough for us. I will not honor him except as one of your servants." The emperor was saddened and then flew into a rage. The bishop continued: "You, a mortal, cannot endure an insult to your son. Do you suppose that immortal God will allow you to insult His Son?" The emperor accepted this and ordered that Arians be persecuted and boldly removed. *Dumbfounded, the emperor ordered that the Arians be persecuted boldly, and he ordered that his sons and princes do likewise. And then he reposed in Christ.*

Following the death of the emperor, a child was born in Emaus, Palestine who had two heads above the chest and four arms. The child lived for two years. When one head ate, the other did not. When one slept, the other stayed awake. And they played with each other, sometimes crying, sometimes laughing. One died two days before the other.

Emperor Arcadius[66] was sensible and restrained. Underneath his royal purple he secretly wore a hair shirt, and he liked clerics. In this period, John Chrysostom went to Constantinople in great glory, a powerful figure when it came to speech, miracles, and doctrine. *Arcadius had John Chrysostom of Antioch in Syria brought to him, for he was desirous of seeing John because of his reputation. When Arcadius saw him, he found his eloquence, miracles, and holiness to be ten times more than supposed. Arcadius made him bishop of Constantinople.* But there were some who scorned John because he did not speak polished Greek. He was of Asori lineage and had been schooled in that language, Syriac. He died in exile in Armenian Comana, having lived 50 years. For seven years he was bishop in Constantinople and for three years he was in exile. After baptism, he did not swear or make oaths, lie

---

66 Arcadius, 395-408.

THE CHRONICLE

or curse anyone. He did not drink wine or laugh, or eat with folk. *Nor, when exalted, did he seek more honors.* When he went into exile, he struck the church with his hand and said: "Stay well, blessed Church, dwelling place of the Lord's glory. With the blessings I received from God I have put 12,000 homilies into the treasury of the Church, which are 800 books."

After this, Arcadius grew ill and had his eight-year-old son *Theodosius* declared emperor. Now since Honorius was sonless, Arcadius' son[67] was the sole heir. Arcadius feared for his son. *For this reason* he made a will entrusting his son to the king of Persia, Yazdgird. When Yazdgird learned about this, he was overjoyed and sent as a tutor for the boy a wise man named Antiochus. He also sent warnings to all the Imperial Houses of the Romans for them to regard the boy with fear and awe. Then Arcadius died, having reigned for 13 years. There was then peace between the Persians and Romans; and the Christians in Persia grew in numbers and were viewed without suspicion, through the efforts of Bishop Marutha.

Then Honorius died sonless in Rome and Constantine[68] ruled. The latter was slain by some autocrat. There remained only Theodosius after Honorius, who had reigned for 13 years. In that period Theodosius designated as *caesar* his father's sister's son, Valentinian, and sent him to Rome with his mother. After this, Theodosius sent Valentinian a crown. Valentinian reigned for 32 years. Theodosius was a blessed man whose table held vegetables, but no oil or wine during fasts. After the death of the bishop of Hebron, he took the deceased bishop's *filthy* hair shirt and wore it every night. He was merciful and lacking in hatred, to the point that when asked "Why do you spare those condemned to death?" he replied: "Would that I could turn to life those who are dead, let alone kill the living. That is God's work, to kill and to let live. *It is for God to grant life or death. I am begging the Lord to return to us from the dead; why, then, should I add to the dead?*"

---

67 Theodosius II.
68 Constans III.

In this period, Yazdgird, king of Persia, died and his son, Bahram,[69] reigned for 22 years. *He rescinded his father's treaty and made war against Theodosius.* The friendship between the Byzantine and Persian kings ended, and the Persians were hit many times through the emperor' prayers. *Theodosius, through his prayers, defeated the Persians, killed, and took captives.*

In this period, virtue was displayed by Acacius, bishop of Amida who ransomed those captured by the Persians, even giving the Church vessels, made of gold and silver, to purchase the slaves. He said: "Our God has no need of gold and silver vessels." His faith was praised among the Persians. The Persian king wanted to see him and greatly exalted him, to the glory of Christ. In this period, the noteworthy clerics were Symeon the Stylite in Antioch and Mor Barsum on the borders of Lesser Armenia.

The heretic Nestorius

In this period, Nestorius was patriarch in Constantinople. *In this period Bishop Nestorius moved from Antioch to Constantinople.* He had a priest named Anastasius who one day enunciated a new heresy from the pulpit—that Mary was the mother of a man, not of God. The people *were indignant and* expected Nestorius to censure him. But Nestorius not only did not blame Anastasius, but he even took the heresy from him and spread it. *However the foolish Nestorius, aided by the demons, was pleased with what had been said and promulgated it throughout the land.* For this reason a great council was convened at Ephesus—the First Council of Ephesus—in the 41st year of Theodosius, which is 742 of the Syrian Era,[70] and 423 years from the time of Christ. Two hundred bishops were present there. Seven of them were anathematized, leaving 193 Orthodox bishops. The great Sahak of Armenia, being occupied, wrote a letter agreeing to whatever they stipulated. A multitude of priests and clerics were assembled there, principal among them:

69 Bahram V, 420-438.
70 A.D. 431.

Bishops Arcadius and Proctius of Rome, representing Celestine, Pope of Rome; Cyril of Alexandria; Memnon of Ephesus; John of Antioch; Acacius of Melitene; Juvenal of Jerusalem; and others who anathematized Nestorius. But John of Antioch and 26 bishops with him did not sign the anathema of Nestorius, and then they themselves were anathematized along with him.

Nestorius went into exile. Then John of Antioch was with Cyril and confessed his ignorance, not knowing of Nestorius' wickedness. *By order of the emperor, Nestorius was exiled to Persian Khuzistan. John and his supporters repented and remained with Cyril, confessing their ignorance of Nestorius' heresy. Having consulted together, they recognized true Orthodoxy.* Thus they confirmed the Council and said: "After this, should any council, bishop, or king create a new faith or definition of the faith, let them be anathematized. Rather, let the decisions of the Council of Nicaea be kept firmly by the blessed Church until the end of the world."

Here are the names of those who were exiled with Nestorius: Theodoret from the city of Cyrrhus; Andrew of Samosata; Alexander of Manbij;[71] Arianus of Tyre; John of Cilicia; Ut'rios of Taron and others with them. They installed Maximus of Constantinople in Nestorius' position.

In the 29th year of his reign, Theodosius heard some clamor about Flavian, bishop of Constantinople and the archimandrite Eutyches, and ordered that a second council be convened in Ephesus, 18 years after the first council, which was under Cyril. The emperor wrote a letter to Dioscorus with this import:

> We the triumphant kings the autocrat Emperor Theodosius and Valentinian to you, holy father Dioscorus, archbishop of the Apostolic see of Alexandria:
> Be it known to your holiness that Nestorius' bitter root apparently has spread its tendrils into

---

71   Mabbug, Hierapolis, Bambyce.

Flavian, and that the beliefs of Mani have influenced the monk Eutyches. This we have heard. This task is fitting for you—to cleanse the Church, the pure bride of Christ. Therefore, make haste to relieve the sorrow of your Mother on her heavenly couch. Bring with you ten metropolitans and ten other educated bishops capable of lighting the torch of Orthodox faith and placing it on a chandelier to the joy of those in heaven and on earth. Bring along too an additional ten bishops from Palestine. Bring Juvenal, bishop of Jerusalem since he was opposed to Nestorius and the heretical Leo. Do not bring with you those who sickened in the faith along with Cyril, namely Theodoret, bishop of the city of Cyrrhus and others of his ilk. Julian the Roman is here with us, filling the place once occupied by Leo in Rome, for Leo manifested symptoms of the disease with his Tome. Also bring the great hermit and father of the desert, Mor Barsuma, representing all the Eastern monastics, since he greatly labored against Nestorius and the Tome of Leo.

The blessed Dioscorus took the emperor's letter and did as he was ordered. He came to the council at Ephesus with 128 bishops. The principals were: Dioscorus of Alexandria, Juvenal of Jerusalem, Domanus of Antioch, Eustacius of Beirut, Theodolus of Armenian Caesarea, Eusebius of Caesarea,[72] Vasilius of Seleucia, and Mor Barsama, head of the monks. They held many investigations. Eutyches showed repentance in form, but not in substance—for which he was not accepted and was anathematized, as he claimed that the incarnation of Our Lord had happened in a fantastic manner. Now Flavian had written a confession of his faith which they brought forth and read. It contained Nestorius'

---

72 Palestina.

beliefs. In it were found the signatures of Vailius, bishop of Seleucia; Julianus, bishop of the Romans; Eudocus of the Cyprians; and Seleucus of the Emesians. When the entire assembly heard this, they cursed it saying: "Get rid of it, destroy it, burn that godless document." With anathemas, they removed Flavian from his episcopal throne and with him Eusebius, Domnus of Antioch and five bishops who were his colleagues, and Irenaeus of Tyre, Akamius of Pepul, Theodoritus of Cyrrhus. Ibas of Edessa, Severus of Thrumo, and Daniel from Harran. Moreover, the Tome of Leo—which had been scorned by the first council—they did not deem fitting to read.

Then a letter arrived from the emperors Theodosius and Valentinian telling them neither to add to, nor subtract from, the Orthodox faith of Nicaea, Constantinople, and Ephesus, but rather to confirm the same doctrines. For this reason, they confessed one Lord, one Christ, one Son, one Person, and one Nature after an ineffable union, both fully God and man, united in spirit, body, and mind, truly and not in semblance.

After the council was dissolved, when envoys went and told Leo what had transpired, Leo was moved to anger. He sent and summonsed Flavian, heard his confession, and was satisfied. Then Flavian further roused Leo against Dioscorus, saying: "He insulted your Tome and said that you are Nestorian." Leo was anguished and sought a means of deposing Dioscorus in return for his insults.

In this time, Empress Theodora and her sister Pulcheria went to Rome on pilgrimage. Appropriately, they were honored by Emperor Valentinian *who was the cousin*[73] *of Theodosius the Younger* and the entire population of Rome.

Valentinian took them and went to the cathedral of the Apostles Peter and Paul where their relics were located. *They were taken to the cathedral of the blessed Apostles where the clergy came to greet them, but Leo did not. Rather, he had thrown himself to the ground behind a curtain and began to cry.* When Leo heard about this, he

---

73 *Father's sister's son.*

threw himself on his face on the ground, behind a curtain, and did not get up and go to greet them.

Then they lifted the curtain and saw Leo heaving and sobbing and they *tenderly and with respect* asked the reason. They took and seated him and he said: "Dioscorus has rent the Orthodox faith and the throne of the blessed Apostles is insulted by him." They comforted him and said: "Let it be as you wish, whatever you command." Leo got them to be intercessors with Emperor Theodosius to order convened another ecclesiastical council to overturn Dioscorus. They swore that they would do this. Now when the emperor's wife and her sister Pulcheria returned, Leo sent with them a letter begging that a council be convened with greater attendance than Dioscorus' so that his Tome be examined correctly and that he not be associated with the evil Nestorius. But when the emperor heard this, he rejected the request, saying: "I believe and accept the determination of Cyril and Dioscorus who judged the Tome of Leo to be parallel to the doctrines of the accursed Nestorius."

Emperor Theodosius, having lived in Orthodoxy, died at age 50, having reigned for 42 years, since he began to reign at eight years of age.

Then Theodosius' sister's son Marcian reigned,[74] selected by Pulcheria. He was an ignorant, uneducated old man who reigned for six years and five months. It is said that he had engaged in adultery with Pulcheria earlier *when she was a nun*. Now in the first year of his rule, a letter of entreaty came from Leo, with the same content as the one he had sent before about convening another council. It was sent to Marcian and also to Pulcheria, reminding her of her earlier promise. Leo also sent his Tome to them so that they would forcibly and authoritatively have it circulated around to the bishops in the Asiatic land *to all the bishops in the province of Asia* for them to sign prior to the assembly. They agreed for two reasons: first because of Pulcheria's promise and vow, and second because it was the law that an emperor should not be seated in

---

74 A.D. 450-457.

Constantinople without the consent of the emperor of Rome and the patriarch. This had already occurred without them and they were afraid of turbulence. Thus, they wrote a letter full of entreaties and threats from the emperor and Pulcheria and by princes and the bishops sent by Leo, they sent the letter throughout the land. They got the signed agreement of 446 bishops.

Now when the emissaries returned and took Leo's Tome to the emperor and Pulcheria on which were 446 bishops' signatures, they were overjoyed and signed it themselves.

Thus, they ordered convened an assembly embracing all the countries under their sway except for Armenia which was not under their rule. *Next, they sent invitations everywhere except to Armenia which was not under their control and whose patriarch had recently died. They had not yet put anyone on his patriarchal throne, and so did not send a representative. All this happened through God's providence so that a recollection of the past be preserved among them.* In the second year of Marcian's reign, 700 bishops assembled. Then principals were: Tromopicus, Lilopas, Likinisus, and Ascolion of Rome, representing Leo; Juvenal of Jerusalem; Dioscorus of Alexandria; Domus of Antioch; Basil of Seleucia; Peter the Iberian, the bishop of Gaza and chief bishop of Palestine. They placed at the head of the assembly Theodoritus whom Cyril had anathematized at Ephesus. And Dioscorus remarked: "What impiety is this? Saint Paul said 'If I rebuild something which has been demolished, I, too, am guilty.' How could such a man, tainted by anathema, be the head and builder of a dead thing?" Juvenal at first supported him and moved everyone to be with Dioscorus. They said: "Cyril anathematized anyone adding new things to Orthodox doctrine and we concur. We anathematize anyone introducing new definitions. Let them also be cursed by Cyril." Following this, the emperor served in person and went about flattering, beseeching, and bribing. He gave to Juvenal three districts in the land of the Palestinians and, with pleading, brought him into agreement along with the 440 bishops who had previously signed the circulating document.

Those who kept to Orthodoxy with Dioscorus were 254 clerics who endured anathemas, bannings, harassment, and death, but did not depart from the love of Christ. The majority of attendees accepted the Tome of Leo with two distinct natures for Christ and, deceitfully, the virginity of the Mother of God. Yet as those wicked men separated the nature of man from her, how could she be the Mother of God? The entire world became filled with agitation and blood. The council lasted for two and a half years. Those who previously had been exiled and anathematized by Cyril and Dioscorus returned to honor and rule, fortified by troops and imperial edicts. Juvenal, among them, went to Jerusalem.

Then there was great disturbance in Jerusalem as they did not accept Juvenal. They ordained their own patriarch, Theodorus. But Juvenal wrote to Marcian, who sent a military commander with troops, and they removed Theodorus and established Juvenal. And he again circulated through the land of Palestine and the Philistines and turned Christians to heresy, while the Orthodox were beaten, persecuted, and had their belongings seized. Many of the Jews circulated around destroying the Orthodox. Now there was a man named Peter who was the venerable bishop of Gaza. It is said that he was son of the king of the Iberians who previously had been sent to Constantinople as a hostage. There he willingly practiced severe asceticism, became renowned for his virtue, and was forcibly made a bishop. Peter upbraided Marcian, cursed the Council of Chalcedon and departed in sadness. No one dared to reproach him, because of his supreme virtue. This Peter wrote to the Armenians, congratulating them on not attending the council and adding: "At Chalcedon, they apostatized Christ. Remain firm in your patrimonial faith which the Lord bestowed on you and your land. For just as once the seed of humanity spread from there throughout the world, so has the seed of Orthodox faith been preserved among you. And it will spread from you to many others. My sons, stand firm on the ineffable rock of Christ."

We, who believe in Almighty God the Father, the Only Begotten Son, our Lord and Savior Jesus Christ, and the Holy

Spirit of the true God, glorify the Holy Trinity and the One God, now and forever, for all eternity. Amen.[75]

In the sixth year of Marcian, which was 769 of the Syrian Era,[76] Valentinian, the emperor of the Romans was killed. Then the kingdom of the Romans split away from Constantinople. Just as Marcian had taken the throne without the consent of Rome, so now did they do the same. And so also was peace disturbed for the Church after the Council of Chalcedon. Marcian died, cursed by the blessed men of the age, after ruling for six years. That same year, one of Marcian's princes, Leo of Thrace, ruled in Rome. In the same year, Peroz[77] ruled in Persia, initiating persecution against Christians and war against the Romans. Emperor Leo gave his daughter in marriage to prince Zeno, and designated him as ruler of the eastern parts of the empire. He made Basiliscus the *stratelat* in Thrace, and Murinus, *Caesar* in Rome. Soon afterwards he was slain by Ricimer, and Anthemius and Lucarus[78] were proclaimed *Caesar*s.

In this period, Callinicus—which was known as Ragha—was built up by order of Emperor Leo,[79] who gave it his name, Leontopolis. At this time there was a fire in Constantinople the likes of which had never been seen. It burned the place from sea to sea. The emperor left the city and was not able to reenter it for six months. Leo published an edict to the effect that on Sundays, young and old should assemble in the churches for prayer and study, and that other work should not be done on that day.

In Leo's day, for a month after the conflagration, the air was full of particles of ash which covered the ground to the depth of a palm, and especially in Constantinople. The land was terrified, since there was also an earthquake and flames escaped from the ground where it had been torn asunder. Many places were burned down, and the end of the world was anticipated. From the earth-

---

75 We omit the translation of the following 72 numbered paragraphs denouncing Chalcedon.
76 A.D. 458.
77 Peroz, 459-484..
78 Perhaps Glycerius.
79 Leo I, 457-474.

quake and the fires, the city of Cyzica disappeared and many cities and villages in Thrace were ruined. Emperor Leo died of an affliction of the bowels. He died after reigning for 18 years. During this reign there was never an end to disturbances and destruction in the land and in the Church. All wise folk realized that it was due to the Council of Chalcedon and its unholy profession of faith that the Holy Spirit of God had become angry.

At Leo's order his six-year-old grandson, Leo, was enthroned. This boy was the son of Zeno, emperor of the East. A year later the boy's father came to do homage to his son. The boy's mother tricked the young lad, telling him: "When you see your father, put the crown on his head and prostrate yourself before him." The boy did as he was told, and the father took over the empire and ruled alone. And after a short time, the boy died, and many were deeply saddened. Now Zeno was Syrian by nationality. Leo the Great's queen, Verine, entreated Zeno to adopt the Chalcedonian heresy and, when he refused, she plotted against him. She and her advisors had his brother Basiliscus declared emperor and his son Marcus, *Caesar*. To that time, Basiliscus had been in rebellion against Leo in Araklia. Now Zeno, who was warned in time, fled to his people in Syria. He entered the fortress of Salame and stayed holed up there. His wife Ariadne secretly joined him there.

Basiliscus and his son reigned for two years.[80] He was a foul, diabolical man and a persecutor of the Orthodox. He raised the supporters of Chalcedon to the pinnacle and was hated by the multitude. The latter went over to Zeno and grew in strength.

Now Basiliscus sent his general Harmatius to make war on him, however Zeno got him to make common cause with himself, promising to make him *caesar*. Zeno[81] took his troops and went to Constantinople where he was received with joy. Basiliscus and his sons fled to a church. Zeno stripped him of the imperial purple, then sent him to Castle Limnes in Cappadocia. There, confined in a tower surrounded by walls, he died a miserable

80 475-476.
81 474-491.

death. Then, Zeno appointed general Artemis and his son as *caesars*. However, shortly afterward Artemis was killed and his son became a reader in the Church.

Then the emperor, through the agency of Acacius, patriarch of Constantinople, began to reestablish Orthodoxy. He sent to Peter, patriarch of Antioch, and to Timotheus, patriarch of Alexandria, who were in prison in Constantinople and inquired after their confession of faith. In writing, they gave a restatement of the doctrines of the Councils of Nicaea, and *of Constantinople*, of Cyril and of Dioscorus, which the emperor had circulated throughout the land and which had been signed by 700 bishops. Peter and Timotheus remarked: "We accept these. But we anathematize the Tome of Leo, the Council of Chalcedon, Acacius, and Nestorius which tore the faith apart, and we also anathematize those who refuse to anathematize them." The emperor received this document, and agreed with it happily. He then sent Peter, called "The Washer," back to his see in Antioch with great honor. He died there.

Timotheus was sent back to Alexandria. It was he who had been ordained patriarch by the Orthodox after Proterius, and then exiled *by Marcian.*

In this period the Samaritans rebelled and established a certain man named Justus as their king. He killed many Christians, entering the church in Caesarea[82] and shedding blood. They pulled down this church *and built a temple in its place.* The Byzantine troops went against them and broke them. They sent *the head of* Justus, whom the Jews had made king, to Emperor Zeno; and the temple which the Jews had built they consecrated as a church in the name of the blessed Mary. The Jews found in Antioch also were destroyed.

In these times, there was an earthquake and the city of Nicomedia was destroyed—for the sixth time by the same means. Then Emperor Zeno died at the age of 60, after reigning for 16 years. Peroz, the bitter persecutor of Christians, died a wicked death and was

---

82 Palestina.

succeeded by Valash who ruled for four years.[83] In his day, there was peace with Christians. Anastasius,[84] *a good and pious man*, reigned after Zeno. During his reign he discovered vices within the schools in Constantinople and in a rage ordered all the students of the schools destroyed, *a deed which greatly saddened the capital*. Anastasius rebuilt the city of Dara, which had been ruined at the death of Darius. He renamed it Anastasopolis. In his day, Nicopolis was demolished by an earthquake. After Valash, Kawad ruled in Persia[85] but his brother Zamasp chased him out and ruled for two years.[86] However, Kawad again grew strong, killed his brother and ruled for an additional 30 years.[87] Then the Huns rose and conquered the Persians. Now the Persians thought that there had been some collusion with the Byzantines, so they invaded Mesopotamia and destroyed many cities, *and then departed*.

Then Timotheus, a very wise and virtuous man, was elected as the 20th patriarch of Constantinople. He wrote to the emperor and established throughout the entire country that the words "Who Was Crucified" should be included in the Trisagion *and that Christ God should be described as having one nature*. Anastasius was overjoyed and stipulated this for the entire country. But among the Nestorians in Constantinople there was great disquietude about saying that the Trinity had been crucified. They threatened Timotheus and killed one of his priests. Furious, Timotheus left the city *and entered a retreat*.

Felician was the brilliant archbishop of Manbij who had been ordained by Peter of Antioch. He wrote extensively about Orthodox doctrine. Emperor Anastasius learned about him and had him brought to Constantinople with bishops and doctors of the Church. One of the doctors of the Church was Severus and there were 200 priests with him. *A great multitude of the proponents of Nicaea and Chalcedon assembled there.* The emperor ordered that

---

83 A.D. 484-488.
84 491-518.
85 First reign, 488-496.
86 496-498.
87 Second reign, 498-531.

an inquiry into the faith be held. The victors were those espousing the Orthodox doctrines of Felician and Severus against their defamers. Then the emperor ordered that the Tome of Leo and the formulations of the Council of Chalcedon be taken from the tomb of the martyr Euphemius and burned *in his presence*. Now Flavian, patriarch of Antioch, did not support this action, *and he blamed the emperor*, thereby demonstrating that he was pro-Chalcedon. He was anathematized and sent into exile. Then Felician ordained the great Severus in Constantinople as patriarch of Antioch. He was a spiritual, educated man, who was very familiar with theological literature. On the day of his ordination, he delivered the homily which begins: "Those who divide the unity of the Son, *the Word* of God," in which he demonstrated the fallacies of all the heretics, which the Greeks have. They always read this because of its clarity in upbraiding them. *The emperor sent* Severus to the city of Antioch in great glory. Severus had been a student of the blessed bishop James of Seruj who possessed a divine grace and had been schooled by the Holy Spirit, and not by man.

Now the Holy Spirit spoke through the mouth of James when he was just a child of seven years. When the patriarch Athanasius heard about this prodigy, he visited the boy's father's house in order to test the lad. Seated at table, Athanasius picked up an egg and asked: "Which came first, the chicken or the egg?" And the child replied: "Do not deceive me, for the Father does not have precedence over the Word of His Son." Enchanted, the patriarch on another occasion took the boy to church and had him mount the pulpit. And he said to him: "My child, tell us about the mysterious throne which Ezekiel saw." Then James began with the words "You, who repose on the throne in heaven are the Word..." and then he interrupted this to announce that the Persians had taken Amida and that the imperial palace in Aleppo had been swallowed up—facts which subsequently were confirmed. Then the patriarch kissed James, saying that indeed the Holy Spirit was speaking through his lips. James delivered some 800 homilies during his lifetime, illuminating the souls of many people, including Severianus.

Simon the Potter, who wrote homilies and hymns of Orthodox doctrine, also was active in this time.

In this period, Kawad, the Persian king, mustered troops, went to Mesopotamia, came to the city of Karin, and captured it. He made peace rather than destroying it because during the besiegement of the city, the defenders had not disrespected him. In the fall, Kawad then turned and went to Amida, which he put into great straits. Yovhanne's vanakan of Kart'ma went to them and urged the rich to have compassion on the poor and he said to the crowd: "Purify yourselves through fasts, tears, and evening vigils." An angel of God appeared to him and said: "This city will be destroyed because of its sins, but you will die and not see its ruination." Rain poured down and the Persians, with their long garments, were hindered by it and weakened. Now the Persians had constructed wooden siege towers and had moved them close to the city walls. But the clever folk among the city's inhabitants created a flammable liquid with anise, sprayed it on the siege towers, ignited it, and reduced them to ashes. At this point, the Persian king said that if they gave him gold and other things, he would depart. But the city's inhabitants insulted him because of their success and did not repent their wickedness. Then, the Lord grew angry and betrayed the city to the Persians, who killed 80,000 people and took the rest captive. The greatcathedral there was filled with people. But at the request of the Armenian head of the Iranian troops, they were spared both death and enslavement. The Persian king entered the church and saw a painting of the Savior on the altar. He inquired: "Who is that?" When they replied: "He is the Christian God," the king kneeled before it and said: "He appeared to me in a vision and said: 'Do not leave, I will deliver the city into your hands.' Thus it was not I who captured this city but their God who gave it to me, because its people had sinned."

Taking many captives King Kawad went on to Edessa, but was unable to capture it. He returned to his own country, leaving at Amida *a small garrison and 3,000* cavalry *under two of his trusted commanders*. When the Byzantine troops learned about his departure, they came and besieged the city, but to no avail, since the garrison was under the command of an extremely capable and intelligent man named Eglon. *The Persians were defeating the Byzantines.* But then a man named Gadan from the village of Kartha came to the Byzantines and told them what he planned to do. He went and tricked Eglon, saying: "Take 400 horsemen with you and we shall go and take 500 of their horses which are grazing out in the open." As soon as they departed, Byzantine soldiers sprang out of ambuscades and killed them. When the Persians learned about the man's treachery, they were furious. In reprisal they confined 10,000 Christians in a certain spot and so deprived them of food that they were eating their own shoes. The Persians then rose one night and departed for their own land.

In the 22nd year of Anastasius' reign, the emperor sent troops[88] to the land of the Armenians and, taking them under his protection, got them to distance themselves from the Persians. *For seven years, the Persians ceased their depredations.* After ruling for 27 years, Anastasius died on the 29th of the month of Tamuz. *The 14th year of his reign corresponded to the 6,000th year of Adam's expulsion from the Garden of Eden.*

In 832 of the Syrian Era,[89] Justinus[90] from Thrace ascended the throne. He is regarded as the first of the emperors of Greek origin. He was born in the village of Bederiana which he subsequently turned into a city and named after himself. It is claimed that the water there is so foul that, if boiled for a long time, it turns to blood.

Justinus was a simple, uneducated man. Many of the Thracians had secretly preserved the Chalcedonian heresy among them, and now they fooled him, saying: "If you accept the doctrine of Chalcedon, the entire world will submit to you. Let the fourth council that of Chalcedon be added to the preceding three as valid." Overjoyed, Justinus issued a proclamation to the entire empire, delivered by armed cavalry, saying that the decrees of Chal-

---

88 Or, *an ambassador.*
89 A.D. 521.
90 Justin I, 518-527.

cedon should be preached as Orthodox. *This was done by bribing the troops and the military commanders. And the whole world was filled with strife.* The Orthodox were persecuted and were deprived of their ecclesiastical thrones. Severus, the patriarch of Antioch, *was outraged.* He went to Alexandria in the sixth year of his episcopacy and anathematized the emperor and removed from the priesthood all the clerics who had accepted the doctrines of that wicked council. When Severus quitted Antioch, fire fell from heaven and burned the royal palace in that city. Nor did the fire cease for six years. Indeed, it burned the entire city, to the point that it seemed that the fire itself was alive. A year after Severus' departure, a certain Jew named Paul, a vessel of wrath, was seated on the *patriarchal* throne in Antioch. He assembled all the Syrian bishops and harassed them to make them accept the Council of Chalcedon. Those who accepted were sent back to their thrones, but those who refused were sent into exile.

Here follows a listing of the names of those who were exiled and remained Orthodox, according to John of Asia: Antiperus bishop of Anazarba; Julius of Hagoni; John, metropolitan of Mopsuestia; Paul, of Iberia; John of Hieropolis; Paul the younger of Alexandretta, which is Iskanderun; and Nicholas of Tarsus. From Cappadocia: Proclus bishop of Colonea; Masinus of Armas; and Nicephorus of Sebastia in Armenia. From Antioch in Syria: Constantia, bishop of Lourginia, who because of his virtue and sanctity had his throne placed close to that of the patriarch, and whose name was remembered after the patriarch's name at all the masses. Antonin of Aleppo; Philoxenus, archbishop of Manbij, who was burned alive in a lime kiln at Gangra after many torments and tortures; Patra of Apamea; Theodorus and Onesimus of Zeugma and Urema; Nonus of Seleucia; Isidorus of Qeneshirin; Maras of Amida; Thomas of Damascus, a hermit who ate no bread but only vegetables for 28 years; Alexandrus from the city of Abel; Thomas from Nargab; John of Turer; another John of Ahuran; Sargis of Cyrrhus; Thomas of Germanika, which is Marash; Paul of Edessa, who subsequently weakened and returned to his throne;

John of Harran; another John of Emrin; Eustathius of Perrhin; Petrus of Ras al-Ayn; Nonus of Circesium; Paulus of Callinicus; Marion of Roman Rock, which is Hr'omklay; John of Tella; Thomas of Dara; and Aaron of Ashumusha. From Asia: The chief bishop of Caria, Euphemius; Minibanus of Pisidian Antioch; Zoxis from the city of Eldka; Peter from Elanta; Julius of Halicarnassus, who subsequently fell into heresy; Thousepeos of Ephesus, who accomplished marvels in Constantinople, standing in silent prayer vigil for three days and giving his soul to an angel of the Lord. His body radiated a heavenly light day and night which astonished the city. *Trembling*, they wanted to bury him with the martyrs, but a voice spoke from his body, saying: "Put me on my throne and bury me at Neocaesarea of Lerins." Elaphet of Casturan; Theodorus of Ulibio; Luke from the city of Mirin; Eusebius of Jedronus; Patre of Malud; Pikatur of Philadelphia; Patre of Manke; Agathadorus of Ason; Pelaginus of Mantar; Photinus of Absenia; and Alexander of Kankar.

We have omitted the bishops from smaller places, as well as the innumerable priests and deacons who, along with the senior clerics mentioned above, were sent into exile, *imprisoned, and placed in chains in Constantinople and Alexandria*. After many investigations, threats, and tortures, those who still refused to accept Chalcedon were strangled.

Here is a list of those who did not go into exile, but were killed *in situ*, in the land of Syria:

Oprinus, from the district of Antioch, and Acriane from Masuptone, were assassinated by a general; John the savant, who fled to the monastery of Blravank' in Selucia and was slain along with other monks; Cyrius, superior of the monasteries of Antioch was put to death with all the brothers of the monastery; Monks at the monastery of T'lhat were slaughtered there after being tortured. The monasteries of Saint Romanus, Saint Simon, of the apostle Silas at Kessoun, were put to the sword, and Eghnat—the head of all the monks, after many arguments with the Chalcedonians— was slain with all the others. The *monks of Sasun* John the abbot of the monastery of Kapra was slain in his place, as were the monks of many monasteries in the Edessa area. The same fate was visited on the monks at the monastery of Saint John in the eastern part of Harran, the monastery of Makanos, the monastery of the blessed Sargis, the great monastery on the mountain which, it is said, the apostle Thomas built.

The great monastery of the blessed Sahak, the grand monasteries of Mipos, Vizale, Begugel, plus seven others founded by apostles were destroyed together with their bishops and clerics in the Amida country. Similarly martyred were the monks of the monasteries of the blessed Ananians, of the blessed Abraham, of the blessed Daniel, and of the blessed Samuel. The monks of the monasteries of blessed Sabam and of T'ra, close to Ras al-Ayn were killed *after much torture*. What more shall we add? The *villages and cities of the Orthodox in the* area from Ras al-Ayn to Baghdad *and the Euphrates* was turned into a desert. As for those who fled and temporarily saved themselves, they were hunted down later and killed.

Here are the names of those doctors of the Church who encouraged the faithful and did battle with the enemy in their writings: Eghia of Scaune and Sami, Cosmas, John, and Maron from the East, Cathpa, Saint Sargis the wonder-worker, Anton and the other Eghia, Simeon, Gayshe," another Sarkis, another John, another Simeon, the holy bishop Ananias, a man of God and miracle worker.

After encouraging and defending the desolated country, all of them went together to the emperor and reproved him *boldly. Now Emperor Justin, that abode of Satan*, brought forth many theologians to counter their objections. However, when they had been defeated by the blessed men, he had all of these wondrous men slaughtered. *Justin had them secretly strangled, and this deed was covered up.* He also destroyed the monasteries in the vicinity of Rages, namely St. Zacharias, St. Aba, and St. Moge, with all their bishops and monks. Now there was a stylite named John[91] there

---

91 Or, *named Simon.*

who throughout his life had not eaten delicate foods but instead had dined on roots *in winter* and vegetables *in summer* which his students gave him. And there was another holy man named T'e'odorite' who spent his time contemplating the wonders of God and who went to Simon and had discourse with him. There was another stylite named Thomas of Dara, a great doctor of the Church *and a miracle worker* whom even the angels respected. These men too were executed after much interrogation.

Paul, the impious false bishop of Edessa, who turned back to the Chalcedonian heresy *and who was infested with demons* filled Mesopotamia with blood and caused many folk to flee to Persia where they were killed. Others, like wild animals, circulated around hiding in the mountains summer and winter, naked, barefoot, and hungry. No one could set down in writing that man's foulness. He summoned to him the blessed James, bishop of Seruj. After praying that his journey would be according to the will of God, the latter arose and went. *En route* he came to the monastery called Persians where an angel appeared to him, saying: "Turn around and bid your students to stay Orthodox, for in two days' time you will be die." And he turned and made preparations for his death. He cautioned his flock and his students and two days later, just as the angel had said, he died.

In these times, the Persian king Kawad demanded that Justin furnish 5,500 gold *centinares* to give to the general guarding the Gate of the Huns. Justin did not want to do this. As a result, the king of the Persians invaded Mesopotamia and went as far as the Antioch area. Among the captives he took were 400 virgins whom he sacrificed to his idol, Uzi. *Then Kawad turned back. And thus did Justin wreck the country, physically and spiritually.*

In this period, the waters of Shiloh vanished for 15 years. In this period too fire fell from the sky and burned the city of Baalbek—which Solomon had constructed on Mt. Lebanon—and the palaces located there. However, there were three stones which Solomon had placed there to the mystery of the Trinity which were undamaged. In this same period a woman appeared *in Cili-*

cia who was a cubit taller than any man, and who did not speak any language. She ate human food, however. She maintained herself for a long period, receiving money from all the shops. But then she suddenly disappeared. And some said that she was a nymph.

In 836 of the Syrian Era,[92] Asclepius, *a wicked and depraved man*, was bishop in Edessa and he harassed the faithful to accept the impious Council of Chalcedon. He rounded up 20 wondrous cenobites, tortured them wickedly and threw them into prison. Now it came about that in the second hour of evening, a major flood poured down from the mountains. It clashed against the city walls and retreated. The second time it came, it demolished the walls and coursed over the city, killing man and beast alike by carrying them into the Euphrates River. Asclepius saved himself by fleeing to the city's citadel as did a number of others. They wanted to stone him to death *because they knew that he was responsible for this evil*, and so he fled to Antioch. There, his co-sectarian Ephrem, patriarch of Antioch, stated: "Behold, brothers, our second Noah has escaped from the flood—which came due to some people for the sin of not accepting the Council of Chalcedon." Justin sent a great deal of gold to rebuild Edessa. As they were digging, they found an inscription written on a rock which said: "Three times will a flood visit Edessa." This was written in Chaldean script. Thirty thousand dead bodies were recovered from this flood, while the figure given by the city's residents for those known to have been carried away by the waters was 200,000.

Asclepius and Ephrem amused themselves by polluting Antioch with that foul heresy. This visited on the city more of God's anger. A fifth earthquake rocked the entire city and all the buildings, homes, palaces, and churches collapsed. *A completely new phenomenon was observed, for the wind delivered the punishment of Sodom. The river boiled over, and up from the depths came black waters* bearing crustaceans, turtles, and the bones of wild animals. The earth vomited up fire and water. And fatal fumes arose which brought death to man and beast through different ailments. For some days

---

[92] A.D. 525.

THE CHRONICLE

fire, like rain, coursed down through the air. Everyone could hear the wails of the injured, but no one dared to approach. For one and a half months, the earthquakes and the fiery rain continued without cease. The great basilica which Constantine had built shook for seven days like a stalk in the wind until it cracked and fire arose to burn the church. Only twelve hundred and fifty souls survived these disasters. Suddenly there appeared a luminous Cross in the sky which disappeared after three days. And the people cried: "Lord, have mercy, Lord, have mercy." The cries of despair from people trapped under the rubble could be heard until their last breath.

Asclepius and Ephrem, however, were nowhere to be found. They were sought for to provide advice and prayer. Now some of their intimates claimed that God spared them from this divine wrath by taking them up to Heaven. However, *because of the shaking of the ground they had been hurled into* a copper vessel used for making tar. And it was in this vessel that their bodies were later discovered. The flesh had been cooked off their bones and their bodies had been reduced to skeletons, while their heads still were visible outside the vessel. This is how they were identified. Other areas also were ruined: Syrian Seleucia by the sea, and the city of Daphe, as well as an area of twenty *mil* about Antioch, and Anazarbus, the metropolis of Cilicia, and Corinth, the metropolis of Greece. *Thus were many men and buildings lost during the wicked years of Justin's reign.*

My dear ones, listen now to this. There is a land called the country of the Himyarites which is located to the east of Egypt and north of India. In the period of Justin,[93] a certain Jew ruled over them as king. He learned that the Romans were harassing the Jews in their own district[94] *and became enraged.* In revenge he began destroying Roman merchants travelling to India, and he closed the throughways. Now Ella-Asbeha, king of the people of Cush, that is, the Ethiopians, sent to him blaming him for killing the merchants, and the Jew made a contrary reply. Then did Caleb

---

93 Justin I, 518-527.
94 Or, *under their jurisdiction.*

amass troops and vowed to God that if he should conquer the Jew, he himself would become a Christian. Caleb went against the Jew, defeated him three times, and expelled the Jews from that country. Next, he sent two princes to Justin and acquainted him with what had transpired. He also requested from him a bishop, to convert them to Christianity. Delightedly, Justin sent to him a bishop by the name of John, who was his co-sectarian Chalcedonian. John went there, baptized them, and the country, *that is, Ethiopia*, became Christian. Further rejoicing in Christ, Caleb put the country of the Himyarites under his sway and enthroned a king named Abraha. Now there were numerous Christians in Himyars. Thus, King Abraha sent to Timotheus, patriarch of Alexandria, requesting a shepherd for this flock. Timotheus sent them an Orthodox bishop and priests who opposed the Chalcedonian bishop John, defeated him with Scriptural doctrine, and removed him from his position. Then they transformed to Orthodoxy the land of Cushites and Himyarites.

One should know that *there are seven kingdoms in those parts*: India is composed of three kingdoms, and the Cushites have four kingdoms. These are in the south, and occupy a greater part of the country in the south and east. The world is divided into 24 zones, of which the Cushites, who are the Ethiopians, *and the Indians* possess fourteen. *By the grace of God, they are Orthodox and profess one nature of Christ and God.*

Nonetheless, the clamor of Chalcedon reached even here, causing conflict between the king of the Indians, Ek'santon, and Intsuk' or Hndak'. In this strife, the Jews grew strong once more and put their king over the country of the Himyars. He began persecuting and often killing Christians, encouraged in this by Justin who had sent to the Jewish king, saying: "Rid yourself of that heresy Monophysitism, for its practitioners are not my people. Nor are they yours. As we see things, you and I are of the same mind about Christ. You say that your forefathers in Jerusalem crucified a man, and we say that too, that the Jews killed a man. Those heretics there, however, claim that God was crucified. *Now these words* should not surprise you, because after the Council of Chalcedon, the Jews in Palestine wrote the same thing to Emperor Marcian. We, indeed, discovered this letter and reproduce its contents below.

> "To the Emperor and Caesar Marcian, lord of land and sea, we Jews, the children of Abraham, always wish for your success. We now must express our deep thanks to you for freeing us from the undeserved contempt of the Christians who curse us saying that we are descendants of God-killers. We now hear that you, with learned men and the brilliant senators, have stipulated that no one should dare to say that our fathers were God-killers, rather, that they killed a man. We implore your highness to impose upon us merely the price of a man's blood that was shed by our fathers. And we will pay that and free our fathers and ourselves from this insult. Be well."

Such is the letter we found that the Jews had written to Marcian, which Justin alluded to in his own letter. The Jewish king took heed of Justin's word and went against the city of Nigran where he killed the Christians living there, as other histories confirm as well as the remaining correspondence from Justin and the emissaries. For emissaries also went to Mundhir, king of the Tachiks[95] to preach about the Lord and they wrote to Justin a letter with this import:

> Your Excellency, know that under the Lord's protection, we came to Het'eta, the capital city of the Arab kingdom. However, the king whom we were seeking was not there. And so, we arose with a guide and crossed a sandy desert for ten days until we came to a mountain where we encountered

---

95 Arabs.

King Mundhir *enthroned in venerable glory. We delivered your gifts to him.* As soon as he saw us, he began to ridicule us and say, jokingly: 'Where is your Christ whom you have made Lord and God of Heaven and Earth? We have heard that you have taken from him not only his divinity, but the Roman Empire as well, claiming that he was a man who died and returned to life.' While he was engaged in this levity, emissaries arrived from the Jewish king bringing this news *written down in a letter*: 'Strengthened by the God *of Israel,* we have killed the Galilean and his followers as well. We went to Najran and, after swearing a false oath, took that city. We broke the oath, knowing that God would forgive us since we were crushing his enemies. But we cannot tell you just how much they love their Christ, for we have not been able to turn a single one of them away from him, not a child, not a woman, not a servant. Indeed, there was in Najran a royal woman with four daughters whom I spared and attempted by every means to make abandon Christ. I said to her: "May the Lord not make me destroy your beautiful face. Only say, as the emperor of the Byzantine says, that Christ was a man and that it was a man who was crucified." She spat in my face in fury. And I cruelly executed her and her daughters. Now do not make friendship with the Byzantines. On the contrary, let us go and destroy the Byzantine empire. We are sending this letter to you via the priest Abraham, who happened to be with us, *to give you advance notice* but I do not know what your response will be. *Be well.*"

It was after this that the Arabs and the Persians united and came as far as Antioch and enslaved Apamea.

It was in this period that there was a disturbance in Constantinople. A judge was slain, and simultaneously the great cathedral church was burned down. All this was the fruit of Justin's wickedness. We have given merely a sketch of the acts committed against the land and the Church *by this wicked and stupid old man who left behind him a legacy of curses. When he was nearing his end*, he made his sister's son, Justinian, a *caesar*. He gave him authority over the empire and sent him against the Persians. Now when Justinian reached Manbij, he heard about a priest's virgin daughter and he wanted to marry her. The priest, however, did not want to give her in marriage. He said: "First, abandon that heresy Chalcedonianism." And so Justinian vowed to him that "she shall keep her *Orthodox* faith with her own bishop and priests, and should it be possible, I will preach your confession throughout my country. *You, on your part, pray that this comes to pass.*" The priest therefore gave him the girl, who was named Theodora. Through her agency the Orthodox experienced much relief. Justinian took her to Constantinople with her bishops and priests. Three months later that impious old Justin died, after ruling for nine years. The young Justinian[96] assumed office and reigned for 38 years and seven months.

In that period, the Persian king Kawad sent his son to a Manichean school in their country where he learned their doctrine and pledged to his teachers that if he should come to rule he would uphold their heresy. The Manichaean teachers said: "We will pray that you reign." Now the boy's mother urged Kawad to enthrone her son during his own lifetime. The king understood the reason for this and was frightened that other kings in future would heed the Manichaeans and that people would say that it was during his rule that Magianism had been destroyed. And so Kawad convened a great assembly and invited to it all the Manichaeans with their bishops and destroyed them. As for those discovered outside, he had them burned alive, and gave their churches to the Christians. *This became known in Constantinople* where there were also many Manichae-

---

96   Justinian I, 527-565.

ans. And an attempt was made—unsuccessfully—to turn them away from their heresy. They too, were generally burned to death.

At that time, General Belisarius was sent to Persia with an enormous force on the great feast of Pascha. The Persian suggested that: "We should honor the feast day of the Jews and the Christians who are among us *and refrain from fighting until the holy day has passed.*" However the Byzantines did not heed this request and began to battle on the great feast day of Easter itself. God's wrath fell upon the Byzantines *who were defeated by the Persians*, for many died in the river and many others were slain by the sword, *and only a few returned home*. After this *victory*, when Kawad died,[97] his son Khosrov[98] ruled. His mother was tormented by demons and the mages *and sorcerers* were unable to heal her. She went to the hermit Moses, *became Christian*, was baptized and healed.

In that period, the Jews of Samaria set up a leader over themselves, destroyed Nicopolis, and did much damage. The Byzantine troops arrived and wiped them out. Then Queen Theodora began beseeching the emperor about Orthodoxy. Consequently, the emperor sent a letter to hermits in the Egyptian desert asking them to come and, through God's grace and their own prudence, examine and establish what is correct and pleasing to God doctrinally. Justinian also sent to the blessed Severus who was at Alexandria to come forth and serve the Church. The blessed Severus and a great multitude of cenobites came to Constantinople. Similarly, bishops from various districts, partisans of both sides, the Orthodox and the schismatics, convened and examined the matter for a full year. The Orthodox gained—to the point that the persecutions against them ceased. Even Anthimus, patriarch of Constantinople, was converted to Orthodoxy through its correctness and virtually the entire multitude of the city's population confessed the truth *when they saw the miracles wrought by the holy men*, with the exception of certain clerics who, devoured by ambition, heaped insults on this correct theology.

97 A.D. 531.
98 Khosrov I, 531-579.

Now while this was occurring, news came of an invasion *of barbarians into Thrace*. Twenty thousand *armed* men went off to war, in the joyous hope of returning everyone to Orthodoxy. The emperor arose to accompany the troops *outside the city*, then returned to a church and prayed. The entire city was stirred up. The streets, terraces, roofs, porches of the church filled up with men and women shouting: "Pious emperor, let there be one confession of the faith, make everyone hold to one faith." The emperor wept for many hours and then answered the people: "Let it be as you wish." Then the crowd cried out: "Emperor, make haste during your lifetime to bring peace to brothers divided. We shall all unite in the one nature of the Word God." And then again did the emperor cry, sobbing loudly. He exclaimed: "Go and let it be as you will." For the faith, *affirming One Nature*, preached and practiced by those monks—the ones with the heavenly behavior, with the divine speech, and the miracle-making—that is the correct faith.

Now the emperor indeed wanted to restore Orthodoxy, since he knew that the Chalcedonians were schismatics. However, Chalcedonians secretly visited the emperor and instilled fear in him, both physical and spiritual. They said: "It would be hateful to God and to mankind if you believe your wife in matters of doctrine. For 636 bishops in unison have condemned and anathematized those who did not accept their Chalcedonian doctrine, and this confession has been proclaimed as Orthodox throughout the entire land. The adherents of Chalcedonianism will not tolerate your doing this." And so the emperor was frightened and in doubt about what to do. *And so, with the threat of excommunication and even of threats against his life, the emperor was constrained to silence.* When Severus heard about this he said: "Truly to Peter was given the authority to bind and to release. Now those who lack the confession of Peter do not have such authority. Quite the contrary, they themselves are guilty and should be anathematized. Peter himself professed One Nature of Christ, not two, when he said 'You are the revealed Son of God.'" Now when the hermits saw that the emperor was prevaricating, and that doctrinal peace would not be established, they said: "Oh emperor, our faith is not young nor recent that it will mature, it is not old and in need of rejuvenation, nor is it lacking and in need of supplementing. It is neither too much nor too little. Rather, it is the same faith that the Holy Spirit through the prophets inculcated, that the Apostles assembled for, that Our Lord Jesus Christ God correctly realized and established. And there is nothing that will make us turn from it, neither gifts nor bribes, neither death nor prison. On the contrary, we stand before man just as we stand before God. *O emperor, you should think about your own faith.*" After saying this, they returned to their desert retreats, while Severus, taking Anthimus along with him, went to Alexandria.

The blessed stylite Mar Zohar who lived in the Amida area heard about these developments and went to Constantinople with ten of his students to challenge the emperor. When he was face to face with the emperor, Mar Zohar asked: "How long will the evils of the accursed Council of Chalcedon endure? Why do you not eliminate it and cleanse the Church?" The emperor was infuriated at this insult and cursing of the Council. With his hand, he struck the holy man's breast and demanded: "By what sign or miracle do you know that your doctrine is correct? And why, in my presence, do you dare to curse the blessed Council?" Mar Zohar retorted: "I anathematize it and may those who believe in it be anathematized. And since you want to see some sign, I trust that the living God will visit such a sign upon you." Mar Zohar furiously quitted the emperor's presence. This seemed like a gross insult to the emperor and he immediately had it written that thereafter whoever cursed the Council of Chalcedon should be executed. This command was promulgated.

Then an angel of the Lord appeared to the emperor in a vision, striking his head with his hand, causing the emperor to fall down, have the wind knocked out of him, and to lose consciousness. Then did Empress Theodora go and fall at the feet of the blessed Mar Zohar, begging him to come and put his hand upon Justinian and, should he be restored to life, he would do as asked of him. The holy man came and touched him and prayed, and Justinian was immediately revived. And Mar Zohar requested that a council be held to restore Orthodoxy. Severus and Theodosius the patriarch of Alexandria, Anthimus and many others arrived for this. *The wicked patriarch of Antioch, by means of the wise Sargis, informed* Agapetus, Pope of Rome[99] about the council and he joined them as well. The emperor and the city exalted him upon his entry into Constantinople. But three patriarchs, Severus, Anthimus, and Theodosius, did not go before him in welcome. After a few days, Agapetus began to blame the emperor, saying: "Who is that deceiver Zohar who has altered your faith in the blessed Council of Chalcedon *and strained it through a sieve?* Hand him over to me *and I will advise him.*" The emperor so ordered. However, the blessed Mar Zohar had secluded himself in vigils and prayer, because it was the first week of Lent. Three times a messenger was sent to him, but there was no reply. Then Pope Agapetus sent to him saying: "Either you come to us here, or the emperor and I will come to you." At that point, Mar Zohar replied: "Until Maundy Thursday I will not go out to see anyone, nor will I receive anyone here." Enraged, Pope Agapetus held a meeting and anathematized the blessed Severus, Anthimus, Theodorus, and Zohar, and professed the doctrine of the two natures as well as the heresy of Nestorianism. The wrath of God fell upon him immediately, for his tongue grew swollen and heavy and his mouth could no longer contain it. His tongue hung out of his mouth. Three times doctors tried to ameliorate the problem, but they were unable to reduce the swelling or to stop the progress of the ulcer which made him suffer miserably throughout Lent. He died wickedly on Holy Thursday. Then the *weak* emperor *merely* lifted his declaration about killing those who cursed the Council of Chalcedon, and the holy men returned to their own places.

In this period, the remains of the blessed Marinos were discovered in the village of Djantaris in the district of Antioch. The body was intact in a wooden coffin, and it was covered with

---

99 Agapetus I, 535-536.

wounds. It effected many cures *to the glory of Christ*. It was taken to Antioch.

In these days the Persians came *into Mesopotamia* and captured Aleppo and Antioch and even took away the marble columns. The Byzantines came and took revenge by plundering Persian territory. After this, the Persian king Khosrov himself came against Edessa but was unable to capture it. After enslaving Seroudj and demolishing Antioch, he withdrew.

In this period, two bishops of the Chalcedonian heresy in Constantinople, Isaiah and Alexander, were seized as homosexuals. At the emperor's order, they were cut in two and their bodies were hanged up on poles for the city to see, with town criers proclaiming: "Such is the punishment for such a deed." The word of Paul was realized here, that "Since they did not see fit to acknowledge God, God gave them up to a base mind and improper conduct."[100]

In the fifth year of Justianian, the Persians arose and enslaved Delimiton and Callinicos, and destroyed Beth Balas. From the latter city, they looted and took to their country the relics of Saint Bacchus, as well as the gold they found in the tomb of Saint Sergius.

In the year 848 of the Syrian Era[101] an event occurred that is beyond belief. Had I not known about it from many different writings, I myself would not have included it. The sun was eclipsed for 18 months. For three hours in the morning, it would give light, but a light that resembled neither day nor night. During that year, fruit did not reach the point of maturity, and all the land became as though transformed into something half alive, or *like someone suffering from a long illness*. An unprecedented plague ensued which began in Constantinople where the first day 5,000 people died, the next day 10,000, the third 15,000, the fourth 18,000—figures reported by the auditors that the emperor had placed at the gates of the city. They counted up to 300,000 people dead and then left off counting. The epidemic first attacked the poor class of the population, then

---

100   Romans, 1:28.
101   A.D. 537.

the merchants and the nobility including the Imperial Palace. The trouble began with a wound that formed in the palm of the hand, and progressed until the afflicted one could not take a step. The legs swelled, then the buboes burst and pus came out. The city began to stink from the unburied corpses and so the bodies were thrown into the sea, but the bodies kept resurfacing. The emperor ordered that 40 *dahegans* be paid to people who would carry a corpse out of town, but often the bearers themselves fell dead in the street. Furthermore, it even happened that someone would enter a deserted house and gather up its treasures to steal, but would end up dying at the door, on the way out.

The plague spread to Egypt where one city was wiped out in this manner: only seven men and a boy remained alive there. As they wandered around the city, suddenly the seven men died on the spot. Then the lad saw the angel of God in the guise of an old man. Seeing the child weeping, the angel removed him from the city and said: "Go now and weep not, for this punishment is the payment for heresy and sin."

In one city in the country of Palestine, demons appeared and said: "Go and find that buried bronze image and bow down to it and you will be spared." The people looked around, unearthed it, paid homage to it, and every single one of them died. This same pestilence, the wrath of God, reached Armenia and Persia. The city of Hems, however, where the head of John the Baptist was located, and it inhabitants who sought refuge in it and its intercession—these were spared.

In the 19th year of Justinian,[102] barbarians took and pillaged Rome. It was damaged to such an extent that those remaining moved to nearby areas since the city was uninhabitable for a time. In this period, the blessed Severus died in Alexandria and was buried with honor. The Orthodox installed the hermit Sargis as their patriarch at Antioch. In this period, the monastery of the blessed Symeon in Antioch burned down and its monks dispersed. In this period, the date of the celebration of Easter was upset. In the 23rd

---

102 A.D. 546.

year of Justinian, the river at Tarsus rose and flooded the city. In the same period, the city of Laodicea with 7,000 of its inhabitants was destroyed in an earthquake. The city of Pompeiopolis[103] in Mysia sank and its inhabitants, still living, were sucked into the pit. Their cries were heard for days, but no one could help them. In Phoenicia the cities of Tripoli, Byblos, and Trovas sank together with all the cities of Galilee. Then the sea retreated by two *mils*, and boats became stranded on land.

In these days, Petra was captured and fortified by the Persians. When the Byzantines learned about this, they went and besieged the city for seven months before retaking it. In the same period, a catastrophic famine took place to the point that a person might eat five *ltrs* of bread, swell up, and still be famished. For two years animals were dying of epidemic throughout the country and the labor of oxen fell off. There was also an earthquake in Constantinople which lasted for forty days and many homes became the tombs of their residents. Numerous churches were demolished and a part of Nicomedia was destroyed. In the 30th year of Justinian, two of Constantinople's walls—those built by Constantine and Theodosius—fell into ruin. The city of Rhegium collapsed, and for ten days the country shook like a leaf. In this period lived the blessed James called Kurdnkar.

In this period, the Christian Arab king named Harith sent to Justinian blaming him for destroying Christianity with the Council of Chalcedon and for turning the Trinity into a Quaternity. Justinian sent some sages to make a reply to him.

When they arrived and the king saw them, he asked: "Are you students of that accursed Council? *Then I shall not greet you.*" They replied: "Why do you command that your kingdom do such things as to curse 636 holy men? Were they merely lay people, it would be a serious matter, to say nothing of the fact that they were leaders of the church and blessed people?" King Harith retorted: "I am a barbarian who does not know how to speak properly, and I am illiterate. But let me ask you something: If a mouse

---

103   Or, *Pentapolis*.

falls into the food which will be eaten by multitudes of people, has that food become corrupted or not?" And they replied: "Yes. It has become spoiled." King Harith continued: "By the same token, have not those 636 bishops been corrupted by the Tome of Leo, which converts Christianity into Judaism?" After much additional discourse, those men made answer. "Let us celebrate the liturgy and take communion together as a display of the friendship between your kingdom and ours." Harith replied: "We shall not take communion with you nor administer it to you." He ordered that the meat of unclean animals *such as donkey and camel* be prepared for their meal. When the food had been served, he said: "Eat." And they replied: "We will not eat such food, for it is unclean." The king asked: "How then would we not be corrupted by eating the flesh of a man, for that is your mass." Then he released them in disgrace.

In this period Empress Theodora of Orthodox confession died, and she was buried by the patriarchs Anthimus and Theodorus.

In Justinian's reign several heresies were uncovered. They are: (1) a group of heretics derived from Manichaeism who came from Persia wearing the clothing of monks. They communed using the blood of a white hen and that of a slain boy. Once a year, they perpetrated these Manichaean crimes; (2) that of Stephen of Edessa, who claimed that after a certain amount of penance for sins, one could become the equal of the just; (3) that of John of Apamaea, who claimed that the essence of God was matter like any other element; (4) that of Julian of Halicarnassus, who claimed that Christ took the body of Adam before his corruption and sin, and that Christ's body was uncorruptible as the Orthodox believe. For Adam was the second or a double, the first lacked the mixture, but after his sins it mixed with corruption. Severus upbraided him, citing theological literature, but he did not recant and remained in his cult; (5) that of John of Hareth, who claimed that the godhead had three natures. He had been a student of Samuel of Ras al-Ayn. Emperor Justinian summoned him into his presence, listened to his heresy, and persecuted him. John of Hareth went and sought support for his heresy in the Bible; (6) that of Photinus of Antioch, who also claimed that the godhead existed in three natures, beings, and personalities. He also produced some writings in Constantinople; (7) that of Theodorus the Cappadocian, which claimed that the deity of Christ was not the same as the Father; (8) that of Athanasius, grandson of Empress Theodora, who had studied with Simon of Edessa and then with the priest Sargis who became patriarch of Antioch. Theodorus preached the heresy of John, claiming that the Trinity had three separate natures. The emperor urged the patriarch Theodorus to make him a priest, but he did not agree to this. After the death of Theodorus, he wanted to make Athanasius patriarch of Alexandria and wrote to the Alexandrians, but they did not agree. Kaynon, the bishop of Tarsus and Eugenius of Seleucia increased the heresy of Athanas and because of that sect got all the other heretics opposed to the homily of Theodorus, patriarch of Alexandria. (9) Ninth was the heresy of Anthimus of Constantinople who said: "Those who do not confess three distinct natures of the Godhead are Judaizing and opposed to Orthodoxy."

In these times, Harith, king of the Arabs, came to Justinian, bringing with him a statement of the faith drawn up by the eastern bishops of Greater Armenia, James Kurdnkar, and the patriarch of Alexandria. He said: "Those who do not subscribe to this are heretics and wicked." Now many did not subscribe to it and Harith grew angry at Justinian, saying: "O you unaware and foolish man, do you not know that all the heavenly wrath which has poured down on this country is because of this evil council?

Why do you not eliminate the cause of God's anger?" And Justinian answered: "I beg you not to be angry. I cannot do what you say and also continue to reign. However, because of your complaint I will not permit the Chalcedonians to deal so pridefully and assuredly with the Orthodox, and the persecution of those with your Orthodox confession will end. For I shall use you as the reason for these changes, so that no one will blame me over what constitutes Orthodoxy. The Orthodox will grow and flourish and God will see to their rehabilitation at the proper time and under the proper emperor."

Then King Harith summoned to him Orthodox bishops and James and had ordained in Constantinople a patriarch of the Orthodox, similarly in Antioch and Alexandria *and in Jerusalem. He then dispatched them,* and warned that no one should bother them. After this, Harith returned to his kingdom. Then the Orthodox said to the Chalcedonians, "You have confirmed the heresies of Nestorius, Theodoret and Theodorus." For this reason, the emperor convened an assembly of numerous bishops to respond to the Orthodox.

The patriarchs were Domnus of Antioch, Apollonaire of Alexandria, Eutyches of Constantinople. Vigilius[104] of Rome was then in Constantinople because Rome had become a ruin. But he did not want to attend the council, pridefully claiming that he was not one of their colleagues. *They barely managed to get him to the conference.* When they wanted to anathematize Nestorius, Theodoretus, Theodorus of Mopsuestia and the other Theodorus from Tarsus, Vigilius forbade it, saying: "One hundred and thirty years after their deaths it is improper to anathematize these blessed men *who had been deemed praiseworthy by our predecessors*." And since they were not anathematized, no one accepted this *proposal, and they returned to their homes.*

In this period the heresy of Julian of Halicarnassus revealed itself in Ephesus, the disciples of Julian claiming that Christ's dispensation was an illusion. Bishop Procopius came among them and was reprimanded by many but did not repent. The people asked that he, because of his age, select some one of his students as a replacement bishop for themselves. But he refused, saying: "I am only one person and it is impossible to do this because three bishops are required for an ordination." Now when Procopius died, his students selected someone named Eutropius and placed the deceased Procopius' hand on his head, making him a bishop *without a single bishop being present.* Eutropius then ordained ten other

---

104 Pope Vigilius, 537-555.

bishops and sent them throughout the country to spread this heresy. One of them, Sargis, went to the country of the Himyars and deceived many people. He made one Movses their bishop who died after three years. Others, in various places, slandered the blessed Severus, claiming that he had said that Christ's body was corruptible and had decayed in the grave.

However, Severus had said that Christ had taken our corruptible body and made it incorruptible, not that it corrupted in the grave, and he in fact anathematized those who described the corruption in this manner. The Julianites claimed that Christ had taken from the Virgin's womb an immortal and incorruptible body and that his passion and death were apparent and not real. One of these sectarians went to Alexandria and mingled with other heretics, the Pantiaks and Lakinatsis where they ordained their own patriarch. He in turn ordained many bishops and sent them *throughout the world.*

However, eventually they turned against one another. Two of them were in jail in Nisibis. The Persian king requested them, and they were released. Now one of them went north *and east* and misled many people. He arrived at Arzn in Armenia, but the Armenians did not receive him. Rather they sent letters to the patriarch of the Orthodox in Antioch, Theodorus, *asking his opinion of the sectarians, whether to receive them or not.* However, he had just died. Then the Chalcedonians wrote a letter as did the Orthodox testifying to their disagreement; the heretics were persecuted. Nonetheless, they managed to deceive many people in Cappadocia and, it said, a remnant of them remained among the Armenians until finally the evil was eliminated.

In this period, Emperor Justinian wanted to renovate the Church of the Apostles and the mausoleum of the emperors. During the digging they discovered three lead coffins which bore inscriptions to the blessed Andrew, Luke, and Timothy. The discovery of the relics of Christ's Apostles brought great joy to the city. The *sebastos* of Caesarea Palestina sent to Constantinople the right hand of someone said to be John the Baptist.

THE CHRONICLE

Although there was some questioning about this, it was placed in a golden reliquary. Justinian constructed 12 monasteries and 96 churches, nor did he cease building churches, hostels, and places for the poor.

In 871 of the Syrian Era,[105] the Armenian Era[106] began. *This was in the 34th year of Justinian[107] during the tenure of the patriarch Nerse's, during the reign of the Persian king Xosrov. Others claim that the Armenian Era of dating was initiated during the tenure of Catholicos Movse's after 40 years of our persecution over Chalcedon.*

After 40 years of persecution and incubation of the Chalcedonian heresy, the city of Amida experienced severe famine for eight months. After eating bread, people would experience a year of diabolical madness and frenzy bereft of their senses, to the point that they would not recognize their own belongings and their own homes. Rather, they entered their homes accidentally, and they committed fornication in public and in the churches. Then they would quit the city and begin barking like dogs, calling out like dumb beasts or roosters. They would strip and run away with no reason, exclaiming "The Persians are coming. They are coming, flee!" People from the surrounding district and from Edessa would come and encounter them and ask for God's mercy. After a year, the afflicted would regain their senses, don black garb, and go on pilgrimage to Jerusalem and elsewhere. After this, an epidemic spread which killed 36,000 people.

Emperor Justinian accepted Chalcedon throughout his entire reign but rejected the letter of Ibas of Edessa, nor would he believe people when they told him that the Council of Chalcedon had accepted Ibas' letter. Now when the pope of Rome, Vigilius, declared that the Council of Chalcedon accepted the letter of Ibas, the emperor rose and declared three times: "The Council of Chalcedon is accursed." Nonetheless, Justinian was deceived by the

---

105 A.D. 560.
106 A calendrical system.
107 *A.D. 552.*

MICHAEL THE GREAT

heresy of the Julianites, through the bishop of Apamea. He wrote to Athanasius, the patriarch of Antioch, informing him about the heresy and insisting that a council be convened about it. A council of 195 bishops convened in Antioch but they not accept it. They wrote to the emperor adducing written proofs that this was a foul heresy, comparable to the torment of our Lord. This document was brought before the emperor. Now some say that when he had read it, he repented about both heresies and turned his face away from the doctrines of Chalcedon and of the Julianites, and died Orthodox, having reigned for 38 years and five months. When Justinian was dying, one of the marvelous religious men had a vision which he related: "I saw an enormous field and in its midst a furnace breathing flames. And I asked: 'For whom are these bitter torments?' And someone told me: 'This was prepared for Justinian.'

However, because of his love for the Church and for the poor, he did not allow himself to die a heretic. Rather, he turned to Orthodoxy and has gone to the place of the Orthodox.'"

After Justinian's reign his sister's son, also called Justinian,[108] ruled along with his wife.[109] He was a formidable military man who did not permit dissension, and so all malefactors fled. He was from Thrace, and a valiant man. His feet, however, pained him. In the first year of his reign a blazing flame appeared in the sky and many said that it portended bloodshed. The emperor had specialists brought from Zamron and Mamcon *who anointed themselves and* were able to walk on burning wood without getting burned. Once again, fire appeared in the northeastern sky. Many died after looking at it. It brought with it the smell of burning reeds or burning paper. Many people gathered in baskets what had fallen from the sky. The emperor, terrified, went to the church to plead as did the entire city. At the ninth hour a fiery cloud appeared with a Cross visible on it. When the multitude saw this, they begged: "Lord have mercy, Lord bestow on us your great mercy." Then the patriarch said to the emperor: "*Fear not.* Do you see what has

---

108 Justin II, 565-578.
109 Sophia, regent 573-574.

occurred in your own day, that a flaming Cross has appeared as happened during the time of the great Constantine? *The Lord has honored you.* Send to Apamea of the Syrians and have brought here the piece of wood from Christ's Cross which a certain bishop keeps." *The emperor sent troops there under a military commander* and had the Cross forcibly taken to Antioch. *There was considerable resistance to this from the local people who believed that this Cross, their pride and protection should not be taken from their country. But after great opposition, it was taken* and split into two parts. One part was left in Antioch and the other was taken to Constantinople. The city and the emperor came out before it and reverentially brought it into the city where they put it into the cathedral church.

In the second year of Justin's reign the patrician John was sent with gifts to the Persian king Xosrov out of friendship. He went and returned in honor. In this period there was no king of Armenia since they had entered under Persian rule. Xosrov, king of the Persians, began to harass the Armenians to worship fire. The Armenians rebelled and sought troops in assistance from Jusin. They triumphed over the Persians and drove them from the land. Xosrov sent to Justin, saying: "Do not help the Armenians. Order them to return to Persian sovereignty and to pay taxes. *If you care so much about them, then pay me their taxes.*" Justin replied: "Give me Nisibis, which is Christian, and in friendship I will return them to you?"[110] Xosrov was silent *and frightened* after hearing this. The patrician John got an order from Justin to discuss unifying the faith of the Armenians and Syrians with their own. He went to Callinicos and had discussions with James Kurdnkar and then held an assembly. John *wanted them to accept the unholy Council of Chalcedon* but they did not, and the Armenians ridiculed them.

In the fourth year of Justin's reign a disturbance broke out over the date of Easter, and they celebrated a false Easter. In this period, Bishop John of Sarmatia, a corrupting man without fear

110 Or, *Why do you speak about Christianity? Are you unaware that, using the Armenians, I will take from you Nisibis and whatever else you hold in Mesopotamia?*

of God, persuaded the emperor to torment the Orthodox by depriving them of their sees, churches and freedom, putting them in chains and prison, and putting them to death *if they did not accept their Chalcedonian doctrine*. This came after forty years *of exile* and persecution. And so bishops went about with troops, the faithful were rebaptized, other clerics were ordained, and those resisting were either killed, exiled, or imprisoned. The country was filled up with great anger and disturbance. We are unable to write down the disasters this brought about or what the Holy Church endured because of it. After thousands and tens of thousands had been slain by the godless John, who was the patriarch of Constantinople, the emperor wearied of the calamities and said to John: "Give me a signed confession of your faith." John wrote this and gave it to the emperor who, upon reading it, realized that he was a Nestorian. He became enraged at him, removed him from his see and sent him into exile. Then he said to his military commander Anastas: "Quickly bring back from exile those Orthodox who are still alive, and do not allow any Chalcedonians to appear before me in future." But can one ignore all the things that had happened before this?

The great man of God, the renowned John, who wrote books about the Fathers and many other books which he gave as ornaments for the Church had been exiled and was then in a prison in Constantinople. The emperor and the patriarch John sent to him for him to be released from prison and to serve as an intercessor in bringing peace to the Church—if he would accept the Fourth Council. But instead, he cursed the Council, the patriarch and the emperor. They became furious, deprived him of visitors, and threw him into a damp cell. The blessed one suffered from pains of the legs and the head, and lice and inflammations caused wounds on his body, while flies and wasps bit him day and night. He was unable to cover himself and lay for hours like a corpse. After a long time, a young man wearing a beautiful robe visited him, apparently one of the emperor's commanders. He was of Orthodox faith. He kissed the prisoner and who started to feel relieved of his pains.

Then he departed. He returned bringing wine. John drank and then blessed him, saying: "Blessings upon you, my son, for caring for me." Thus for eight days did this youth serve, heartening and encouraging him, saying: "Be patient, father. Blessed are those who bear such tribulations for the sake of Orthodoxy." He cited examples from Scripture concerning the faith and patience shown by his predecessors *such as Job and Daniel.*

John was delighted with his wisdom and asked: "Young man, whence does such complete wisdom come to you as a lad, wisdom which I, in my old age, do not possess?" The man replied: "Father, everything is possible to the Holy Spirit. Rejoice for you shall emerge from this place and enlighten many people." After this the patriarch's archbishop came and said to him: "Holy father, hear and obey the emperor so that there will be unity in the members of Christ." The holy man responded: "May Christ God curse you. Have you no shame? Even if you are sincere, after causing such grief to the Church of God, who would reconcile with you, leaving aside the fact that you are a heretic and hateful to God." The archbishop departed. *He went and narrated all this to the emperor and the patriarch.* Then, at the emperor's command, people came and removed John from prison and took him to an island inhabited by idol-worshipping barbarians. He was thus exiled there. Through his doctrine and miracle-working he converted *many tens of thousands of* people to belief in Christ, to the glory of Christ our God Who is blessed for all eternity. Amen.

News of the persecution of the Orthodox reached the country of Persia. The mages *and the chief mage* assembled and went before their king Xosrov, saying: "Why do you not do what the Byzantines do? When people do not turn to their faith, they kill them wickedly? In your kingdom live those who do not worship the sun as you do." When the Persian king heard this, he began a great persecution throughout all parts of his realm. He had three bishops taken and flayed alive, killed many others through diverse tortures, and demolished many monasteries. There is no tallying the slain. He sent to Armenia to build fire-temples there. Enraged, the Armenians, encouraged by God, slew them without mercy. The great Catholicos who resided in Dwin went to Constantinople to secure troops to resist the Persians. The Byzantine patriarch and the entire city came out to greet his arrival in Constantinople. When the people in Armenia learned about this honor shown by the Chalcedonians and that the patriarch was keeping the Catholicos with him constantly *because the army was not ready*, they were worried that he might be tricked. Thus they sent this message to him: "Do not accept their belief because of our need of their protection, for our hope is in Christ and we shall not change our Orthodox faith out of fear of death. *Return to Armenia with us.*" This letter was taken and delivered. However, the *Catholicos* had already realized the wickedness of the heretics, had separated himself from them, and was staying by himself. While he was delayed in Constantinople, he passed away in Orthodox faith and was prepared for burial by the Orthodox. *By the order of the emperor, he was buried with great honor in the Orthodox cemetery in Constantinople.* This was to be a great support and confirmation of the faith and pride of the Orthodox, for the Armenians would remain with the truth, standing apart from both sides, from the Persians and from the Chalcedonians. For it is God alone, not man, who can strengthen and aid people.

Now the empress Sophia, who was the niece[111] of the empress Theodora, had been raised Orthodox and was a virtuous and pious woman. She was to have a religious vision. Presently, she took communion from the formerly Orthodox priest, Andreas. This man had been persuaded to exalt Chalcedon and to take communion with them, *and for a year he had been taking Sophia with him to the Chalcedonian church. This went on for about one year.* Then the blessed Virgin Mary appeared to Sophia and said: "My daughter, why have you abandoned me and followed after heretics?" And she replied: "It is because I do not know the correct doctrine. Teach me." The blessed Virgin said: "It is sufficient that you say 'the Father, the Son, and the Holy Spirit *have mercy on me*'

---

111 Sister's daughter.

and not accept communion from the Chalcedonians." When she had seen and heard this, Sophia left the Chalcedonians and did not taken communion from them.

Now around this time, in the eighth year of his reign, the emperor Justin made his cousin Marcian[112] a *Caesar*, and sent him against Nisibis. Marcian, going to Dara, sent troops into the country of the Persians. These troops raided, and returned to Dara with an enormous amount of booty. The Persians were terrified.

Through bribes and servile humility, the Persian *marzpan* who was at Nisibis kept Marcian away from the city until additional provisions could be brought to it, and their king could be informed, and the city's Christians could be removed. On the feast of Easter they surrounded the city and commenced fighting on all sides and were about to capture it. At that point Acacius arrived with the emperor's order that he was to remove and replace Marcian. Marcian said: "Give me two more days *and I will capture the city*." But this plea went unheeded, Marcian's honored status was removed and rudely. The army was saddened and left off besieging the city. Many thought that the emperor had died. They stopped fighting and dispersed, while the city fortified itself. The cause of Marcian's removal is worth mentioning.

The country of the Tachiks[113] is divided into two parts. Half, under a Christian king, was Christian while the other half, under the Persian monarchy, was pagan. At this time the Christian king was Mundhir, who had succeeded his father, King Harith. They were always friends and allies of the Byzantines traditionally *because of their Christian faith*. Now it happened that Mundhir went to the country of the Persians, took captives, and then went and pitched his tent in that part of Arabia which believed that he was the Persian king to whom they were loyal. Thus, people went to him unarmed. Mundhir killed them, and took that portion of Arabia. He looted and enslaved it, and returned home with an enormous amount of booty. When the Persians learned about

---

112 Mother's sister's son.
113 Arabs.

this, they held a great meeting, and resolved to go against Mundhir's land. When Mundhir learned about this, he sent to Justin requesting a lot of gold to purchase mercenaries to fight against the Persians. Justin was saddened by the request, thinking that it was a demand for taxes.

Then Justin wrote two letters. One was addressed to Mundhir which said: "Go to Marcian *in Nisibis and provide him with aid. Then he will help you keep your country.* I have ordered him to provide you with *as much* gold and troops *as you want.*" Justin wrote to Marcian: "When Mundhir comes to you, secretly behead him and send the good news to me." It was God's will that the letters got mixed up. What had been written to Mundhir went to Marcian, and the letter to Marcian was delivered to Mundhir. When Mundhir read the letter, he received he said: "In return for what wickedness are they planning to do this to me?" And he thanked prescient God for saving him from Justin's evil plot. *He wrote to Justin, revealing that he had learned about his evil intentions.*

When Justin found out what had happened, he suspected that Marcian had sent his letter along to Mundhir, and that the two had become friendly. Thus, he sent Acacius to put Marcian in irons.

Now it happened that the Persian troops learned that Mundhir had separated from Byzantine alliance and that he was not arriving to help the Byzantines who were besieging Nisibis. Therefore they returned to Mesopotamia, destroyed the Byzantine forces and put others to flight. Then they continued on to Antioch and Apamea, enslaving all of Mesopotamia which was under the Byzantines. Then they went against Dara. The multitude of Byzantine troops which had fled were seeking safety from the Persians there in Dara. The Persians went and besieged the city. *But the Byzantines displayed great bravery there. Consequently, deceitfully, the Persians behaved as if they were giving way and departing. The exhausted Byzantine troops left off guarding the wall and went to relax and eat some bread. At that point, the Persians sol-*

diers returned, struck at the wall, scaled it with ladders on all sides, got inside, and began killing. Then they departed to their own land with great joy. Now the Persian king Xosrov selected some 5,000 young virgins from among the captives. He prepared troops and sent them to the country of the T'etalats'ik' in T'urk'astan with a lot of treasure to persuade the T'etalats'ik' to come to his aid against the Byzantines, Armenians, and Mundhir's forces. The girls watered the road with their tears as they traveled along, for they were the lambs of Christ who would be food for wolves. They came and descended by a large Persian river. There the girls took counsel with each other and came up with a plan. They said to the soldiers: "Have pity on us and go off a ways and avert your eyes so that we may bathe after our wearying journey." They agreed with this request and distanced themselves. Then the virgins began to pray: "Christ God, salvation of Christians, the crown and blessed bridegroom to virgins come to us and take us under your blessed veil and do not give us who confess you to the wild beasts. By the prayers of your immaculate mother, the blessed Virgin, the Mother of God, and the intercession of all your saints, by the blood of our parents who were martyred for you, slain by the impious ones, receive us." Then all of them went onto the bridge, jumped into the water and died.

When the troops realized what had happened, they approached but could not find a single one of them alive. They *wept for many hours and then sadly* went and told their king. He was astonished *and did not blame the soldiers*, but that plan of his came to naught. The Persian troops besieged the city of Dara for two years. The Byzantines displayed great valor there; however, the Persians were able to take the city by deceit. The Byzantines had become tired and left off guarding the wall to sit down to eat and drink. Then the Persians suddenly struck, encircled the walls with ladders, took the city, and destroyed it.

After these developments, Justin became reconciled with the patriarch John. *The Chalcedonians claimed that everyone would soon accept their doctrine.* Encouraged by John and by other Chalcedonians, the idol-worshipping emperor resumed persecuting the Orthodox using death, various tortures, and insults which the pen cannot describe nor the ears listen to. So God sent to the emperor and the patriarch angry demons who seized control of their minds. They became enraged and began barking like dogs and meowing like cats and tearing out their hair and beards with all ten fingers. Other ailments were visited upon them, leading them toward death. Now after many insults and humiliations, both of them were removed from this life by the demons, choked to death. But before the emperor's death, during a slight break in the demonic possession, people asked him: "Who will sit on the throne of the kingdom?" The emperor frequently named a Thracian notary named Tiberius. Thus, they made him emperor. He was of Greek nationality. From the time of Gaius Julius Caesar until the last Justin, fifty emperors had been of Roman nationality and the army was called "Roman." This had been because of Rome and also because of Constantinople, which Constantine had named "the new Rome." The two were mixed together by language and writing, and did not separate until Tiberius. With him begins again the reign of Greek emperors. For from ancient times, from the time of the Macedonians, there were 38 emperors who were called Greeks, from Cronos the Macedonian to Perseus in the year 288 of the Syrian Era.[114] The second period of Greek emperors began in 886 of the Syrian Era[115] which corresponds to the year 15 of the Armenian Era.[116]

Now at this time the Persian king, Xosrov, was elated with his triumph in Mesopotamia. He then went to the country of the Armenians where the Armenians displayed great valor, with the support of the Byzantines. Thus, for the second time, Xosrov departed in shame. But on the third attempt the king massed troops and, marching north toward the mountains and bypassing Armenia, entered Cappadocia. The Byzantines resisted him. He went

---

114   B.C. 23.
115   A.D. 575.
116   A.D. 566.

to Sebastia, captured and burned it. *The Byzantines then retreated somewhat.* The Byzantines *got reinforcements and* went to war again, seizing one of the Persian camps, and the fire-temple which they carried around with them. This they pulled apart. Indeed, had there not been discord among the Byzantines, they could have completely eliminated the Persians. But due to the dissension, the Persians were able to gain strength. They went and took Armenian Melitene and burned it. The Byzantine forces sent word to the Persians: "What is this destruction and burning you are doing? Such is not your king's rule. Rather, if a territory is captured in war then it belongs to you. We do not commit such destructive acts in your country, even though our emperor is not with us." *Now come and fight us.* When the Persian commander heard this, he was ashamed and took his stand by the eastern side of the city. The Byzantine troops went and took up position opposite them and there was no fighting from morning until the ninth hour. Then the Persians went and started retreating by crossing the Euphrates and the Byzantines went after them. Hurrying as they crossed, many Persians were drowned. After this the Persians went to Armenia and then to their own country. Then Xosrov made it a law that a king should not go in person on raiding and looting expeditions with the troops, only if it involved a battle with another king.

The Byzantine forces headed northward to war with a part of the land of Armenia and to loot it *because of the Armenians' anti-Chalcedonian Orthodoxy.* Since they were Christians, people from the monasteries and villages went out before them preceded by the Cross and the Gospel, *to inspire the Byzantines with respect and affection by these signs of Christ the Redeemer.* The Byzantines impudently hurled those crosses to the ground, stripped the clerics and laity of their clothing, killing or enslaving them, raped believing virgins, and tore women's earrings from their ears. Bracelets which were difficult to remove they ripped from their arms, tearing the flesh. And they did many other wicked things. Taking the booty, they turned back joyfully, as though from a major victory. Leaving their horses and removing their weapons, they sat down to eat and drink. It was then that the Persian troops turned around, and then that the rage of God fell upon their heads for the evils they had visited upon the Christians. The Persians came and destroyed them. They seized all the horses, weapons, and everything the Byzantines had, and departed in great triumph.

At that time there assembled the bishops, priests, and monastics of Mesopotamia and Armenia who were under the rule of the Byzantines. They went to Tiberius to ask for peace so that they might practise their faith freely *and in exchange they would serve loyally. "Otherwise, slay us with your sword," they said.* Some of the Chalcedonians attempted to get the emperor angry with the Orthodox. However, the emperor *silenced them*, held an assembly and loudly declaimed:

"Hear all that I have to say. Most of you do not know how Emperor Justin died since you were not present, whereas I was there with him, morning and evening, as many of you can testify. The emperor was suffering from horrible pains *and I was attending him. I saw the angel of the Lord who stood by his head. At times the angel would threaten the demon who tormented him and reminded him of his cruelty toward the Orthodox, and sometimes the angel would let the demon torment him*. The emperor said: 'Merciful God, requite those who made me persecute the Orthodox.' Then he said to me: 'My son, Tiberius, do not follow in the footsteps of one who, when given the kingdom by God, tried to remove Him from it. Do not imitate my evil ways. Rather, revere God, revere the Orthodox whom I persecuted, revere the empress who raised you and has been a mother to you.' These and other similar things he said to me, while he endured the torments he had earned. As he was dying Justin said to me: 'There are two things you must do, my son. First, reinstate those whom I have persecuted and follow their doctrine. Second, obey Sophia who was your own regent and has become your mother.'"

Now, said Tiberius: "Let none of you try to turn me towards Justin's wickedness through your own wicked advice, because I will not heed words that lead to destruction." And he said

THE CHRONICLE

to the Orthodox who had assembled: "My blessed fathers, go in assurance and live in peace observing your own faith. And pray for us."

Empress Sophia would not allow Tiberius' wife into Constantinople. The patriarch said to Tiberius: "Repudiate your wife and marry the empress." Saddened, Tiberius replied: "Now I know that fear of the Lord does not exist in your sect, Chalcedonianism. You say that I should leave my lawful wife, who has borne me three children and shared my poverty when in exile, and arouse the wrath of God?" The patriarch departed in great shame. Sophia heard about this and had Tiberius' wife brought to the city, loving her and calling her by her name of Helen. During the emperor's illness, Tiberius had been a *Caesar*. He was a generous and merciful man, and when he became emperor, he disbursed 72 *centenarii* to the poor, on a daily basis.

At this time Mundhir learned about the death of Justin and the elevation of Tiberius. He went to him and there was great joy. But Tiberius blamed him, saying: "Why did you let the Persians attack us?" Mundhir took out and gave to him the letter that Justin had written to Marcian regarding having him assassinated. Tiberius read it and was greatly astonished. Then Mundhir added: "It is because of the friendship you have made with the Orthodox that I have become reconciled with you and have come here. I beg you to proclaim that Orthodoxy may be practiced freely throughout the entire land." Tiberius so ordered and it was written that Orthodoxy could be preached. Mundhir then visited Antioch, since Orthodoxy had been established there initially, and spoke with the patriarch Gregory. While matters were at this pass, a letter arrived from Mundhir's sons saying: "The Persians are about to come against us." Thus Mundhir left for his own country, *and the Persians halted their activities*.

In the fourth year of Tiberius' reign the Slavs came *unarmed, horseless, and naked* and took much booty in Thrace and Thessalonica. They seized the royal herds of horses, weapons, and weapons factories *and thus became an army*, armed and armored, for up to that time they had neither horses nor weapons nor trained cavalry. They went and besieged Sirmium. Then they sent to Tiberius saying that he should either come and fight or give over the city to them *so that they might dwell there in peace.* The emperor delayed for two years, expecting the Lombards to arrive. But when they did not come, he was forced to give the city to them, that is, the city and the goods but not the people. The Slavs entered the city and found the people forsaken and weak from hunger since they had been eating dogs and cats during the siege. They showed them great humanity, providing bread and wine. But some died from eating and drinking so quickly. Seeing this, the Slavs nourished them with lighter food in smaller amounts. And when the people were better, they put them outside the city and they themselves inhabited it. A year later, the barbarians set fire to the city and then departed.

In this period, Tiberius made Maurice *caesar* and sent him to fight against Persia. He went and discovered that a large bridge over a river had been destroyed, and believed that Mundhir had informed the Persians about his expedition. He went to Tiberius and bad-mouthed Mundhir, and they were looking around for a means of seizing him. One of the princes named Magnus undertook to capture him. He took troops and departed as though he were heading for Persia. Magnus then sent to Mundhir asking him to come to discuss some matters *relating to the Persian campaign.* Without any suspicions, Mundhir went to him, and they engaged in a great deal of feasting. Now in the night they seized him *while he was in his cups and careless* and sent him to Tiberius. He was put into prison. When his son Numan heard about this, he came with troops into Byzantine territory to take treasure and livestock but not to hurt people. The Byzantines planned some wickedness against him, intending to capture him. Now when Numan realized that they were not going to release his father, out of concern for his father he risked his own life and went to Tiberius swearing that if his father were freed, he would stand with them against the Persians. Tiberius agreed and they swore an oath. It was then that the impious Maurice said: "It would be a sign of the sincerity of your vow if you take communion with us." Numan replied: "I cannot do that since many of my people would become angry with me.[117] I will speak the truth even if it means death since I do not want to be hateful to God *as you are*. The Byzantines, hearing this, became enraged. They seized him and sent him into exile by his father. Now when this bad news reached the Arabs, they split into fifteen different factions and selected leaders. Nor did they agree with one another. Some were bribed by Persian gold and went under Persian suzerainty. Others united with the Himyars, *a very few* others put themselves under Byzantine suzerainty. Thus, as a result of the wicked Council of Chalcedon, that marvelous kingdom was eliminated.

Tiberius, however, was full of charity. He gave a quarter of his total wealth to the poor, and eliminated some taxes throughout his realm. He was a decent, optimistic, and sincere man who reigned for four years and then took ill. *Now some claim that he ruled for only one year. But do not believe them, for we have confirmed from many books that he ruled for four years.* He gave his daughter Constantina in marriage to the *Augustus* Maurice, making him emperor. Maurice hailed from the village of Arabissus in Cappadocia. Then Tiberius died, leaving a good portion of the land grieving. And Maurice became emperor.[118]

Rome, however, rebelled against Maurice and seated Germanus as their own emperor. *Previously he had been successful in warfare against the Persians.* Then the Persian king Khosrov died and his son Hurmazd[119] reigned. Now Maurice sent emissaries to Rome so that they would recognize him as emperor, but the Romans refused. Instead, they went to the country of Persia and took captives, sending 3,000 to Maurice. Germanus subordinated himself to Maurice, who was delighted. *And so he agreed to let him rule the Roman sector of the empire, under his authority.* Maurice ordered that the city of Arabissus—whence he himself hailed—

---

117 Or, *would stone me to death*.
118 582-602.
119 Hurmazd V, 579-590.

should be enlarged. This was located in Second Armenia, *and so some said that he was of Armenian origin.* Four years later the city was devastated by an earthquake and was rebuilt with the greatest care, better than before. But it was hit by an earthquake yet again.

Maurice then placed his brother-in-law, his sister's husband, Phillippicus, as military commander and sent him against the Persians. The Persians had sent much treasure from Nisibis to Martyropolis and took that city. Philippicus went and retook it and killed the Persians who were there. That same year, the Persians turned against their king Hurmazd and blinded him. He died in the eighth year of Maurice's reign. In the ninth year of Maurice, Hurmazd's son, Khosrov, was enthroned.[120]

Maurice made his son Theodosius a *Caesar* and held a grand ceremony with the patriarch placing the crown on his head. The same year[121] the Persian prince Vahram revolted against Khosrov. Khosrov was frightened and went to Edessa. From there he sent to Maurice asking him to be his father and help him to retake Persia. Maurice sent Thracian and Armenian troops which took and established him on his throne. They returned with gifts and the Persians returned to the Romans Dara and Ras al-Ayn. Maurice gave his daughter Maria in marriage to Khosrov, sending her along with bishops and priests. Khosrov built three churches in Persia for his wife and the patriarch of Antioch went and blessed them. One was named for the Mother of God, one for the Holy Apostles, and the third for Saint Sargis. And great peace prevailed.

Maurice reigned for 20 years. He became careless about the army and reduced its gifts and stipends. Now it so happened that the Bulghars had entered Thrace. The Byzantine army went against them, chased them out, then arrived at Constantinople with a message for Maurice: "God has granted you peace during your reign. However, an army does not live on peace alone but on honor and pay. Now either you restore to us our proper respect and money, or you should regard us as your enemy from now on." But Maurice

---

120 Khosrov II, first reign, 590.
121 590-591.

hardened against them. Then the troops spoke to his brother, saying: "We shall kill your brother and make you the emperor." The brother went and told Maurice about this. Maurice, horrified, fled to Chalcedon. The army went there and killed him. They enthroned a certain one of the military commanders named Phocas.[122]

Khosrov, the king of Persia, heard about the murder of Maurice and his sons. He was deeply saddened, donned mourning black together with all the Persian houses, and wept for many days. Then he acquainted people with the good things Maurice had done for the Persians. "It was he who established me on my throne, which had been usurped. Now tell me, who among you will exact vengeance for his blood, so that my heart will be eased?" A certain one of the great princes named R'omizon stepped forward and said: "*If you give the order* I shall go and work your will on the Byzantines and I shall fill their country with the blood of any Byzantine I encounter." *King Khosrov was delighted and said: "I have confidence in you.* Henceforth you shall no longer be called R'omizon but rather Shahrvaraz, for you are a brave man." And he sent him off with the entire Persian army. Shahrvaraz *came to Mesopotamia* and captured Dara and Ras al-Ayn and Merdin and then wintered in Mesopotamia. After that he took Harran, Aleppo, and Antioch. *The cities were willingly given over to him since* he hurt none but the Greeks *and Romans.* In the eighth year of Phocas, all Mesopotamia was in Persian hands. Then they passed on to Cappadocia and Galatia, to Ancyra and Asia, and went raiding as far as Chalcedon *shedding a lot of blood.* For Khosrov had in mind that he would rule over even more of the Byzantines, since he had been adopted by Maurice and also was his son-in-law.

Emperor Phocas, *who was weak and womanish,* executed many military leaders and soldiers on mere suspicion, and was loathed by everyone. It happened at this time that there were two patricians in Africa who were prominent and valiant in warfare. One was named Gregory and the other, Heraclius. These two men planned to kill the emperor. They assembled troops and sent

---

122 Phocas, 602-610.

their own sons with them, one by sea and the other by land. Heraclius' son had the same name as his father. It had fallen his lot to take the sea route, while Gregory's son was to go overland. And they vowed that whichever of them reached Constantinople first would become the emperor, while the second to arrive would become *caesar*. They also wrote to the city and to the court revealing their intentions so that the Constantinopolitans would kill Phocas and enthrone as emperor whichever of their sons arrived first. Now it came about that Heraclius arrived first, due to favorable winds. When the addressees saw the letter, they immediately killed Phocas. Then they enthroned the brave and prudent Heraclius, and there was great rejoicing for all and also peace.

When the king of the Persians had conquered Mesopotamia, he sent Nestorian and Chalcedonian bishops to them from Persia. The chief of these was named Ashximia. However, the Orthodox in Mesopotamia did not accept them and wrote a letter to the Persian king begging him not to overturn their patrimonial religious arrangements. King Khosrov heeded them and called the bishops back. They asked Khosrov to order that a council be convened to investigate why it was that the miaphysites rejected them. *This proposal was quite agreeable to Khosrov since, for some time, he had been keen to know what this conflict among the Christians was about.* Khosrov sent letters to Armenia and to Mesopotamia that wise and ranking clerics should go to him and reply to the Chalcedonians and Nestorians. Nerses, the great Catholicos of the Armenians, and the Syrian patriarch of the Orthodox, Athanasius, and his brother Severus. The latter had been called to the priesthood by miraculous signs, as we shall now relate.[123]

A pious and God-fearing man of Samosata died and left two sons, Athanasius and Severus and their mother Mani. He also left a great deal of property. Their mother Mani exhausted all her

---

123 The 1870 edition (pp. 305-307) here describes the theological debate between the Miaphysites, Chalcedonians, and Nestorians. An expanded version of the debate appears in the 1871 edition (pp. 288-291). We omit this part. The narration returns to the biography of the patriarch Athanasius, who was one of the prominent attendees at the theological debate.

wealth, giving it away to the poor. *She dedicated her sons to God*, and reared them with prayers and faith, to the point that when she saw a bishop, priest, or monk, she would say: "Make the sign of the cross over me." Then she would extend her arms out before her as though holding a parcel, go to her home, and pour what she held in her arms over her sons' heads. When the boys asked: "What is that, mother?" she replied: "It is a blessing, my sons, which I have got for you from the holy men of God." Mani sent her sons to school. When the children grew older, they went as students to the monastery of Saint John.[124]

Then the king honored the patriarch of the Armenians, Nerses, entrusted his son to him for tutoring, and he placed the entire land of Armenia under his command. King Khosrov also gave very grand gifts to him and to Athanasius and gave over the land of Persia to them to look after the Christians there in accordance with their doctrines, to appoint bishops, priests, and deacons, to construct churches and promote church life. Thus does God glorify those who glorify Him. Glory to Him forever.

Heraclius[125] reigned in the 21st year of Khosrov. He sent to Khosrov, to reestablish friendship, saying: "We have slain Phocas, the one who murdered Maurice. Make peace with us." However, Khosrov did not accept this. Instead, he arose and came to Armenian Caesarea, to reinforce his troops. He captured Caesarea, and killed myriads of people, *and then turned back*. In the fourth year of Heraclius, the Persian general Shahrvaraz subjugated Damascus to the Persians. The next year he took Galilee, and in the sixth year of Heraclius he took Jerusalem and killed 90,000 people in it. *At first, he did no harm to* the Jews who had purchased captured Christians at a low price and then killed them, out of their wickedness. The Persian general took the Cross of Christ and sent it to Persia along with Zacharias, the patriarch of Jerusalem who

---

124 We omit the translation of the next section which describes the miracles that attended Athanasius' rise to the patriarchal seat, his invitation by King Khosrov to participate in the religious debate, and his defense of Monophysitism. At the conclusion of the debate, Khosrov is won over to Miaphysitism.
125 A.D. 610-641.

was Chalcedonian. Subsequently, Shahrvaraz exterminated all the Jews in Jerusalem and the surrounding areas, and then sent the captives on to Persia. The next year Shahrvaraz went to Egypt and conquered it and then subjugated to Persia all of Libya as far as the Cushites.[126] That same year, yet another Persian general, Shahe'n, came against Chalcedon, and took and destroyed it. He turned back, conquering Cilicia, and then returned to Persia with a large number of captives and loot. They even took to Persia marble columns and vessels made of copper and iron. And then the entire kingdom of the Byzantines, from sea to sea, was obedient to the Persians. Heraclius proclaimed his son Constantine *Augustus* and sent him against the Persians.

In was in this period that Muhammad,[127] son of Abdullah, appeared in the city of At'rape' in Arabia. Arabia extended in the north from the Euphrates River to the sea in the south, and in the west from the Red Sea east to the Persian Sea. Its inhabitants are called Ishmaelites, after Ishmael; Saracens, after Sarah; Hagarenes, after Hagar; and Madianites, after Kendura's son, Madan.

This Muhammad rose from the city of Medina and, involved in commerce, travelled from Palestine to Egypt. There, he became acquainted with an Arian cenobite who brought him to a belief in God through his sermons. *In Palestine, he became acquainted with Jews who taught him their laws, and he believed in God.* Then, Muhammad went and preached to his own clan. Some of them he convinced, *but others chased him away, regarding him as a fanatic.* He rose and went with his supporters into the desert. He enslaved and ruined those who would not submit. Many folk adhered to him and they went on expeditions to areas of Palestine, capturing and bringing back their booty. They became rich, and their army grew larger. Muhammad's renown spread. The Jews united with him and gave him a woman of their people. *The Jews liked him and took him with them, and, using him, they harassed the Persian troops.* And the Arabs harassed the Persians

---

126 Ethiopians.
127 c. 570-632.

and ruled over many lands. Muhammad first appeared in the 12th year of Heraclius,[128] in 933 of the Syrian Era,[129] and in 67 of the Armenian Era.

In this period, there was a half eclipse of the sun which lasted from the month of *Areg* in the fall until the month of *K'aghots'* at the beginning of summer. And people said that the sun would never come out of hiding.

In the 15th year of Heraclius, the Persians seized the island of Rhodes. The Persian generals Shahrvaraz and Kardarigan descended upon Constantinople. The Persian troops had already spread into Thrace and some were on the western side, and they besieged Constantinople which had no hope from any quarter.

But suddenly relief came to them in this fashion. It happened that certain Persian officials accused Shahrvaraz in Khosrov's presence, saying that Shahrvaraz had grown arrogant in his activities. They claimed that Shahrvaraz had said: "That womanizer Khosrov sits *inebriated* among his concubines and harlots, thinking that he is king. He does not realize that it was I who took territory from the Byzantine empire and added it to Persia, thereby giving him ease. *And he thinks that I am going to give him the country I have conquered through my own labors.*" When Khosrov heard this he was enraged, and sent a letter to Kardarigan, the second general, saying: "As soon as you see this message, behead Shahrvaraz and send his head to me." This letter fell into the hands of Heraclius' servants. *They brought it to Heraclius who secretly informed Shahrvaraz of its contents. Shahrvaraz came to Heraclius and made a pledge to him.* The servants told general Shahrvararz about it and even showed him the letter. Shahrvaraz took the letter and cunningly altered it as though the new contents had come from Khosrov. Here is what it now said: "Shahrvaraz and Kardigan, *my loyal men*, as soon as you receive this letter you are to kill the following three hundred princes in your entourage" and the names of each were listed. Now Shahrvaraz showed this to Kardigan.

---

128 622.
129 622.

The matter became known to the grandees[130] and they were moved to fury against Khosrov. They rebelled from Khosrov and established friendship with Heraclius. They gave him Shahrvaraz's son as a hostage, and then departed for Persia, leaving Byzantine territory. Heraclius then sent to the king of the North, the Khagan, promising that he would give him his daughter Eudokia as a wife if he would provide 40,000 cavalry for an expedition against Persia. The Qaqan promised to fulfill his request, and sent the troops through the Caspian Gate, *for, he said, I have some work to do in the area, to destroy the city of Tiflis.*

Heraclius rose and went to Armenia *to meet the Northerners' troops, since it was with them that he was going against Persia.* When the Persian king heard this, he massed troops, put them under a commander, R'uzi-Bahan, and sent them against Heraclius. *Heraclius took the Northerners and went against Rozibahan and completely defeated him.* Hearing about this, Khosrov fled to his fortress of Sagarta. Khosrov's son Shiruya,[131] who at that time was in prison, was released by the will of the Persians. He killed his father, and acceded to the throne. Heraclius went to winter in Assyria *at Nineveh.* Shiruya sent to him seeking friendship and pledged that he would remove his troops from Byzantine territory. Heraclius accepted this. Heraclius sent his brother Theodorus *to Edessa in* Mesopotamia in advance. However, the Persian troops at Edessa did not accept Shiruya, while the Jews—due to their hatred of Christians—aided the Persians and did not receive Theodorus at Edessa. Theodorus fought and defeated the Persians and then took the city. Now it happened that one Jew had descended the wall and went to Heraclius at Tella. *Theodorus took the city and killed many Jews there.* The Jew who had gone to Heraclius brought an order not to kill the Jews, for up to his arrival many of them had been slain. *Now Heraclius went to Theodosiopolis where he weakened the Armenians doctrinally through the ignorance of their patriarch, Ezr. But he was not able to turn everyone*

---

130   *i.e*, the princes in the list.
131   Shiri, Shiroe, Kavad II, A.D. 628.

to his views, since the anti-Chalcedonian Armenians looked to God Who remembered the sweat of the martyr Gregory.

Then Heraclius arrived at Edessa. An enormous multitude of clerics, and monks from the monasteries on the mountain of Edessa came out to meet him. Their number is said to have been 90,000. Heraclius was astounded at the crowd and bowed down before them. But when he learned that they did not accept the Council of Chalcedon, he said: "It is not worthy to reject the prayers of such a multitude over the Council of Chalcedon." On the feast of Christmas he entered the Orthodox Church of Saint Sophia and greatly respected the clergy with gifts. Now when it was time for communion, Heraclius stepped forward to receive communion. At this point, the archbishop, Isaiah, stopped him and said: "First curse the Council of Chalcedon and the Tome of Leo." The emperor was greatly angered by these words. He took that church away from the Orthodox and gave it to the Chalcedonians.

Heraclius then journeyed to Manbij.[132] Here, the patriarch Athanasius came forth to greet him together with twelve bishops who had originally come from Antioch and had remained. The bishops' names are as follows: T'uma of Tedmor, Basil of Emesa, Sargis of Aris, John of Cyrrhus, T'uma of Manbij, Daniel of Harran, Isaiah of Edessa who had come to the patriarch in advance of the emperor's arrival; Severus of Qeneshirin, Athanasius of Arabissus, Cosmas from the city of Epiphania in Cilicia, and Severus of Samosata. *Now Isaiah of Edessa had gone to Antioch while Heraclius was at Manbij. The Monophysite clerics of Manbij then went before the emperor and told him: "Our beloved emperor, do not glorify the Persians' doctrine,[133] and do not dismiss the truth so quickly."* The emperor received them and then they held discussions for twelve days. The emperor requested a written statement of their faith, and they presented him with the Orthodox formulation. Heraclius praised it and thanked God, saying: "This is the true confession. It curses the Council of Chalcedon and the

132 Hierapolis/Bambyce.
133 *Nestorianism.*

Tome of Leo. *We find no heresy in your doctrine, however we shall retain our own."* His court bishop opposed this, and the emperor commanded that his nose be cut off. Then, the patriarch Athanasius was released with great honor.

After some days Heraclius went to Antioch. The Chalcedonians and the princes assembled and gave him this advice and counsel: *The princes and clerics of the city conferred with each other and with men from the royal court and told the emperor: "Unless you visibly fight against that heresy which both the Greeks and the Romans loathe, your reign will not be a long one, and God will be dissatisfied with you. He will not let you overturn the efforts of so many men who had supported Chalcedonian doctrine.* The deluded emperor, who cared more for human comforts than for the glory of God, issued an order that "No one should appear in my presence who does not hold the Chalcedonian doctrine. Moreover, let there be no trial for those who kill, rob and persecute. And let them not dare to enter the cathedral. *I will now convert Greater Armenia, and then who will dare to resist me?"*

They assembled in Theodosiopolis[134] and Heraclius turned many Armenians to his heresy through the agency of the greedy Armenian Catholicos, Ezr, whom he had bribed. However, the Eastern monastics and the wise bishops did not submit to him *and removed the title of Catholicos from him*, and many lands kept their Orthodoxy unshaken. This situation continued until the true Orthodox ended this evil heresy by means of that miracle-working wise man of God, Yovhannēs Odznets'i.[135] This was 84 years after Ezr had ignorantly accepted Chalcedonianism. Yovhannēs Odznets'i, Catholicos of Greater Armenia, adorned the Church with splendid arrangements through the prayers of Saint Gregory the Illuminator of Armenia and his blessed sons.

Shiruya, king of the Persians, died after reigning for nine months. Then his son Artashir[136] ruled for two years. And then

---

134 Erzurum.
135 Catholicos (717-728).
136 Artashir III, 628-629.

Shahrvaraz killed him and ruled, keeping friendship with Heraclius. However, Kardarigan also had some partisans and tore the Persian monarchy apart. Heraclius aided Xorean and Kardarigan was killed. Xorean ruled for a year, and he too was slain. Khosrov's daughter Boran ruled for a few days and then died. Then her sister Zarmanduxt ruled. Following her there ruled Shahrori, Daburan Khosrov, Peroz, Zruanduxt, Ormazd—all relatives of the Persian king and all of them dying within two years.

In the meantime, Heraclius added to his wickedness by marrying his brother's daughter, Martina, in his old age. She gave birth to a son of impiety named Heracleonas.

Muhammad, after ruling over many lands for seven years, died. *Muhammad tyrannized over many districts preaching a religion according to his own wishes, and establishing laws as he willed.* Then rule of the kingdom was taken by Abu Bakr for two years and five months.

After Abu Bakr, 'Umar ruled. He sent many captives to Arabia. He took Basra from a Syrian prince, and destroyed numerous cities. 'Umar sent a *large* army to Persia and found them in turmoil since some supported Yazdgird[137] as king and others supported Ormazd. Eventually, Ormazd was slain and Yazdgird reigned. The Arab army, after taking a great deal of booty *and prisoners*, turned back. *On the way home they struck at the Byzantine army and its general Sargis.* And they strengthened against both Byzantium and Persia, *and became a great power.*

Heraclius sent his brother Theodoricus against the Arabs. The latter came to the Antioch country, to the village called Ko'sit. Now it happened that there was a stylite named Symeon dwelling there who belonged to the Chalcedonian sect. Theodoricus and his princes paid him a visit. Symeon said: "Vow to me that when you return triumphantly, you will eliminate those who do not accept the Council of Chalcedon, and I will believe that God will grant you the victory." They so vowed to him, and added: "Indeed, we have such an order from the emperor, to ruin and

---

137 Yazdgird III, 632-651.

kill such people." Now one of the princes who was very Orthodox became greatly saddened at this, since he realized that the wrath of God was about to descend on them. Indeed, Theodoricus' troops set off full of swagger and when the wrath of God struck them only a few managed to flee. The remainder fell to the Arabs' swords. The Arabs also seized all their war materiel. The emperor's brother escaped by a hairsbreadth and, out of shame, did not dare to meet anyone's eye. Once again Heraclius massed troops and put them under a military commander named Sklaros. He also brought out Xor'ean's son and sent him against the Arabs with 70,000 troops. They went and fought by the river of Damascus, and the Byzantines were defeated. They lost 40,000 cavalry. Xorean's son managed to go to 'Umar in Hems and said that if he would entrust him with troops, he would go and conquer Persia for him. But it happened that the Persian king Khosrov's daughters were there among the captives and said to 'Umar: "This man is the son of a rebel. He will go and *destroy your troops* and reign in opposition to you. Do not trust him." *Umar believed them* and sent and had him killed, crucified on a cross. After this he took Damascus and its surrounding districts and cities *and resided there*. And he became extremely powerful.

In that period, the Arab general Sad arose from Yathrib and pitched his camp over the city of K'ubar. Yazdgird, king of Persia, heard about this and arrived and encamped opposite him on the Euphrates. In the fierce battle which ensued, the Arabs conquered the Persians and chased them as far as Ctesiphon. Now the Persians were many in number and armed, while the Arabs were few and unarmed. Indeed, it happened that there was one Persian prince who was heavily armed who went fleeing before a naked and unsaddled Arab horseman. Many times, the Iranian turned around and shot arrows aiming at the Arab's heart, but none of them hit the target. Now as he went along the prince espied a hoe lying in the road. As a test, he fired at the hoe, but the arrow missed. Then he realized that it was God Who was responsible and he fell from his horse, was killed and robbed by the naked Arab. And some say that the Arab told them: "There was a piece of horseshoe in my breast pocket, and the arrows struck that ten times and did me no harm."

In this period, the feast of the martyr Symeon took place, and the celebrants assembled there. The Arabs learned about this and went and massacred them. Many Christians were confounded and asked: "Why did God betray us?" But they were unaware that they had broken the rules established by the ancient celebrants who prepared for the day by fasting and with tears of faith. Today, however, it was done with eating and drunkenness, with other sinful carryings on, *which displease God and lead to sin and personal ruin.*

The Iranian king Yazdgird arrived at the Tigris River. The Arabs also went there. Now when the Persians saw their multitude, they destroyed the bridge. Seeing this, the Arabs cried: "Come, let us cross over. For God Who aided us on dry land will aid us in the water." And they crossed without any casualties. They struck the Persians and put them to flight. Yazdgird was to go against the Arabs four times, and was defeated each time. At that point he realized that his destruction was upon him. He fled to the Sistan country of Maragan, which borders on the Turks, called Sagastan. He hid there for five years. Then he was killed by the Turks. And in such fashion was the Sasanian Persian kingdom ended. It had lasted for 418 years. The Arabs took over the rule of Persia.

Now while the Arabs were growing stronger, Heraclius started robbing the Christians in the area from Antioch to Constantinople, saying: "Better we have the loot than the Arabs."

Umar then went to Egypt. Bishop Cyrus came before him promising to give him 2,000 *dahekans* annually if he would not enter Egypt. *Umar agreed to this,* and so he turned back. Heraclius was furious at this, removed Cyrus from the episcopacy, *exiled him,* and sent a military commander—an *ostikan* of Armenian nationality named Manuel—to hold the country. When the Arab tax-collectors came to collect the tax, Manuel said: "I am not Cyrus, who would give you gold. He had a pilon, what I have is a sword." *When 'Umar heard about this* he took the Arab forces to Egypt and captured it. Then 'Umar went to Jerusalem. Sophronius, the bishop of Jerusalem, came before him. When he saw that 'Umar was wearing old clothing, a worn fur, *and a worn and coarse sheepskin*, he brought him costly clothes and beseeched him to put them on. But 'Umar replied: "God put into my hands the entire Persian treasury at Ctesiphon, as well as the treasuries of the Byzantines, Damascenes, and Egyptians *and many others*, and still I did not change these clothes of my poverty so that I would not become proud and forget myself." And so saying, he did accept the clothes from him. 'Umar *honored the bishop* and gave authority over that land to him.

The bishop requested that the Jews be removed from Jerusalem and 'Umar gave him an edict to that effect. 'Umar also ordered that a mosque be built on the site of the Temple. Then he went to Syria. There Heraclius' military commander in Edessa, John, went to him at Qeneshirin and gave him 100,000 *dahekan*s, the taxes for one year, to prevent him from invading eastern Mesopotamia. Now when Heraclius heard about this, he was furious and ordered that John be put into fetters. For God, Who had willed the loss of the land from Heraclius, gave him over to bitter and imperious ideas. *This was the reason that* when the next year arrived, the Arabs came and entered Mesopotamia, *took and ruled it*. When he went to Edessa, the clergy affectionately came out to meet him. In their wisdom they removed the Byzantine military which was there. *The Byzantine troops departed peacefully*. Thus, the Arabs came to rule over Mesopotamia. But the cities of T'lmo'z and Dara did not submit peacefully and were taken by force, and the troops in them were broken. And in that year the Muslims put a head tax on all the Christians under their rule. In that year Heraclius died,[138] having reigned for thirty years and five months. His son, Constantine, then ruled for four months. Now Heraclius had three sons: Constantine, Heracleonas, and the youngest, Heracles. Heraclius' wife, Martina, killed Constantine with poison and enthroned her own son, the young Heracleonas. But the nobles were

---

138 A.D. 641.

displeased with this and killed Heracleonas, and then enthroned Constantine's son, Constans, grandson of Heraclius.

'Umar,[139] after his triumph over the Persians and the Byzantines, was slain by one of his servants. This man had beseeched 'Umar for a decision on some matter on which 'Umar had demurred. And so, one day when 'Umar was at prayer, this servant killed him with a dagger. 'Umar died after reigning for 12 years.

Following this, 'Uthman took power. *Then they bestowed the dignity of Caliph on 'Uthman.*[140] He was a greedy *and cruel* person who went beyond all his predecessors in this respect. The princes thought to kill him. *They warned him to stay in line.* 'Uthman learned about this and begged them to forgive him, promising to remain within the bounds set by his predecessors. And they left him alone. They designated Mu'awiya as military commander. Mu'awiya came with his troops to Caesarea Stratonean,[141] taking it and destroying the Byzantines there, *and putting it under taxation. From there he proceeded to Amasia. After taking much booty, he turned to Cilicia and subjugated it.* Then, in the fifth year of Constantinianus, he looted the country and departed. Emperor Constans[142] massed troops, dividing them into two parts. One he entrusted to an Armenian named David[143] *who chased the Hagarenes out of Cappadocia*, and the other to Valentinianus. The latter went via Cilicia and was slain by the Arabs who had come to subdue Cilicia. They appeared before him and wasted the Byzantines, leaving a few to flee. David went to the upper lands and the troops who were with him were in no way less active in robbing the Christians, taking gold, silver, and precious clothing. They even disgraced women in front of their men. Someone went to David and said: "Why do you let your troops work such evil? What answer will you give before God?" David became furious with the Byzantine troops, saying: "Here is the reason for

139 634-644.
140 A.D. 644-656.
141 Caesarea Palestina.
142 Constans II, 641-668.
143 Sahar'uni.

the ruination of the Christians for there is nothing to differentiate our deeds and lewdness from those of the unbelievers." He took the troops and returned to Constantinople *not wanting to lead such troops.*

In that period, the patrician Grigor rebelled in Africa. The Arabs suddenly entered Africa, and took and enslaved it. Grigor, having submitted, went to Constantinople.

In the same period, at Mu'awiya's order, 1,700 ships assembled in Egypt. He took them and went to the island of Cyprus where he demanded taxes from them *in exchange for which he would spare them.* But the people had fortified themselves in their cities and did not want to give taxes. *Those fortified cities of theirs became their cemeteries.* The sword of Hagar fell upon them and a very great multitude were killed. Then Mu'awiya went to the city of Constantia, which was the capital of the island, full of people and treasure. He besieged and then destroyed the city, filling it with blood *and thoroughly looting it.* He also committed abominations in their cathedral church, which had been built by Saint Epiphanius, because they did not hold to the Orthodox faith practiced by Epiphanius or to the canons he established or to his works. After filling up with *an incredibly large amount of* booty, the Hagarene troops, gave a portion of it to those who had come from Egypt, and then sent them back to their own country.

In these times, the blessed patriarch of the Orthodox Syrians, Athanasius, wrote to the blessed Catholicos of the Armenians, K'ristap'or, that he should concern himself with the Persian areas and the Syrian Christians to warn them against the heresy of Nestorius and the Chalcedonians.

"*My lord and father K'ristap'or, rejoice in the Lord. We have heard that the doctrinal carelessness of Ezr did not please your holiness, and so we have glorified Christ God for His grace upon you.* For we have found," he said, "a letter of the blessed Marutha, *your compatriot,* describing how, through the grace of God, your Armenian people survived the corrupter Barsauma. Here is how this is related in the letter. Barsauma was one of Nestorius' students and he was at Nisibis or, *he was at Edessa.* When the Council of Ephesus was convened, during the reign of Theodosius, Barsauma did not attend the meeting, saying instead: 'I am under the authority of Catholicos Pawi whom the Armenians ordained in the land of the Persians. *Barsauma told them: If he attends, I will too.*" And so they sent two monks from Ephesus to Persia requesting the presence of Pawi, *Barsauma,* and other bishops who were under him. *Pawi who was impotent did not attend. Instead,* wrote a letter with the correct confession of faith and sent it to *the Council at* Ephesus in the hands of two monks. In the letter he also said: 'Do not blame us for not attending, for we are under the authority of impious folk *and evil masters* and we are afraid that it might become a cause of problems for us, and that the sword which killed our fathers will be turned on us *and on our flock* as well.

Whatever you designate as Orthodox, we will accept.' The letter carriers returned to the wolf Barsauma in Nisibis. When he saw the letter he took it, and turned them back, saying: 'I will deliver this letter. You should now return so that there is no thought that the Romans are engaged in espionage.' In their naivete they went home and the Catholicos did not blame them. Rather, he told them: 'You did well to heed what our brother said.' *Meanwhile, Barsauma selected two of his own people, disguised them, and sent them on with the letter, as a substitute for attending.*

When *that wily snake* Barsauma learned that Nestorius had been anathematized, he became angry and went to the Persian king. Barsauma said to him: 'There was a man Nestorius in Constantinople who was a leader of the Church. He wanted to have lasting peace with the Persians, *and to bring the Church closer in faith to the Persians* and to prevent the Byzantines from making raids on Persia. For this reason, they *slandered him before the emperor and* sent him into exile and the doctrines he professed were condemned. This Catholicos is a spy among you for the Armenians and the Byzantines. Behold, here is the letter in which you are described as impious and bloodthirsty.' The king believed him. Barsauma then requested of him: 'Give me authority over all the Christians under your sway so that I may confirm in Iran the faith of Persia's friend, Nestorius. I will also fill your treasury with the wealth] of those who do not accept Nestorianism.' The Iranian shah gave him that authority and *as many* troops *as he wanted*. Then Barsauma said: 'Let me have that Catholicos.' And the shah gave him an edict to do as he wanted. Barsauma went to the Catholicos and said to him: 'Profess the doctrines of Nestorius.' He replied: 'I have heard that Nestorius has been anathematized, and may he be anathematized!' Then Barsauma became enraged and cut out his tongue *and sent it to the king claiming that he had cursed him*. The king heard about his and was saddened. He summoned Barsauma and asked: 'Why did you do that?' Barsauma replied: 'Because he cursed you.' The king said: 'If that's the case, go and behead him as well.' And he went and decapitated him.

Barsauma next went to Baghdad and made them submit to Nestorianism, and from there he continued on to Nineveh. There, he seized the archbishop Martiros along with twelve bishops and ninety priests and said to them: 'I ask nothing of you but this: either give me communion or accept communion from me.' They responded: 'We do not give the sacrament to a dog, nor do we accept it from a dog.' Enraged, Barsauma killed the priests and took the bishops to Nisibis. There he incarcerated them in the home of a Jew.

Subsequently, he had them killed by lapidation by his troops and had their bodies suspended on poles. A sign of heavenly glory appeared above them, and the Jew became a believer and was baptized. Barsauma then arose and wanted to enter Armenia. When the Armenians heard about this, they went and chased him away and threatened that if he repeated his attempt, they would burn him and his troops with fire. Then Barsauma wrote to the king in Persia, saying: 'The Armenians have rebelled against you.' The Persian king sent to the military commander in Armenia saying that it was the order of their king to come to Persia, even if the Armenian king was unwilling. Similarly, he wrote to the king *and to the Catholicos* ordering them to come to Persia and answer questions regarding their faith. The king of the Armenians replied, saying: "We are not obliged to come and answer your questions regarding our faith. However, should you go against the barbarians, we shall indeed come with our priests and our crosses to participate in the fighting. Such was the oath you and we swore to uphold *which stated: when the Armenians come to us to go and fight against our enemies, let them come with their crosses and priests, and practice the traditional faith of their fathers.* If you do not want to abide by your agreement, we also will not honor it. *And should that Barsauma come to us, he and his troops will not return to you."* Then the king was silent.

  And in such a fashion the sword of Satan and the second deluge of the world did not enter Armenia, rather it turned upon the Syrians because of our many sins. Barsauma held three meetings *as opposed to the three holy Councils*—in Ctesiphon, Gatr, and Grawmia—and wrote a document defining the canons of Nestorius' impious beliefs. Those who did not accept this were *robbed, persecuted, and* mercilessly slain, or, more accurately, they were martyred, with more radiant haloes than those who were killed by the idol-worshippers. For, as we have heard, he killed a total of 7,800 bishops, priests, and deacons of the Church, and as for the laity, there is no knowing their toll. We beseech your holiness to go as a good physician where there is sickness, and to fulfill the words of the Apostle that 'Whoever among you is able should raise up the weakest of the weak', so that the grain of holiness which was harvested not be completely denied to the multitude. *Due to numerous dangers besetting me, I am unable to tend to the remaining Orthodox in Persia and the Nineveh area, which is under the authority of my see of Antioch, and so am entrusting them to your holiness' sympathetic care to send preachers and doctors to those places especially where the sick are to be found. Ordain shepherds for them as is fitting and provide brotherly aid to them]. This is our plea to you. We greet all of our co-adjutors in Jesus Christ our God, forever."*

MICHAEL THE GREAT

Now we shall return to where we left off in our previous narration. In the year 965 of the Syrian Era,[144] Cyprus was ruined again by the Arabs, for they had heard that the inhabitants had assembled there once more. Abu'l Hawar, military commander of the Arabs, went there, took it, and tore the place apart, not leaving any valuables untouched. However, he did spare a few people who pledged an oath to him. *He placed under taxation those who had remained from Mu'awiya as well as others who had gathered there, and then departed.* Meanwhile Mu'awiya went to the island of Rhodes which he took and ruined. Thence he went to Crete which he quickly captured, and he also took the very well-fortified islands of Aradus and Cos. He had the fortifications pulled down. On the island of Rhodes he saw the bronze statue of a man which had been considered one of the seven wonders of the world. He toppled it—not without difficulty—using ropes, and found that it measured 105 feet in height. He lit a fire under it and melted its attachments, then cut it up. It made 3000 loads of bronze. A Jew from Emesa bought it *and took it back to his home.*

In this period, there was a severe famine which led to cannibalism and other loathsome things. In Germanica, which is Marash, there was *an imposter monk, a villain* named Elisha who dwelt in a cave. The famine did not cause him to quit his impiety; rather, he stole children and ate *fifty-one of* them. Then he went and consoled the children's parents *for the loss of their children,* since they believed that he was a monk. After this, he was discovered and hanged. *He was punished in this world and will eternally suffer the punishment he deserves.* In this same period, a fierce wind blew from the north demolishing many churches, destroying *many fortresses and cities,* and uprooting forests.

In the days of Constantine's son Heraclius, there appeared in Constantinople a man named Maximus who professed a heresy. He claimed that Christ had two wills and two operations. Even though this was not accepted, it was not denounced in Rome. In

---

144 A.D. 654.

the days of Constans' grandson Heraclius, in Armenian Comana, a count by the name of Theodorus asked the Pope of Rome, who was named Agatho, to hold an inquiry about this matter since some folk were whispering about two natures and two wills. Agatho convened an assembly and confirmed Maximus' confession, one hundred twenty-five years after the Council of Chalcedon. For they said that Christ's nature with it's two parts also required two separate wills and operations. We say that they needed yet another person to fulfill the measure of their wickedness, and so that they would not be distant from Nestorius.

In the year 966 of the Syrian Era,[145] which is 93 of the Armenian Era,[146] 37 of the Arab tyranny,[147] the 10th year of Constans, and the 9th year of 'Uthman, the military commander Mu'awiya ordered that an enormous fleet of ships be assembled at Tripoli to sail to Constantinople. Among the overseers were two soldiers who were sons of believers. They removed all the Frankish slaves with them, killed the other troops, and set fire to all the ships. They themselves *who were of Frankish nationality* then boarded a boat and headed for Rome. When Mu'awiya learned about this *he was furious*, and had more ships *than before* readied. He organized the troops and entrusted them to the command of Abu'l Hawar to go to Constantinople. When *Emperor* Constans[148] heard about this, he *assembled as many troops and ships as he could,* came to Acre in Phoenicia *by land and by sea*. His brother, Theodosius, came by sea with a multitude of ships. As soon as the Hagarenes learned about this, they brought their ships against them. On the evening before the battle, Emperor Constans *awoke from sleep and* summoned an interpreter of dreams and told him: "In a dream I saw myself in Thessalonika *at a feast*." The interpreter of dreams replied: "Would that you had not slept and not had such a dream, for 'Thessalonika' signifies victory for the other side." The emperor

---

145 A.D. 655.
146 A.D. 644.
147 A.H. 37 = 659.
148 Constans II.

scorned his words *and became angry, and the man was silent.* The next day, an enormous battle took place at sea, and intensified until the air was filled with dust, as though the fighting were on land. Constans was defeated and barely escaped with a few men. The number slain who were found by the shore was 23,000 men. The Hagarenes wanted to go on to Constantinople, but at the emperor's command, *prince* Ptolemy came *to Mu'awiya* and agreed to pay taxes *if he would not go to Constantinople.* He was lying about it, however. The Hagarenes therefore departed for the country of Syria. *Mu'awiya agreed and withdrew.*

But *Constans broke his oath, and did not send the tribute he had promised. Therefore, the Hagarenes went and raided Syria.* Ptolemy then brought taxes for three years and his son Grigor as a hostage, and then left, *thereby removing them from the country.* Now Constans, fearing for his reign, slew his own brother, Theodosius, and became so hated by everyone (*by the troops*) that he went off to Rome, whence they called him back to Constantinople. Leaving Rome, he came to Syracuse, a place he liked. From there, he summoned his sons Constantine, Tiberius, and Heraclius. However the troops would not let them go. Rather, they designated them *caesars* and kept them in Constantinople. As for the emperor, he did not dare to quit Syracuse, for he had heard that they were calling him a second Cain, for murdering his brother.

In these days, the Arab caliph 'Uthman was killed in the city of Yathreb because of his foul deeds, and his rule was split in two between Babylon and Egypt. Muhammed's son-in-law, 'Ali, ruled in Babylon and Syria,[149] while Mu'awiya ruled in Egypt *and in the other lands that he himself had conquered. And they warred with each other once and then twice and many were killed on both sides. Subsequently, one of Mu'awiya's servants went and treacherously killed 'Ali, and then everyone submitted to Mu'awiya.* Mu'awiya transferred the seat of the kingdom from Yathreb to Damascus and ruled for twenty years.[150] After seven years of peace, Mu'awiya

---

149 656-661.
150 661-680.

went and ruined the districts of Galatia, Asia, and Bithynia. *And all the countries were afraid of him.*

In this same period, the stratelate Andre killed Emperor Constans at Sirmium while he was bathing. Constans had shut his eyes while his head was being lathered with soap, and at that moment Andre stabbed him with a dagger and he died. They enthroned a patrician of Armenian nationality named Mzhezhius,[151] who was a pious man. However, Constans' son Constantine[152] gathered a force, killed Mzhezhius, and himself ruled along with his brothers. At the start of their reign, some 80,000 souls were enslaved by the Arabs in Africa. The Arabs then went to Lebanon where they were defeated by the Byzantines and lost 30,000 troops. This was their first defeat. In this year, a man from Baalbek named Callinicus, who was of Syrian nationality, was the first to discover Greek fire and was able to burn ships on the sea that were filled with Arabs. In this same period, a rainbow appeared in the sky *after the sun had set* and completely covered it for an entire night. And the entire world was terrified. In the ninth year of Constantine, some *villainous* troops arose from the Byzantines, went and dwelt at Mt. Lebanon and were declared rebels. The Syrians called them *Chur'chans*. They seized all the territory from Mt. Lebanon to the Black Mountain. (Perhaps it is for this reason the Iberians are called Chur'chans *by the Franks*, since they had rebelled from service to the Armenians and from religious unity with them). The Arabs rose and wiped out these rebels.

In this year, Mzhezhius' son, John, pursued Constantine for seven months because of his father's murder. But then he himself was slain. Constantine became arrogant with his victory, scorned his two brothers and deposed them from ruling. Then Prince Leo, *who was furious, since the brothers were his friends,* said to him: "I will not allow you to rule alone." Through bribes, Constantine swayed the troops and had Leo's tongue, hands, and feet cut off. He himself had a son named Justinian.

151 Gnuni.
152 Constantine IV, Pogonatus (668-685).

MICHAEL THE GREAT

Now after Muʾawiya his son, Yazid,[153] ruled the Arabs for three years and six months,[154] and then died. Then Mukhtar rebelled in Babylon. He was a false and dishonest man who claimed that he was a seer and a prophet. Meanwhile, Abdullah ruled in Yathreb, and in Damascus people thought to enthrone Yazid's son. Consequently, there was warfare. Then it happened that an old man from Yathreb went among them and pleaded for peace. He advised them to write the three candidates' names on three arrows. One of the names was his own. Then the arrows were released, and a lad was to select one arrow. Whichever candidate's name was on that arrow, that man would rule. The lot fell to the old man himself.[155] He ruled, but died after one year. Once again they were divided. Then, Marwan's son ʿAbd al-Malik ruled.[156] In this year, Constantine died and his son Justinian ruled.[157] Now because ʿAbd al-Malik was troubled by rebels at this time, he made peace with Justinian for ten years, and promised to give him yearly 1,000 *dahekan*s, a horse, and a servant. Cyprus was to pay taxes both to the Arabs and to the Byzantines. The Armenians helped the Byzantines. For a second time Lebanon became the dwelling place of rebels, this time 12,000 of them, *cavalry*. The Romans removed them and brought them to Rome.

In these times lived the blessed *vardapet* Jacob of Edessa,[158] *a gracious and scholarly man*, who was from the district of Antioch. He learned the language and letters of Greek and Hebrew, going among the Jews and covertly translating their secrets from Hebrew into Syriac. *He did this by pretending to be Jewish.* He wrote interpretations of many writings, became bishop of Edessa, and ended his life in the Kessoun country in the monastery called Saint James *after his own name*.

---

153 Yazid I, 680-683.
154 Or, for four years.
155 Marwan I, 684-685.
156 685-705.
157 Justinian II Rhinometus, 685-695, 705-711.
158 c. 640-708.

THE CHRONICLE

'Abd al-Malik subdued the rebels. In that period Justinian conquered Cyprus, and there was discord between the Arabs and the Byzantines. 'Abd al-Malik sent Muhammad, emir of Jazira, to the Caesarea area. The Byzantines, with mercenaries from the Slavs, arrived to battle against Mehmet. The Byzantines were defeated, while the Slavs *requested an oath and* came under Arab rule. There were some seven thousand of them, *cavalry*, which the Arabs settled in Antioch and Cyrrhus, giving them women and goods.

In 1006 of the Syrian Era,[159] the Byzantines came to the Antioch country to battle the Arabs. Many of them died, while the rest fled; however more fell from the Byzantine side, and thus the Byzantines were conquered. The number of those slain from both sides was put at 400,000. This battle occurred on April 3rd, and the site was Pushirik'. To this day one may see their bones strewn across the fields. In the year 75 of their calendar,[160] the Arabs removed images from their dirhems and *dahekan*s, and minted coins which lacked pictures and had only writing on them. This was done due to their hatred of image-worship. In this period, Justinian became very severe and killed many princes and soldiers. They seized this wicked man,[161] cut off his nose, threw him into prison, and enthroned a certain man named Leo.[162] Now the general Apsimar who was in Cilicia, came and removed Leo and himself ruled.[163] He subdued the Slavs and then went against the Arabs at Samosata, killed 5,000 of them, took booty, and returned.

At that time, 'Abd al-Malik appointed two military commanders, Muhammad and Hajjaj, *godless men* who were merciless and exercised their authority mercilessly. The latter treacherously assembled the Armenian nobility at Naxjawan and tried to turn them to his religion. When they refused, he placed them in a large church and set it on fire, burning them to death. *In their struggle and triumph, they shared the martyr's crown with the blessed*

---

159 A.D. 695.
160 A.D. 696-97.
161 Emperor Justinian II.
162 Leontius, 695-698.
163 Tiberius III, Apsimar 698-705.

Ananians. May Christ God through their prayers look with compassion on their nation and Church.

In this period, there was a wise and pious man of Edessa named Athanasius, son of Goumaye. *He was praised before 'Abd al-Malik.* They took him to 'Abd al-Malik who exalted him and placed him in his home as administrator of the house and all its belongings. He was given 60,000 *dahekan*s on a yearly basis and received a *dahekan* from each soldier in addition. Athanasius effected many easements for Orthodox Christians. In Edessa, he constructed two churches. One was named for the Mother of God and the other for Saint Theodorus whose relics had been brought from Ewxayita, which is Ablastan and placed there. Between these two churches, he built underground chapels where he concealed the shroud of Christ which he had bought from the Arabs for 50,000 *dahekan*s. And he built a staircase by which people descended to it and then came up again. On its holy day, it was taken out and displayed to the people, until the time of the patriarch John. The latter secured it in an even deeper spot, putting it between two walls, in a place where no one would find it. John then wrote truly about the concealment, saying: "I have placed it where it would not be found, out of fear of the infidels." *Let no one go hunting for it, since they will not find it.* Now as to what Shroud it is that the Byzantines possess, I do not know. In this period, 'Abd al-Malik's son Maslama ruled as king in the Qeneshrin country, which is Aleppo. In the 19th year of his reign, 'Abd al-Malik sent Maslama against Mopsuestia and took it.

In the same year, Justinian was released from prison after ten years' confinement. He went to the king of the Khazars, the Qaqan. The latter received him with the greatest joy and gave him his daughter in marriage. With support from the Bulghars, Justinian came to Constantinople. Apsimar fled. Justinian killed Leontius, destroyed many at court, exiled others, and generally emptied the court. He located 6,000 Arab captives, and freed them to go home in peace. Then he sent many troops to fetch his wife, but they drowned in the sea. When the Qaqan learned about this he was devastated, and sent a message blaming Justinian, which said: "Fool, why did you send such a mass of troops for your wife? Did you think that I wanted to prevent her from joining you? Send just a few and take her." When Justinian heard this, he was very happy and sent and had his wife and son Tiberius brought to him.

In 1015 of the Syrian Era,[164] which is 152 of the Armenian Era,[165] Maslama rebuilt Mopsuestia, expanding it with high and secure walls, and he placed troops there to resist the Byzantines. In the same year 'Abd al-Malik died and Walid ruled for nine years and five months.[166] It was in this period that Justinian persecuted the Armenian people in his realm by means of Philippicus. The Arabs received them happily in Melitene and Mesopotamia. And there was a great strengthening of the Orthodox in Syria against the Dyophysites. They built monasteries, retreats, and Armenian villages which exist to this day. The impious Muhammad had stirred up fierce persecution among the Arab faithful.[167] Muslims seized the Arab Christian leader and tortured him with various torments because of his faith until they killed him. His body was left there for thirty days, but it did not decay nor did birds or animals approach it and Muhammad was shamed. A very great number of Christians suffered martyrs' deaths for the name of Christ, but Muhammad killed them mercilessly.

In this same period Maslama went to Cappadocia and 40,000 Byzantine *cavalry* were killed from Justinian's army, *not to mention those who were taken prisoner*. They captured the city of Tyana. Then Maslama, after taking Darand, came into Cilicia where he captured Djerdjoum and Podanta among many other cities. Henceforth there were Arab troops at Darand. Now Philippicus, *who had grown powerful*, killed Justinian and his son Tiberias and he himself ruled.[168] In these same days, a decree

164 A.D. 704..
165 A.D. 703.
166 al-Walid I, 705-715.
167 i.e., Christians.
168 Philippicus, Bardanes 711-713.

was issued by al-Walid that Christians should be taken into churches and killed if they did not apostasize their faith. A countless number of Christians died as a result of that order. Philippicus, who was versed in Scripture as well as in secular knowledge, scorned the decisions of the Sixth Council, and the heresy of Maximius, and tried *to have them anathematized*, but those who were seeped in that heresy did not allow it *and the emperor failed because of the stubbornness and arrogance of his supporters*. In this same period Maslama took Amasia as well as Antioch in Pisidia.

After he had reigned for two years, they blinded and exiled Philippicus. Then Anastasius[169] ruled for two years. Al-Walid died and Sulaiman ruled for two years.[170] In the same year, Maslama took the Galatian country and the fortresses in it. Anastasius sent troops to the West which rebelled and killed their commander. They enthroned Theodosius[171] while Anastasius fled to Nicaea.

Maslama went to the country of the Turks and returned with a great deal of booty. He went against Asia where he captured Pergamum and Sardis, and took prisoners. Then Maslama waxed proud *and thought to go to Constantinople.* He assembled 200,000 cavalry and 5,000 fully armed ships. Taking along an additional 12,000 Bulghars, 6,000 camels and 6,000 mules laden with victuals, he had prepared for many years of operations. He appointed 'Umar as military commander and vowed to destroy Constantinople. In addition, there were 30,000 volunteer fighters with him. He had two armies, one of which went by land and the other by sea. *He sent this entire multitude in advance of himself, while he slowly came with 12,000 other troops. He came and besieged Nicaea, promising peace to those troops who crossed over to his side, nor did he harm anyone.* Now Theodosius' general Leo *heard about this and* came to Maslama who vowed to him that should he take Constantinople he would make him emperor. Leo then entered

---

169 Anastasius II, Artemius 713-715.
170 715-717.
171 Theodosius III, 715-717.

Constantinople. The Arabs who passed through the districts and cities made peace with them. Then Caliph Sulaiman himself came after them with 12,000 encamped by Nicaea and besieged it.

Now Emperor Theodosius had learned about Leo's duplicity, seized his family and put them in prison. Leo fled to Sulaiman. Taking 6,000 cavalry, he descended on Amorium and swore a secret oath to the city that "I am falsely[172] circulating around with the Arabs." The city folk went and brought his family and gave them to him. *The emperor sent his family back to him, saying: "Do not blame the city and exact vengeance on it for your family."* Then the troops began to head toward Constantinople on two fronts. As they were advancing, troops arose from the city and went to Leo and submitted to him. *And they sent Theodosius' son to him as a hostage.* When Theodosius heard about this, he cut his hair and became a monk.

Leo told the Arab troops with him: "Stay here. I will enter the city and do your bidding. Then, Leo[173] ruled as emperor. Now when Sulaiman was apprised of this, he rejoiced greatly—thinking that Leo would give the city into his hands. But Leo began to deceive him with words and fortified the city. When Maslama realized that Leo had tricked him, he crossed to the other side, his troops going ahead of him. He came following behind with 4,000 troops. But then the Bulghar mercenaries fell upon them. Maslama himself escaped. He went and joined the other troops and the Arab forces in the western portion of the city, opposite the Golden Gate where warfare took place. Now there were some 30,000 troops in the sea guarding the ships and another 20,000 guarding the Bulghar side, and they fought for the city on land and on sea. Then the Bulghars rose and destroyed many of the Arabs. The Arabs were terrified because winter was approaching and they were seized with fear from the sea, from the Bulghars, and from the city itself. Famine came upon the Arabs, who were eating trash and drinking their own urine. While these disasters were unfolding,

---

172 Or, as a ruse.
173 Leo III, the Isaurian, 717-740.

Sulaiman, the Caliph of the Arabs, died and 'Umar[174] took over. He sent to Maslama to leave the city and return. Maslama thus returned with few troops, while others were destroyed by the famine. Thereafter, 'Umar began to persecute Christians in vengeance, as though the defeat had been their fault *for the prayers they had made in their churches*, and he tried to turn them to his own faith.

In this period, a man by the name of Severus, an Assyrian *who used magic,* began to preach among the Jews: "I am the Anointed. Gather your belongings so that I may prepare an army and go and rule as king in Jerusalem." And they believed in him and gathered up much treasure. When 'Umar learned about this he summoned him, seized the accumulated treasure, and then let him go. *As a result of this,* 'Umar made it law that the testimony of Christians should not be admitted, nor should Christians ride on saddled animals. And should an Arab Muslim kill a Christian he would not die as a result, but could pay a blood price of 1,000[175] *drams.* 'Umar also made the clerics free from taxation so that they not give all their belongings to the court. Moreover, he made it law that Arabs should not drink wine.

When 'Umar II died, Yazid[176] ruled for four years. Now it happened that a man who also was named Yazid rebelled against him in [the district of] Her. He attracted many followers. But Caliph Yazid sent and had him killed. In this period, many lands became depopulated because of famine which resulted from the coming of locusts. Now Yazid sent orders throughout all the lands that images should be obliterated in the churches, removed from clothing, books, *monuments,* and all other goods. Leo, *emperor of the Byzantines,* similarly effaced images from the Byzantine churches.

There was dissatisfaction with him *from many folk who were greatly displeased.* He stirred up persecution against all the races of humanity who did not accept his profession of the faith. Many Jews were baptized and became Christians, *some were*

---

174   Umar II, 717-720.
175   or, 5,000.
176   Yazid II, 720-724.

killed, while others fled. Then Yazid died, and Hisham[177] ruled for 19 years. He was *a wicked and greedy man,* an oppressor and tax gouger *who made the country long for death.* He dug a canal above Callinicos which took water from the Euphrates and irrigated the plains. He went to Neocaesarea *on the Wolf River* and captured it, and in the same year the Arabs took the impregnable fortress called Shize' in the Cilicia country.

In this period, Severus was the patriarch of the Syrians at Antioch and Yovhanne's[178] *the Philosopher* was the patriarch of the Armenians. In places such as Vaspurakan, Sasun, Aghuank and Siwnik', the Jacobite Syrians held the same confession based on Apostolic foundations.

Thus, the Syrians went to the Catholicos of the Armenians and said: "We are of the confession of Saint Gregory," and they received ordination from the Armenians. Nor was there any conflict among them. *They were called "Gregorians."* But then a priest by the name of Barshapuh and a deacon named Gabriel from Mup'arkin arose as slanderers between the Armenians and the Syrians. They went and said to the Catholicos of the Armenians: "The Jacobites claim that the body of Christ is corruptible." Then they went to Athanasius and said: "The Armenians are Julianites." And the two patriarchs, Armenian and Syrian, wrote to one another letters of accusation, and then asked for written confessions of the faith from each other. They wrote these confessions of the faith and saw that the two were the same. However, *here and there many* folk still were mired in the disorders caused by Ezr. Thus, the patriarch of the Armenians, Yovhanne's—a blessed miracle-working man who was extremely learned in Scripture as well as in secular knowledge—requested that a solemn ecclesiastical assembly be convened in the town of *Armenian* Manazkert by the two sides, Armenian and Syrian. *Six bishops and many clerics from the Syrian side arrived there, and together* they held an inquiry into Orthodoxy, *which included* the slanderers, priests and Julianite deacons.

177 724-743.
178 Yovhanne's III, Odznets'i, 717-728.

They found that there were no differences between the Armenian and Syrian confessions except for some aspects of the service, which they did not bother with. However, some of the Syrians said: "In the Acts of the Apostles it is written: 'God raised Jesus from the dead nor did his flesh see corruption *thereafter*."[179] The patriarch of the Armenians was saddened by this and replied: "It says that because previously it was corruptible." Then he requested an Armenian copy of the text and found the truth there and they looked at the Syriac version and found that in both the Armenian and the Syriac versions of that passage the word *thereafter* was nowhere written. Those who had stated that the passage contained the word were embarrassed by their own ignorance, and the others were delighted and the error of Ezr—which some still held—was corrected. Barshapuh and Gabrie'l *and the Julianites* were anathematized and a declaration of love and peace against slander was made between the Armenians and the Syrians. This occurred in 1035 of the Syrian Era,[180] which is 164[181] of the Armenian Era.[182] However, some claim it occurred in 135 of the Armenian Era.[183]

In this year, Egypt rebelled from the Arabs. The Arabs went and destroyed them. Those who escaped this destruction took ship and fled. The next year, Turks arose and came to the Arab country at Artughi and took numerous cities. This was the beginning of the emergence of the Turks. Maslama went against them and thousands and tens of thousands died on both sides. Then the Turks made peace with the cities they had taken for these had been left to them, and they turned back. *And they made peace with each other, and the Arabs left to them the cities they had seized from them, and went back. This was the beginning of the rise of the Turks.*

The same year there were torrential rains, to the point that it seemed the very heavens had opened. Again, the wall at Edessa was demolished and the city was taken. The following year, the Arabs

---

179 Acts 2, 30-32.
180 A.D. 724.
181 Or, 166.
182 A.D. 715.
183 A.D. 686.

went to Byzantium and took the city of Gangra and then Nicaea, which they pulled down. Then a command was issued by Hisham to kill all the captives. There was an inquiry made at Edessa as to whether they were martyrs or not. The truth was not revealed in this, *for doubt remained.*

In the 24th year of his reign, the Byzantine emperor Leo took the daughter of the Khazar Qaqan as a wife for his son Constantine, having her baptized first. Then he gave the kingdom to his son *and died that very year.* Then the emperor's son-in-law, Artawazd, rebelled and entered Constantinople. Constantine fled to Anatolia, and they promised to help him. He arrived at the city of Amorium, and wintered there. Now when Artawazd learned about this, he assembled troops and went against Constantine, striking at him and making him flee. The remainder of his forces went over to Artawazd, and so he reigned as emperor.

After 19 years of rule, Hisham died. He was succeeded by Walid[184] who did evil to the house of Hisham. He made Abas his military commander and sent him forth into the treasury of the Arab caliphate as though he were going into a sea of gold. By distributing treasure to all the military, he took over the caliphate. However, many did not accept Abas because he was the son of a concubine. Moreover, Walid was an evil-doer and a drunkard and they did not accept him, either. Thus, they enthroned Walid's father's brother's son Yazid[185] in Damascus, and he sent and had his brother beheaded and put his head on a pike and circulated it around the city *in a cart* in a container of wine. Now after this, all the emirs rose up against each other, killing each other, each one seeking the Caliphate for himself. Wasid took the country of the Persians; Marwan, Armenia; Sarit, Khorasan; Abdleh, Africa. Five months later, Walid died. His place was taken by Ibrahim, a decent and merciful man. After a short while, he, too, died. Then Marwan arose from Armenia and encountered his brother Sulaiman by the Euphrates. Between the two of them, 12,000 men

---

184 Al-Walid II, 743-744.
185 Yazid III, 744.

perished in their fight. Sulaiman fled to R'utsap' while Marwan went to Damascus and ruled.[186] He brought 3,000 camel loads of the kingdom's treasure to Harran. Then he went on to Hems and took it after four months. He demolished its wall and also pulled down the wall at Balbek. Then he went to Assyria, to Nineveh and to the Parthians at Bahl *whom he conquered.* Ali's son Abdullah came to Khorasan against Azab which is a river in Assyria, namely the Tigris. *And through such infighting among the Arabs, the Byzantines had some peace.* Marwan fled and the Ptoyik' took from Marwan 700 loads of *dahekan*s and *dram*s.

Taking auxiliaries, Constantine came to Constantinople, blinded and exiled Artawazd, and established himself on the throne. He had a son whom he called Leo after his father. The Byzantines ceased their warfare with the Arabs. This was even more so for the Armenians.

In this period, very great signs appeared from the month of March to *the end of* April. The air was full of dirt and dust to the point that day seemed like night. Then there appeared in the north three columns of fiery clouds visible for three days. These rose up and descended. After this, there appeared an unknown star the size of the moon. Each day it rose in the east and traveled to the west, being visible to people for the entire day. There were flashes of the stars all night which flew against the Milky Way. After this there was a severe earthquake and, in places where the earth was torn asunder, fountains arose, the color of blood. After this, there was a huge churning in the Great Sea[187] with waves rising to the heavens, one would think, and boiling down to its depths. Many people and animals near the shores died from the thunderbolts. A fortress that belonged to the children of Ammon and that had been built in the midst of the sea was torn from its foundations. The great tower that had been built with great care by Solomon over a fountain he had discovered in the water collapsed and sank. Following this, there was a great famine and a plague accompanied by sore throats

---

186 Marwan II, 744-750.
187 the Mediterranean..

which killed 20,000 people a day in Basra. It is said that monkeys in the country of the Madianites became enraged and caused great damage by attacking people and animals. When Caliph Marwan of Damascus, who had moved his capital to Harran, saw all of this, he repented, seeing his death before him, and wrote edicts to all his realm urging repentance. The ground trembled, tears flowed, and everywhere fasts and prayer vigils were undertaken. For they believed that these numerous strange signs were omens of the coming end of the world. Indeed, extraordinary marvels occurred. For example, there was a village at the foot of Mount Tabor which an earthquake moved from its place and transported two miles distant without disturbing any structures and without losing a single chicken. The city of Manbij sank in its place. A third of the city of Constantinople collapsed, while Nicaea was completely demolished. Moreover, many cities in Bithynia were destroyed. *However, the Chalcedonians did not repent or cease their evil doing for those living in Antioch* bribed Marwan and established Theophilus —called the son of *Mazman*[188]—as their patriarch. He went to Harran and, again through bribes, took over the church of the Syrian Orthodox. A monk associated with Archbishop Theophilus struck the altar with his hand and declared: "O desecrated altar, tomorrow you will be sanctified by Orthodox blessings and mass." As soon as he said this, he caught fire and burned to death and great fear seized the patriarch Theophilus. That night they gathered up the charred bones and fled, and the city remained Orthodox.

    Now in those days Abdullah, son of Ali came to Harran and Marwan fled to Askelon with six camels loaded with gold and silver. From there he went on to the land of Nubia, with Abdullah following him. Abdullah caught up with him at Aswan on the banks of the Nile River they fought one another. Marwan was slain. All the treasures which Marwan had greedily collected and all his belongings were expropriated by Abdullah who then ruled alone.[189] Now while he was seated in his tent *in a place close*

---

188 Theophlact Bar Qanbara.
189 al-Saffah, 750-754.

to a cemetary, a noise was heard. A large crowd hurriedly gathered which started to head toward the cemetary. Abdullah also went there. There they saw eight *old* men with dyed beards sitting up in their graves. The army remained there for three days and three nights. Abdullah placed guards by them. The men had come to life. Though they were asked questions constantly, they gave no answer, nor did they speak at all. Annoyed by this, by order of the caliph they were buried again. Nothing *as to the meaning of this* was understood.

Emperor Constantine was an intelligent man well versed in Scripture. He secretly practiced Orthodoxy. Now it happened that his wife, who had been the Qaqan's daughter, died. He did not wish to take another wife, as was the custom of Christian kings, yet for three years they tried to pressure him to do so. Finally, he told them: "There is no need for me to rule after a second marriage. However, if you really want me to remarry, make my son the emperor and then I will take another wife." And that is what they did.

Leo reigned as emperor, although his father cared for and concerned himself with the land and the house of the realm. Taking a wife and assembling troops, he came to Armenian Melitene and the surrounding districts. The Armenians and Syrians who had been under Arab rule he took away with him, saying to the Byzantines: "They are Christians. Let them be with us as our brothers and sons." Now when the Chalcedonians saw this, they went to the emperor and asked: "Why do you bring them, for they insult us and anathematize the Fourth Council." Then Constantine requested from them a written statement of their faith. The Armenians and the Syrians then provided written statements describing the one nature, one will, and one operation of Christ. Now when the emperor and all the princes saw this, they were astonished and praised it, saying: "This is true and Orthodox Christianity." Therefore, he ordered that a council be convened to turn the entire country to this confession. And thus, the Council called the Seventh took place. The emperor said: "There are two provisions which I beseech you to remove; namely, validity of the Council of Chalcedon, and the prohibition on the worship of images in the Church." But they were unwilling and fell at the emperor's feet begging him not to tax them with his two requests. *"Even if you put us to the sword, it is impossible for us to do what you ask"*. The emperor, who was greatly saddened, turned and said: "Will you at least eliminate the inventions of Maximus, the accursed Nestorian?" *If not, I will not stay with you.* They heeded him on this and anathematized Maximus who claimed that Christ had two separate wills and two operations. It is for this reason that many of the Byzantines have no consideration for this Seventh Council. However, the emperor secretly practiced Orthodoxy and ordered the Armenians to return to their country "so that after my death, they do not persecute you." He gave them presents and provisions for the journey and auxiliaries to take them there peacefully.

In this year locusts came and devoured numerous districts. The following year hail fell such as had never been seen or heard about before. It demolished many buildings and killed many animals *wild and domesticated*. People weighed one hailstone and it weighed eight *litr*s. In this year Abdla, caliph of the Arabs, died after reigning for seven years. He was followed by another Abdla, Abu'l Abas[190] who ruled over the Persians and the Arabs. And there ruled Abu Jap'r who rebuilt Melitene and the city of Karin which the Byzantines call Kalanike' and the Arabs, Erzurum which means "branch of a tree," *or East* and Kamax which the Emperor Constantine had ruined. In the same year *after rebuilding these cities,* the Arabs took Africa and, from the Persians, the land of Tabaristan and all the surrounding areas, and *the fortified city of Rey.*

In 1073 of the Syrian Era,[191] Jap'r built a city on the Tigris River above the city of Ctesiphon and named it Baghdad, which translates "middle" since it is midway between the Persians and the Syrians. In this year, a group of Kurds *known as Mark'* arose and captured 50,000 souls from Gozan.

190 Al-Mansur, 754-775.
191 A.D. 762.

In the same year, a woman from Bukara became renowned. They say that from the time of her birth she had not sucked a drop of her mother's milk nor had she eaten any food. Yet she came of age and became a normal woman *thirty years of age* without eating anything at all. They brought her to Baghdad to Jap'r. She was tested and it turned out to be so. Jap'r convened an assembly of savants to inquire whether such a thing had ever been known before, and they told him that it was unprecedented *and they could not explain it, but that it was a miracle from the Lord God.*

In this period, the Magians,[192] *deceived by this sign*, revolted and set up their own king. The Arabs went against them and were defeated by the Magians. Then the Arabs went against the Magians a second time, killing 40,000 of them. They subdued the Magians, *killed their king*, and returned home. Then Jap'r turned to Mesopotamia. There he appointed two tax collectors: an Arab named Suleiman and a Jew named Muse'. Together they drained the land of gold and silver. Many folk dug into the cemeteries looking for something to give them since they were harassed and tortured by their violence. *They opened the graves of pagans and gave what they uncovered for taxes.* When the Byzantines heard about this, they too began to dig up the graves of the long dead. Now while they were digging in the city of Nicomedia, they came upon the tomb of Nicomedes, the builder of the city. There was a great amount of gold and *luminous* precious stones interred with him, and they informed Constantine. He went to see this but did not want to take anything from him; rather, he had the place walled up with stones and mortar, and said: "Is there anything more repulsive than for the living to rob the dead and profit from it?" Then he *got angry and* threatened them not to do it anymore.

Due to Jap'r's brutal greed, the land became so destitute of silver that an ox and an ass were sold for one *dram*, while a child fetched five *drams*. After 20 years Jap'r perished and the land rested from his evil pollution. That same year *Emperor* Constantine

---

192 Zoroastrians in Iran.

died after a reign of 34 years. His son Leo[193] *who had ruled with him* was established in his position as emperor. Jap'r was succeeded by his son, Mahdi[194] who ruled as Caliph over the Arabs. He dispersed everything that his father had stored up and gave himself over to witchcraft *which he studied*, and he was guided by astrology. When Leo heard about this, he sent him the sorcerers' books *Janes* and *Jamres* which had been used against Moses. They were received with the greatest delight. Mahdi came to Aleppo where 12,000 Syrian *Christians* came out to honor him. He was astounded by such a multitude *and envious*. Then he seated himself and summoned them, saying: "You have two options. Either die or convert to our religion." All of them, including 5,000 Arabs, died for the Christian faith. Moreover, the wives and children of those who had apostatized left them and fled. Then Mahdi went to the Arabisos country in Byzantium, sending his son Harun to raid. Reaching the Euphrates, he enslaved 7,000 people, losing 4,000 of their own troops.

Leo sent troops to Mesopotamia, gathered up the Armenian and Syrian Orthodox Christians and settled them in Thrace. He travelled the same path as his father, neither revering images nor allowing them to be revered. Nor did he commune with the Chalcedonians. It was for this reason that some of the Greek historians complain about him and call him a Jacobite. After a reign of 10 years Leo died. Then his twelve-year-old son Constantine ruled and his mother was regent because of his youth.[195] *When Harun learned about this*, he came to the country of the Byzantines but returned home in disgrace. In this year Ali, at the command of Mahdi, built the city of Hadath in the Marash country. *But he was not successful in this since* Mahdi died and his brother Musa ruled for two years.[196] Two years after the building of Hadath had commenced, the Byzantines came and demolished it.

---

193 Leo IV, the Khazar, 750-775; 775-780.
194 Al-Mahdi, 775-785.
195 Constantine VI, 776-780; 780-797 Irene regent 780-790, 792-797; Irene 797-802.
196 al-Hadi, 785-786.

Then Musa died and his brother Harun, called Rashid, ruled as Caliph.[197] It was at his order that Abd al-Malik built the city of Rashid. He prepared 2,000 carts and pulled down the churches which were west of the Sanga River which is close to Samosata. They also demolished the church at Kesoun with its fifteen altars, which had been built by the Apostles. And these stones were taken by cart to build Hadath.

In this period, the coffin of a Jew was found in Edessa on which was *a thousand-year-old* inscription: "I believe that Christ will come, born of a virgin, and that He will cause His light to dawn on me." *God physically will be born from a virgin and through a Cross will the light of His glory spread throughout the universe. May His mercy be visited upon me.*

In this year, Constantine learned that Elpidius, the patrician of Sicily, was committing adultery with his mother. He wanted to seize and blind him, but Felix fled to the Arabs. Taking 40,000 *of their cavalry* troops, he went to turn over Sicily to the Arabs. But as they went, they became trapped in the snow. Many of them died while the survivors went to Constantinople where they were treated humanely and departed *with provisions.* Because of his mother's adultery, Constantine disallowed the mentioning of her name in Church. Then Constantine's wife died and he scorned the Apostolic canons and took another wife, thereby becoming hateful to many. He also defiled the daughters of the princes. His mother Irene heard the discontent of the princes, blinded her son's eyes, and herself assumed the rule having as her second the eunuch P'iladi.

In these days *in Edessa* the grandchildren of Athanasius, the children of his son Koma, were digging in their home and found many treasures such as snakes and scorpions made of gold and with the insides hollowed out. These were filled with some chemical, which, when spread on copper, melted it and turned it to gold. It was written on them that the profit from this discovery should belong to the poor and the Church. And they arranged that. After this discovery the grandchildren became very grand

---

[197] Harun al-Rashid, 786-809.

indeed, receiving horses and donkeys, dogs and falcons, and they went out to hunt. News of this reached the Caliph of the Arabs who had them brought to him. He tortured them and took everything they had. They took the snakes, opened them, thought the contents were earth and dumped them out. Only later did they realize the value of the thing and greatly regretted their actions. One of the prisoners was a blessed virgin whom they gave to a Chalcedonian to guard. He had her put in an attic and placed Arab guards around the place. She, fearing that she would be dishonored, threw herself down from the heights and died. When the Caliph of the Arabs heard about this, he was greatly saddened and let the others go.

Then the Arabs began to hate the Byzantines because of the lady Irene, *since they had a woman for a ruler*. Now the troops took counsel and planned to enthrone Nicephorus the Cappadocian. But when Irene heard about this, she wanted to blind his eyes. However, a eunuch concealed him. The troops found him and made him emperor.[198] The latter treated the regent and the eunuch respectfully, but when he heard that they were planning to do him evil, he sent Irene into exile to Athens and forgave the eunuch, not doing any bad things to him because of his own gratitude to him.

In this period, the caliph of the Arabs constructed a city in the country of the Arabs *in Armenia* and called it Sozopetra. Now the Byzanantines came and looted the Arab country. Nicephorus was a mighty and thoughtful man. *He went to the country of the Arabs and returned with a great deal of loot*. Some said that his family was of Arab origin but that they had earlier converted to Christianity because their own folk had scorned them, and that Nicephorus was the born from them. Now after P'ilite' had given Sicily to the Arabs he went and told them that Nicephorus was a valiant man, a man who fasted and prayed. They wrote to Harun. Caliph Harun assembled an immense multitude and went to Byzantine territory. There Nicephorus arose against him. They encamped opposite each other for two months and talked of peace. They made friendship with one another and the troops mingled.

198 Nicephorus I, 802-822.

They swore an oath to each other and ate bread together. Then Harun gave all his tents *and dining vessels* to Nicephorus, and turned back.

Harun built a city above Callinicos and named it Heraclea as he had taken a wife named Heraclea. Nicephorus built Ancyra. Anania, bishop of Merdin, lived in this period. He hailed from a mountain near Nineveh known as Thousands. He built the Ananians monastery. Finding a ruined fortress, he bought it from the Arabs and dug inside, transforming it into a sacristy through much expense. *He built secret and deep chapels there.* He placed in it the remains of the Ananians, brought from Dara, and the remains of the Apostle Bartholemew from Armenia, and the remains of Philip from Manbij. Then he went to Rome *where he prayed* and wept across from the tombs of the blessed Apostles. A portion of the relics of Peter and Paul were given to him. He brought these also to his monastery. Then he went to Babylon where he found the remains of the prophet Daniel, Ezekiel, Shem, who was Noah's son, and many other remains. He brought these and placed them in the sacristy he had built *and hid them.* Over them he built a magnificent church, where to this day prayerful vows are made.

Harun, Caliph of the Arabs, made a count of the value of his treasures and found that he had more than Jap'r had accumulated, a millionfold more. And he was overjoyed. He prostrated himself before God three times and then *wrote a document stipulating that his sons should succeed him in order of their seniority.* He promised his kingdom to his eldest son, Muhammad. After Muhammad, Mamun was to rule and after him Kasim, which turned out to be the cause of the ruination of their kingdom. Harun put Muhammad in Baghdad; Kasim in Syria; and Mamun he took along with him to Khorasan. He gave him his treasure and died there after a reign of 23 years.

Now Nicephorus went with a large force against the Bulghars. He reached the *capital* city of their kingdom and caused great destruction, to the point that he threw their little children on the ground and mercilessly drove over them with his threshing wagons. It happened that a certain Frank became enraged by this *wild and bestial behavior*, struck Nicephorus and killed him *when he was alone and away from his bodyguards.*

Then Muhammad[199] ruled as caliph of the Tachiks. He took his father's treasures from Callinicos and removed them to Baghdad, since Mamun[200] was ruling in Khorasan. This man was learned and intelligent as well. Now al-Amin wanted to create disturbances and violate his father's oath and not give treasure to Mamun. Thus, the two of them, al-Amin and Mamun, began to war against each other. When people heard about this, many of the Palestinians rebelled. Al-Amin mustered troops and put 'Ali as his military commander, and sent them against Mamun. They fought one another. The forces of Mamun were conquered and they fled and some drowned in the river. Then al-Amin was in Samosata where he rebuilt the fortress and secured himself inside. Through Abd al-Malik' he subdued the rebels. He rebuilt the walls of Edessa and Samosata and K'esun with the goods he robbed from Christians. Then the military commander Husayn rebelled, seized al-Amin, put him in prison, and went and resided in Baghdad. Al-Amin sent beseeching Husayn just to let him live, there being no need of him to continue as caliph. Husayn took pity on him, sparing him his life and giving him the caliphate. Al-Amin then went to Baghdad. Mamun then sent his military commander, Hort'om, to go and besiege Baghdad. Rocks were wanting in the city, so they demolished churches and hurled those out. Then that ceased and Hort'om and his troops entered the city. They found al-Amin hiding in a house, and they seized and slew him. Then Tahir, another of Mamun's military commanders, arrived at Callinicos with 4,000 troops, and the rebels started to decline.

In that period, a frightful earthquake took place. The Koghot mountains, which were spread about here and there, moved and became close to each other—something which folk actually

199 Muhammad al-Amin, 809-813.
200 813-833.

observed. Moreover, one mountain collapsed and fell into the Euphrates, blocking the river for a day going upstream. Many other mountains collapsed and many sources of water, bitumen, and naphtha came to light while many others disappeared.

Now there was a line of Arabs called the Qureshis who accepted Ibrahim as their caliph in Baghdad. When Tahir learned about this, he assumed authority in Harran and Callinicos and gave an order that, henceforth, those who were idol-worshippers should make their sacrifices openly. And there were many who did. Tahir put Abdullah in Edessa and he harassed the Christians, saying: "Get up and go to your Christian king so that we may rest. Till now we have been tormented by living and wandering about out in the open, but now we have taken this country by the sword and hereafter it belongs to us, *since the Lord has given it to us*." The *Orthodox* Christians were gravely saddened, as there was *no mercy* and no place of refuge for them. *They placed their hopes only on the hereafter.*

After Nicephorus, they enthroned Leo.[201] Michael, the military commander of the Romans, slew Leo and ruled himself.[202] In this period, Nasr rebelled in Suruj and he sent to Michael to pledge allegiance to him. Then Michael sent emissaries to Nasr. However, his own people led Nasr astray, and they killed those emissaries.

Now Mamun had a prince of Byzantine extraction with him whose name was T'omas. He had come to his father, Harun, saying: "I am the son of Emperor Constantine." They held him in honor *and believed him*, and Mamun gave him troops to go to Constantinople, either to rule over them or to create a disturbance there. T'omas went and besieged Constantinople for six months. Then Michael took his Arab servants aside and promised them freedom if they would wholeheartedly fight against the Arabs. And they fought and made T'omas flee. They pursued and caught him, cut off his feet and hands and took him around the city. But Michael did not liberate his servants *as he had promised*.

---

201 Leo V, the Armenian, 813-820.
202 Michael II, the Amorian, 820-829.

THE CHRONICLE

In these times, Mamun *heard that the Qureshi sect of the Arabs had rebelled in Baghdad and had designated Ibrahim as their king, and so he* came to Baghdad. Tahir came to him and he was sent as prince to Khorasan. Meanwhile, Ibrahim fled and disappeared. In this year the Adriatic Sea threw up onto the shores of the Cilicia country a fish having the length of 40 cubits and a similar width. It was not like a fish, but more like a frightful hill. The country assembled, cut, dried, and ate the fish and extracted a lot of oil from it which they sold in Antioch. They burned this [as fuel] and, *marveling*, ate the meat for a long time.

Now in 1140 of the Syrian Era[203] the Byzantine emperor Michael died and Theophilus reigned as king.[204] Then the Bulghars submitted to him, as did the K'urdank' and a part of the Arabs who are K'urdank' with a separate language. In ancient times they dwelled among the Kurds and had a magical belief that a man named Mahadi would be revealed among them and that he would rule the entire country. Those who believed in him and died would rise after 40 days, live again for a while, and then be transferred to a deathless land. Some claimed that he was god; others, that he was a king. And they waited for him. Now in this period a certain man named Mahadi appeared, and the people thought he was the one. And he himself thought so as well. He put a crown on his head, covered his face with a veil, and his renown spread. *His people gathered around him and they emerged from that country as a great multitude.* Now Mamun was frightened by him. Then Mahadi went and established his dwelling in the Ararat mountains of Armenia, *killing those who did not accept him*. His forces went forth in all directions and he defeated everyone equally, eventually reaching the borders of Jazira, striking and destroying everything. Then Hasan, the military commander of Mamun, heard about him and insisted that he go against him. And he began to defeat Mahadi's forces. The multitude of his mob of followers began to flee from him. As for Mahadi himself, he removed the crown and

---

203 A.D. 829.
204 Theophilus, 821-829; 829-842.

the veil and fled, landing in the territory of the Armenian Sahak. Now the Arabs had seized his camp and turned back. *Sahak went after the Arabs, killing many of them and causing others to flee.* The Armenian prince Sahak seized Mahadi and beheaded him.

The K'urdank' meanwhile had surrounded Sahak's fortress. When the latter had returned from the destruction he found his home thus surrounded, and he killed them. A few of them fled *secretly* and thus came to Theophilus. Now those Arabs who had gone with the K'urdank' also believed in Mahadi, who sometimes said: "I am Christ" and sometimes: "I am the Holy Spirit." Therefore they had believed what he himself had told them. When Theophilus saw the fugitives who had come to him, he was happy. With them he went into Arab-controlled territory. He went to Sozopetra and took and demolished it, and took its inhabitants captive. But at the coming of the next year the Arabs rebuilt Sozopetra.

The patrician Manuel rebelled from Theophilus, came to Mamun, and urged him to invade Byzantine territory. When he went to Harran, he ended the demolition of the churches. Then he went on to Edessa and made inquiry about the revenues of the cathedral there. When he was told that they paid taxes to the Arabs, he issued an order that the Church should not pay taxes *on any of its holdings, and should pay nothing to the court.* In summer Mamun went to Cappadocia, captured four strongholds there and then turned back to winter in Damascus. In April of the following year, he again returned to Byzantine territory. He descended to the fortress of Lulu; however, unable to take it *by siege*, he turned to Kesoun. Patriarch Dionysius came out before him, and Mamum treated him with great honor giving him a document freeing the Church from taxation. Now it happened that while he was speaking with the patriarch, they brought him the glad tiding of the capture of Lulu by the troops he had left at the fortress. And so, he felt even more affection for the patriarch.

In this period the patrician Manuel left Mamun and went to Theophilus. Theophilus sent to Mamun, requesting friendship, to which Mamun replied: "Pay taxes to me and acknowledge me as king over you, and I will establish friendship with you." Then Theophilus made him no further reply. Now Mamun went to Cilicia, and a certain Byzantine came to him claiming that he was the emperor's son. Mamun believed him and gave him a crown costing 3,000 *dahekans*, and told the patriarch of Antioch, Job, to consecrate him emperor according to Christian custom. And this was done. When this was discovered in Constantinople, they anathematized Job. This imposter lived two years among those Arabs and no one bothered with him. Then he apostatized Christ and became a Muslim.

Mamun went to Byzantine territory and through kindly deceit subdued the entire land as far as the city of Tyana, which the Arabs had demolished. And he started to rebuild it through taxes demanded from the country so harshly that every tongue cursed him. This reached the ears of the Lord of Power, and thus God struck him and he died. Then his brother al-Mu'tasim ruled.[205] He burned the building of the city and all its arrangements, then proceeded on to Baghdad which he subdued by force—even though they were not with him. Subsequently, he went to Basra. *Men had come to him from there with complaints, saying that* There is an island called Banat, which had always rebelled and was causing great grief, because the islanders were wont to kill the merchants who travelled from Basra to Ethiopia and India. That island was located in the sea at a place opposite from where the Euphrates and Tigris Rivers join, in the Persian Sea. The caliph sent troops against it but was unable to take it because of the fastness of the place, the ingenuity of the people, and the bravery of the soldiers. And so, the caliph sent to Egypt and Saba and had brought from those places craftsmen and skilled divers who covered their sense organs with the fetuses of children and poured oil into jars with which devices they were able to descend and later emerge from the sea.

Now the caliph had sent the divers along with the troops so that when the inhabitants of the island came forth in boats to fight

---

205 A.D. 833-842.

with the Arab boats, they would suddenly enter the city and burn it. And this is just what they did. The rebels were destroyed, *the fortress was demolished to its foundations* and great ease came upon the merchants and travelers while the land of Basra expanded and was greatly built up.

Al-Mu'tasim built a sumptuous palace between Nineveh and Babylon in the village of Samara. From Egypt he brought balsam trees and many other types of plants and made a beautiful park for walking. *He did the same thing in Baghdad as in Babylon. Now you must not think that these places are the same since they are separated by a four days' journey.* In this period, al-Mu'tasim sent an embassy to Nubia *and reminded them that* from ancient times there had been *a treaty of* peace between the Arabs and the Nubians. The Arabs gave a great deal of wheat, wine, olive oil, and clothing to the Nubians. Furthermore, should a king of the Nubians arise and go to the country of the Tachiks, the Tachiks would submit to him in all matters, just as though he were their own king. The Nubians *annually* gave the Tachiks 300 black slaves, 10 monkeys and a giraffe. This latter is an animal with a tall front section and spots, large as a buffalo, and worth 20,000 *dahekans*. They also gave wood which does not decay. Now when division had fallen upon the Arabs, that treaty had expired. Al-Mu'tasim was seeking to renew it. When an embassy arrived there, it found that *their king had died leaving a daughter as his heir.*

A prince named Zak'aria had given his son Gorg to her as a husband and thereby became king, since among them kingship by law is from the father's side. Now Zak'aria thought it would be agreeable to send his son to al-Mu'tasim. When the caliph of the Arabs learned about his coming, he was delighted and sent a great deal of money, men, and animals to cover the travel expensess. He also issued an order that the Tachik and Christian clerics, laity, *and prominent people* should go out to meet him and the entire land surged forth on the route, to see this novelty.

The Nubian king was a handsome youth of attractive stature in his twenties. He was seated on a beautifully caparisoned camel adorned with a new and priceless saddle surmounted with a golden howdah adorned with precious stones and pearls which had a dome topped with a golden cross. He wore gorgeous clothing which cannot be adequately described and a crown on his head, and in one hand he held a golden apple with a cross, and a golden staff *with a cross* in the other hand. There were four bishops with him, a multitude of priests, and four priests on all sides carrying golden crosses. The troops were also decked out in various costly dress which astonished the viewers. The Caliph of the Tachiks arose and came out to meet him with many troops and accompanied him into Baghdad, where they sat on the same pillow. Patriarch Dionysius was summoned, *asked the king about Orthodoxy*, and then performed the mass. And King Ge'org took communion. The patriarch was astonished at the young man's wisdom and his brilliant expression of Orthodox faith, *since he insulted those who spoke of Christ having two natures*, and the patriarch blessed him. The Arab Caliph gave this Christian king countless gifts so extensive that they could not be weighed, since he realized that prior to himself none of the Arab kings had been so glorified by the coming of a Nubian king. They confirmed the treaty which had existed before *but not, as previously, based on monetary exchanges, but rather based now on complete friendship and mutual understanding*. And they shared the cities named Aswan, and Gawzan on the Nile between the Arabs and the Nubians. And *the handsome King Ge'orgi departed with the greatest glory for his own land*. However, two bishops and many other *troops* from their party died, since they were unaccustomed to the changing temperatures of summer and winter. At this time, two Arab military commanders, Nasr and Babak, who were pleased by the Christian religion they observed in the Nubians, went to Theophilus, emperor of the Byzantines, with many of their troops and became Christians. Inflated by this, Theophilus took them and went with his troops to Sozopetra, which he demolished.

After equally killing Muslims and Christians, he went on to Melitene and enslaved it. Then he arose and went to Arsamosata and Handzit', capturing many people, and departing. Now as soon as al-Mu'tasim learned about this *he was infuriated* and descended into Byzantine territory with two of his armies. These consisted of 30,000 Mauritanians, 30,000 merchants, with 50,000 camels and 20,000 mules bearing provisions. He went and took Ancyra. He proceeded on to Amorium a large and populous city, secure and lovely, unequalled in the country. After a siege of twelve days accompanied by fierce fighting, it was captured through the betrayal of one of its princes, named George. In that city were monasteries filled with thousands of virgins whom al-Mu'tasim gave to his servants. They killed 18,000 people there, and burned the city and its churches. God's judgement is unfathomable, and its depth is impenetrable.

Al-Mu'tasim had a son named Daoud *who was motivated by demons*. He asked that his father *completely* eliminate Christian freedoms: not to let them as pallbearers raise their dead in their arms, nor to ring the bell, not to display the cross outside churches, not to openly celebrate the divine mystery, not to raise hogs or to eat pork. *And al-Mut'asm did this.* So much did Daoud loathe Christians.

In this period, al-Mu'tasim learned that his brother's son, Abas, wanted to murder him. And many princes had pledged that they would get aid from the Byzantines, destroy the Caliphate of the Tachiks, and go under Byzantine rule. Al-Mu'tasim put them into fetters and they died of hunger. And he wrote to all the Tachiks that Abas had wanted to destroy the Tachik authority. For this reason, the Tachiks hate the name Abas.

In this period in the north there appeared for three nights a red cloud which was like fire. This was followed by *a strange* rainfall which previously was unheard of and never before seen. Falling with the rain were rocks which peeled the bark off trees. The downpour denuded the land of its soil. Then the deluge visited Harran where an untold multitude of people and animals drowned, and many villages and districts were ruined. The waters picked them up and carried them into the Euphrates.

After this Emperor Theophilus sent gifts to al-Mu'tasim and sought from him an exchange of captives, that he should give the Byzantines and receive the Tachiks. In return, al-Mu'tasim sent gifts *even more valuable gifts* loaded on 50 camels and said: "It is not the Arab custom to exchange one Arab for a Byzantine since the Arabs have greater value. But if you give up our people then I will return many of your people." Then Theophilus released many Tachiks, and there was peace between them.

In these times in Palestine there appeared a man named T'amam who claimed that he was a messenger of God like previous such messengers. He said: "It is not fitting to tax Christians at the current rate, only four *drams* should be taken from them." The Christians were ecstatic and they assembled—some 30,000 naked and barefoot paupers. T'amam arose with them and went to Jerusalem where he pulled down the Church of the Blessed Resurrection. Jap'r, the military commander of Damascus came there and killed him. Then al-Mu'tasim died and his son Harun became caliph Harun al-Wathiq.[206] That same year, Theophilus died and his three-year-old son Michael became emperor with his mother, Theodora, controlling the empire.[207] Now as for al-Wathiq, he was a man who loved to eat and drink, who knew nothing about past events, or what might befall the land. He left administration of the caliphate in the hands of some other men and then, after five years, he died. Theodora managed the Byzantine empire for 14 years with her son, and then died. And Michael was established as sole ruler. In his day the Tachiks had six caliphs: Harun, Jap'ar, Mahmad, Ahmad, another Ahmad, and Abu Abdla who killed many people for no reason during his drunkeness. He was followed by al-Muhtadi[208] who arose in Khorasan and came to Baghdad.

Michael, after ruling as emperor for 25 years died. Now since he had no son, a certain man named Basil[209] ruled for two years.

---

206 Harun II, 842-847.
207 Michael III, the Drunkard, 842-867; Theodora, regent, 842-856.
208 869-870.
209 Basil I, 866-867.

Then his son Leo ruled for 25 years and eight months. Al-Muhtadi died in his reign, and then Ahmat ruled as caliph for 23 years.

Leo's mother, Theophano, wanted to kill her son and he wanted to kill her, after he had been ruling for 11 years. But then suddenly the mother died, having lived a life full of good deeds. Then a year later Leo's wife died. Trampling on the Apostolic canons, he took another wife and thereby became loathsome to everyone. Then, for no reason, he dropped that wife and took yet another wife. And then he took a third since there was no one to reprove him. And then he took a fourth wife and began to stipulate that every man should have four wives. After that he died of a bowel disease. In this time, witchcraft was discovered in the patriarch of Constantinople. They removed him and put another in his place, only to find that he was a witch and a pagan. He had placed idols behind the altar curtain and revered them during liturgy. This evil was revealed and, as a result, for a long while in the Church the curtain was done away with. They set up another patriarch, and since he, too, worshipped idols, they deposed him as well. He had said: "I learned this from your patriarchs, otherwise I would never have known about it." And this is how they were, for they did not have a thorough definition of the faith and, for that reason, God permitted them to do unworthy things.

After this Leo's son Alexander ruled for a year. He, too, followed the witches. During his reign an earthquake occurred in Thrace which rent the earth and swallowed up many churches and structures. Alexander died from the shocks and his half-brother Constantine ruled for 57 years. Now because he was a lad at his accession, they gave him governors and assistants to counsel him until he was established.

During Alexander's reign, the Caliphate of the Arabs changed from the line of Muhammad to the line of Ali, and Ablabas ruled for 20 years. In this year the military commander of the Bulghars arose and grew stronger than the Byzantines. He sent his troops against Constantinople and harassed it greatly through warfare which lasted throughout the reign of Constantine.

In the 13th year of Constantine's reign, Muhammad ruled over the Arabs for six years. In the 29th year of Constantine, Jap'r ruled for 24 years. In the 53rd year of Constantine's reign, Abunosr ruled over the Arabs for two years. In the 54th year of Constantine, Ablabas ruled for five years. In the 55th year of his reign, Constantine became sick and died, and his brother-in-law Romanus ruled. In that year Simon, the chief of the Bulghars, came and enslaved Thrace. Then he went and besieged Adrianopolis, greatly harassing it for a long while before he captured and then demolished it. Romanus sent to Simon requesting friendship. He got him to agree and they met each other at sea and established peace between them on the western front. And they turned to the East.

From the time of Heraclius *and 'Umar* onward, Armenian Cappadocia and Syrian Mesopotamia and Cilicia were under Tachik control. Now, however, the Tachiks had weakened because of their drunkenness and fornication. And so Romanus' general, Kirakos, went to Melitene in Lesser Armenia. The city asked him to excuse them for 40 days while they sent to their Caliph and asked what he commanded. Kirakos agreed to this. The inhabitants sent an emissary who set out and was seized and brought to Kirakos. Out of terror, the messenger swore with tears in his eyes that he would give the city to them, and then he stayed there with them. Eventually he returned to the city giving them the glad tidings that "Today our troops will arrive. In the evening open the gates so they may enter the city." And they believed him. The Byzantines arranged themselves as though they were Tachik troops, and come evening, they entered the city. The city was thus filled with troops and the Byzantines took it. However, they did not kill the Tachiks since they had sworn an oath. They removed them and departed. Then they took the city of Erzurum *and Kamax* and Kesoun and the entire country.

Thereafter they went to Cilicia and took that, too. Then they arose and went to Antioch by the sea *and they took all the coast there* and then went on to Jerusalem. People quickly consented to their rule, since the Tachiks had grown weak.

MICHAEL THE GREAT

It was at this time that Romanus died and his son-in-law, Constantine, who was a highly literate and benevolent man, became emperor. In the *twenty*-fourth year of his reign Abusahl ruled as caliph over the Arabs. Constantine sent his son, Basil, who came and captured Samosata. But then the bad news arrived that Constantine had died and his *other* son, Romanus, became emperor. *Basil returned and submitted to his brother. Romanus sent troops to Aleppo and captured that city.* That same year Abusahl died and then Abu Lianas ruled as caliph for six years.

As for Romanus, when he reigned, he made gifts to the troops and generously distributed presents. Then he sent a force and captured Aleppo and harassed the Tachiks. Romanus died and the troops enthroned Nicephorus.[210] He was a man hated by the Orthodox, who deceived many people. He went to Melitene, saw the ruin of the city and the land and then took his confidants' advice: "Send to Athanasius, patriarch of the Syrians for him to bring people and restore the land so that should the Tachiks grow strong again it will be good for us if they destroy the Syrians and fall into the Tachiks' hands." He sent to Lord Yovhannēs at Antioch and swore to him that if he would fill the land up with Orthodox folk, either he would turn the entire country to Orthodoxy, or else the dyophysites would be allowed to scorn them. *Nicephorus vowed that he would end the persecution of the Orthodox.* The patriarch believed him. He went and assembled Orthodox people everywhere and, by the emperor's promise, built up Melitene and the country and built numerous monasteries *and villages which he populated with Orthodox people brought from Mesopotamia and Armenia*. And he made his residence at Perit. Now when he had succeeded in this matter, the emperor called him to Constantinople, claiming he had so promised. And Lord Yovhannēs went to Constantinople with many bishops *and vardapets*.

In 1280 of the Syrian Era[211] many dyophysites had assembled there and held an extensive examination of the faith for two

---

210   Nicephorus II, Phocas, 963-969.
211   A.D. 969.

months. The Chalcedonians had so falsified things that there was not even an opinion about the truth among all the listeners. The Emperor again tricked some of them by flattery and promising sees and gifts to the bishops who accepted their Chalcedonian confession, while he threatened those who did not. However, neither the blandishments nor the threats moved them. Instead, they replied: "We do not want to divide the one nature of God into two parts and neither gifts nor fear will make us do it." When the emperor heard this, he became furious with them and had them bound and placed in prison for four months.

God's wrath fell upon the emperor, and he died. And the empire was taken over by John,[212] a military man who was personable. But they say that Nicephorus' wife, Theophano, murdered her husband because he was not married to her. Then she took John, who had previously been[213] Bearer of the Slipper to the Emperor. As a result, he was known as Tzimisces. He committed adultery with the empress and Theophano took him as her husband and gave him the crown. *And they plotted together to kill the Emperor.* He was militarily successful, taking many districts from the Tachiks. And it was he who removed the Syrian patriarch and his bishops from jail. After this they returned to their own districts.

Now it happened that in this period the patriarch of Antioch was a Chalcedonian named Agapius. He persecuted the Orthodox with the connivance of some princes whose sons he had taken as pupils after baptism. He took the Syrian Gospel, the chrism, and the eucharist and three times tried to burn them in a roaring fire. But by the grace of God they were spared and did not burn. This impious man did not regret his deed and viciously claimed that "they did not burn because of witchcraft." As such, he was more wicked than Nebuchadnezzar who, upon seeing that the three children had not burned, repented and glorified God. Agapius, on the other hand, on the feast of the Epiphany made bold to remove from the churches and from the city Armenian and Syrian men

---

212 John I, Tzimisces, 969-976.
213 i.e., bore the title of

and women, *and seized their churches*. They held the feast outside the city. They beseeched God with tears in their eyes and vowed not to enter the city until they had seen their vengeance exacted. God quickly granted their request. He wrathfully struck that impious man, afflicting him with wicked ailments until he died. Then *the Orthodox* were returned into the city sighing and in honor, and glorifying the name of God. This took place in 1285 of the Syrian Era.[214]

Emperor Tzimisces was from the district of Handzit' and had his dwelling in those parts. He freed all the captives, was of a generous and forgiving nature, and beloved by all. He constructed a great church in Constantinople, and it is said about him that he was Armenian by nationality. He ruled for three years and then died. Then there was great mourning all over the Byzantine world. After this they enthroned Basil and Constantine, sons of Emperor Romanus. And they were amicable toward one another. This was because Basil left his brother to rule and he himself went against the Tachiks. He reigned for 55 years and enjoyed many victories during his entire life, and subdued many lands. He stood against the Armenians and the West, and subdued the Armenians and the Bulgars. Then he died and his brother, Constantine, occupied his position for two and a half years before he, too, died. In this period, the Tachiks were ruled by Alp'atl for 29 years, followed by Bubak'r for 19 years, followed by Abul Abbas for 22 years.

After Constantine in the Greek section there ruled Romanus, the brother's son of Constans. He arose in battle against the Tachiks, was defeated and fled. *He had threatened the monasteries on Black Mountain saying that if he returned from battle successfully, he would make them Chalcedonian, as he loathed the Orthodox.* He initiated a great persecution throughout all the countries under his domination and summoned lord Yovhanne's to Constantinople. He went there with six bishops and a multitude of priests. They found assembled in Constantinople 200 Chalcedonian bishops, and they made an examination of the faith. They

214 A.D. 974.

had the Patriarch standing while they themselves were seated. Now the Patriarch was an old man and it was difficult for him to stand. Therefore, two bishops stood on either side and supported him. The Patrarch spoke with Scriptural authority and reprimanded them severely. They promised to give him the See of Antioch if he would only say that there were two natures after the hypostatic union. The Patriarch gave this reply: "I hold the throne of Peter on earth and in heaven, and have no desire for a physical chair. As for what you are trying to force me to say about two natures, what is that other than denial of the Trinity?" Then Theodorus, who was bishop of Melitene, slapped him on right cheek hand and the Patriarch was about to offer the other cheek when a certain Asori bishop arose and hit Theodorus and then stood by the Patriarch. They told him to sit down and he replied: "I see Christ slapped and I rise to my feet. Should I now sit down? ...*I rise to my feet while you stay seated.*"

Then they dismissed the meeting in sorrow, since the emperor and the princes had begun to cry. However, subsequently, they started to conduct inquiries and said: "You do not hold Christianity fully. Accept baptism and the priesthood, and then depart." But the Patriarch retorted: "We already have had baptism in Christ and the priesthood, which were given to us by the blessed Apostles, and which Dioscorus and Severus maintained, and which you do not possess, except for the anathemas which are on your heads." They grew angry and ordered that he be sent to the West, into exile. They took him for 28 days and then repented and returned to Constantinople where they were placed in prison. There great healing occurred, and news of these miracles spread, until neither prince nor commoner had not heard about them. Many blind folk had their eyes opened and many demoniacs were healed, *and many were converted to Orthodoxy*. The venerable patriarch Yovhanne's died there in jail with the solemnity of a martyr, to the glory of God. His disciples took his remains and put them with the other martyrs while his memory was ranked with the saints.

MICHAEL THE GREAT

Then the wrath of the Lord visited Romanus and he died wickedly. They enthroned Michael,[215] who reigned for eight years. At this time, the Caliph of the Tachiks was Ablabas.[216] Now one of Michael's relatives, who was called Michael the Califat[217] planned to rebel. This rebellion lasted for five months, then they gouged out his eyes. In the days of Michael, the Tachik Sulayman gave Edessa to the Byzantines. Then Michael died and there reigned the daughters of Constantine, Zoe and Theodora.[218]

At this point, I must briefly write about the Turks, what people they came from, where they lived, and concerning how and why they came to dwell here among us, in our country.

As *the head of the prophets*, the blessed Moses says in the book of Genesis,[219] "Torgom was the father of Gog and others." It is clear that the Turks, who are Gog and Magog, descend from the line of Japheth. *Japheth was the father of Tiras, Torgom, Gog and others with him. From this it is clear that the Turks are from the line of Torgom, and are called Turks from his name. Gog and Magog, who are nomadic people, descend from them.* After *the destruction of* the Tower of Babel they went eastward and turned north, establishing residence between two lofty and extensive mountain ranges *called the Breasts of the North*. Then they spread and extended from the northeast to the southwest. They held two gates: one gate opened into Persia, and the other was by the Georgians *and Alans*. Alexander of Macedon closed these gates.

Alexander of Macedon also had a gate made a Darpand, employing 3,000 blacksmiths working in bronze and iron for six years. This long wall was constructed between the mountain and the sea and blocked them from entering. The Turks are modest with regard to women, and gentle and moderate in their ways. They worship one god, the sky, which they call *gok tangri*, since *gok* in

---

215 Michael IV, the Paphlagonian, 1034-1041.
216 Al-Qa'im, 1031-1075.
217 Michael V, 1041-1042.
218 1042; Theodora Porphyrogenneta, 1055-1056.
219 Genesis 10, 2-3.

THE CHRONICLE

their language means blue. *They worship one god and call him Ko'k'tanghri which means "blue god," because they believe that the sky is a god.* They eat all sorts of unclean foods and carrion and wear clothes made from wool and hair for lack of other materials. They have no written laws or traditions, since no prophet or Apostle visited them. As a result, the aforementioned doors were closed against them so that they not fill up the country with corruption or ruin the world with their multitude *and their abominations.* The Persians *when they had grown powerful* further fortified the gate which leads into Persia—which Alexander had built with one fortress—by building six fortresses and placing guards in them. Whenever there was a need for troops, the Persian kings took them from there for pay and, once the war was concluded, took them back there.

In the Bible, the prophet Ezekiel says about the Turks that Gog and Magog, the princes of Tubal and Mosokh, will threaten the Jewish people and destroy Jerusalem. On three occasions, the prophet mentions the tribes of Gog and the destruction they will bring. If we search in detail, we learn that indeed there were three times that they arose. The first took place during the time of the Persian king Cambyses *son of Cyrus*, whom some style the second Nebuchadnezzar. He hired troops from the Turks and defeated the king of the Assyrians. Then he sent them under Holofernes, who was one of them, to Palestine. *Now after the conclusion of the battle he led them back to their own territory, and they took back with them [as booty] all the good things of the land: gold, silver, valuable clothing, and fruit.* After Cambyses, others of the Persian kings brought the Turks forth as auxiliaries, from the time of the Macedonians to the Sasanians. Each time, after the battles, they would be taken back, with valuables. And thus, there arose in them a desire to emerge from there permanently, if there was a chance. This took place 510 years before the birth of Christ. Here is how it came about:

Once when the Turks were being led back to their own country as usual, when they got near the gate, *since their escort was small*, they turned on the Persians who were leading them and killed them. They seized a fortress which they retained and made more secure. Then they notified their kinfolk and a group of them arose *to help them*, and seized other fortresses, placing the gate under their own command. *Then they notified some of their distant people, who were their princes and the wealthiest of them.* After that, multitudes of them who had been behind the gate started to come forth frequently. Having accomplished this, they again fortified the gate, rose and came to the Aral country in the land of the Persians (*near the land of the Persians*). Now they say that a white animal, like a dog, led them on. *That dog led them to the next gate and behold, the gate was open and they passed through.* Whenever they started to stray, that animal would bark loudly at them until they came back to him. They worshipped it. And the dog led them from their own land to the Aral. Then it left them and vanished from sight.

There were three divisions of Turks. They cast lots, throwing three sticks into the air. One stick fell to the south, and so one division of them went south toward India and mingled with the Indians. A second lot fell to the northwest, and so the middle division went west to Thrace and dwelled there, calling themselves Cumans after the name of the land. The third lot fell in the middle country and the third detachment came and mixed with the Persians. Afterwards, many others arose. Then they closed the gate again. There were 70 chiefs among them who had come to the Aral. They placed 70 princes in a circle *which they traced on the ground*. Each one held a wand in hand, and it was stipulated that when they threw their wands into the air, whoever's wand fell inside the circle, that chief would rule as king. They threw the sticks. Nine fell shy of the target, but one of them landed within it and, moreover, was driven into the ground. And so, they established nine kingdoms there, eight of which submitted to the one who's wand had stood in the ground. They are well established there and hold the gate. Now the Turks ruled below two mountains called the Breasts of the World, and they likewise ruled many lands beyond those mountains. They always call their leader Qaqan since that was the name of the first king. Group after group came forth. Since many of them mingled with Arabs, they were styled Muslims after them and particularly after the general named Mslim, the leader of the troops who went against Constantinople. They especially cleaved to them since both the Tachiks and they confessed one God. The Turks also learned from them not to worship created beings. As a result, they hate the Cross *and the Church.*

These people,[220] wherever they go, adhere to the religion practiced there. Those who went south to India mixed in with the idol worshippers and became idol worshippers. Those who went *to the south and* west mixed with the Christians and became Christians. The Armenians and Georgians also, in times past, used to call forth Turks as auxiliaries via the other Gate. These folk became Christians. The people called Qipchaq—to use the Georgian word—are from these converts. In their own language "valley" is *xit*, and "vessel" is *chʾax*, and thus, Qipchaq means that they are locked up as in the neck of a vessel and poured out of it as needed.

The first emergence of Turks was during the time of Cambyses, as mentioned. The second was under the Arab kings when they came to Palestine, and as John of Asia states: "There were 4,000 Turks with Abu Ishaq when he took the city of Amorium." As for the third emergence of the Turks, it is still in the future, close to the end of the world. As the prophet Ezekiel laments, three times will they come into the land of the Jews, *corrupting the world as far as Palestine.* And it is also said *and John of Asia says further* that when Emperor Tiberius[221] sent envoys to them—as did Justin[222] and Heraclius[223]—the Qaqan wept upon seeing them. When they asked what occasioned his tears, he replied: "There is among us a sort of prophecy passed down from our ancestors

---

220 The Turks.
221 A.D. 14-37.
222 Justin I, 518-528.
223 Heraclius I, 610-641.

which I heard from my fathers which says that when the kings of the Romans subdue the Turks with gifts and bribes, the end of the world is close at hand." The Qaqan asked: "Do you Romans pay taxes to the Persians or not?" They replied: "On the contrary. The Persians pay taxes to the Romans, for Trajan put taxes on the Persians." *John of Asia also says this*. The Qaqan was astonished *that the Roman empire was so large*. Now the envoys which went to them did not go there by traversing through their own country, but rather *to the Qaqan residing by the gate near Mt. Caucasus as the ambassadors of Justinian and Heraclius narrated* via the gate in the territory beyond Maragha. The Persian shah, Shapuh, had sent 5,000 virgins to the Qaqan who resides in a large area outside their own native land. *The name of the land is Aragh, and they extend to T'etalia which is called Turk'astan. It is to this place that the amir Mahmut led the captives to Khorasan. From this people there ruled as sultans Tughril-Beg,[224] followed by Alp-Arslan.[225] Now they always style their king, "Qaqan."* But they have their own laws in their land, having left aside cannibalism *which had been practiced there. Let us here resume our previous narration.*

Now in the year 1361 of the Syrian Era[226] there ruled over the Byzantines Constantine[227] for 12 years, a great and generous man who suffered from gout. Rule over the Tachiks was held by Abu'l Sevuar.

In this period, the Armenian city of Erznka was deluged by water and there remained unharmed only one house which belonged to a pious believing man named Kirakos, plus a church. And in the same year there was a strong earthquake on the Fast of the Firstfruits. In the same year there was conflict about some matter among the Orthodox clergy. Some of them *half of them* went to the dyophysite patriarch and he turned them to his heresy while he expelled other Orthodox from the city. He also took from them

---

224 *Tuhgril Beg, 1055-1063.*
225 *Alp-Arslan, 1063-1072.*
226 A. D. 1050.
227 Constantine IX, Monomachus, 1042-1055.

a church which had been built on the grave of the evangelist Luke, after taking the church of Saint Peter. But God took vengeance on him during the feast of Easter: *thunder was heard and* fire fell from the sky and burned the church together with the patriarch and his students *while they were worshipping* as well as many other people, such that not even one bone remained which could be removed from the place. And it was believed that this was the Lord's righteous judgement. Then the Orthodox returned to their homes, while those of the apostates who remained after the fire returned to their own confession, and many others turned to our confession and glorified our faith.

After lasting 430 years, the kingdom of the Tachiks *began to fragment into many parts* and the kingdom of the Turks began, in Khorasan. *The Turkish captives which Mahmat had settled on fertile land were left alone; they grew and waxed arrogant.* The name of its ruler was Tughril Beg *who had gained power and became king. Others call him Do'ghlabe'k'. There was some great conflict and he ended up ruling over many lands.* He sent troops to the confines of the Armenians. They came to Melitene, took the city, took captives *and much booty*, and turned back. But then a fierce snowstorm fell on them on Mountain(s) of Sasun and 3,000 people *of the Turks* perished from the cold. But the captives became free and returned since they were familiar with cold, *snow*, and frigid weather and did not die. Then Monomachus died and his daughter, Theodora,[228] ruled for one year. After her an old man, Michael,[229] ruled for one year. He was a blessed man who fasted. Rather than live on the fruits of other people's labor, he made spoons with his own hands and sold them for his livelihood. As soon as he saw that the Turks were growing stronger, *and were coming to ruin the Byzantines' country, and that they already had ruled over the Persians, Medes, and Assyrians, he became frightened*, and removed the Christians on this side of the sea and relocated them to the other side *to a secure place.* And the Turks came, found

---

228 Theodora Porphyrogenneta, 1055-1056.
229 Michael VI, Straioticus, 1056-1057.

the country *of Atalia, Uch, and Iconium* deserted, and settled there. Many blamed Michael, but he had done a humane deed, *saving believers.*

In that year a certain prince Comnenus rose up and seized the kingdom. Michael escaped, shaved his head and entered a monastery. Comnenus[230] then ruled for two years. He was followed by Ducas[231] from the Paphlagonia country who grew stronger against the Turks, built a wall for Melitene, and, after reigning for nine years, died. In this year, Tughril's military commander K'sisari came to Aleppo and took it. This was the start of the taking of cities in deep Assyrian Mesopotamia, from Damascus to Aleppo, and from the far side of the Euphrates to the sea of Adrianople, which is Cilicia. Tughril's military commander went as far as the sea of Pontus. In these days, Satan inspired the patriarch of Constantinople to do a deed loathsome to man and angels alike. He had the writings and holy oil of the Orthodox Armenians and Syrians burned and trampled under foot. They did not respect even the bread and chrism of communion. He had Patriarch Athanasius and 25 bishops summoned to Constantinople. However, before they departed *the wrath of God descended and* that godless insulter of Christ died as did Arius. His replacement as patriarch held an investigation *into the faith* and angrily and heatedly denounced them. *The Greeks were defeated by the Holy Spirit. The blessed Athanasius became furious and anathematized them.* Furthermore, they were exiled to the island of Chios. But at the empress' order they returned to their own places *he returned to his patriarchal throne.*

Now after Ducas, Romanus Diogenes ruled.[232] In this period died the sultan of the Turks, Tughril, whom they call Do'lghabak, and Alp-Arslan became sultan. He came in person among the Armenians and Byzantines. *He subdued them and took Shamshute.* Then he went on to Ani which he took with 100,000 men. There he killed 1,000 men in a ditch and bathed in their blood. Then

---

230 Isaac I, Comnenus, 1057-1059.
231 Constantine X, Ducas, 1059-1067.
232 Romanus IV, Diogenes, 1068-1071.

he turned to Naxjawan. Diogenes gathered countless troops and went against them. The Byzantine emperor came to Kars and burned down an Armenian church and he swore that if he defeated the Turks, he would either completely exterminate the Armenians or convert them to his Chalcedonian faith. The Lord heard him, but did not help him. The Byzantines were defeated by Alp-Arslan and Diogenes was seized. When this was learned in Constantinople, they enthroned Michael.[233] Then Diogenes got free *of Alp-Arslan through oaths and entreaties and wanted to go to Constantinople.* However, the Byzantines blinded him and, on Michael's order, they killed him.

Then Alp-Arslan sent his sister's son, Sulaiman, who came and took the land of the Armenians and ruled as king. Then there were two sultans, one over the Byzantines and Armenians, and another in Khorasan, of Turkish nationality. Sulaiman arrived and suddenly entered Antioch at night, seizing it. And he turned *the senior churh of* Saint Peter into a mosque.

In this period an emir *pious, prayer-loving, and kind* by the name of Danishman arose among the Turks, came and entered the Cappadocia country, *came to Cappadocia with his troops at Alp-Arslan's order.* He seized Sewast and Caesarea. *He took Sewast and Caesarea, ruled them, and grew great.* This was the beginning of the House of Danishmand. *For this was his name. Earlier they had been taken captive among the T'etalik', learned the laws of the Tachiks and thereafter believed in Islam. They became fervent in the faith.*

The history of the taking of Cilicia by the Armenians starts here.

When these developments were unfolding, some 50 Armenians *who had been harassed by the Turks went and dwelt in deserted areas. They armed themselves and harmed the Turks,* beat the Turks, and took from them things they needed. They came to Marash and found there a man of *their own* Armenian nation-

---
233 Michael VII, 1068-1071.

ality named Philaretus. He was a personable and attractive man. He became their leader and they entered Cilicia. At that time, the Turks were ruling there. The Armenians took a fortress from them and made it more secure. Then they took the entire country with its cities and fortresses as well as many lands around Cilicia—Marash, Kesoun, Ablastan, *and Gargar*, Melitene and Edessa on the other side of the Euphrates, and many other places. *The Turks were frightened of him.* The Byzantines learned about this and gave gifts to Philaretus, styling him *sebastos*. Afterwards, Turks from all over gathered against Philaretus and took half his lands. Then he went to Baghdad, to the Caliph and, for the territory, he weakened in the faith and converted to Islam. He received from the Caliph a document saying he should retake the lands. Before he had returned, they had taken the remainder of his lands and did not return it. They say that Philaretus regretted his conversion to Islam and returned to his own faith and, in repentance, *shaved his head and* entered a monastery.

Now in this period, when the Turks were growing strong, the Arabs—who were called Tachiks after one Tayyi, a glorious and wise prince of theirs—submitted to them. The Turks and Tachiks mingled together and became one people *and were called by the same name*. Now they left alone the prince in Baghdad, who was called *Caliph* and was of the line of Muhammad. He received honor from the Tachiks and Turks and they received their faith and honor from him. *And they revered him as though he were Muhammad himself. By writing and through oath, both peoples submitted to him, promising to take their faith and orders from him. From then on it was by order of the sultan in Khorasan and the caliph that those deemed worthy received the honor of emir. Then the Turks came and ruled over lands and districts.* And thus, in this way, there came to the Armenian areas an emir named Sukman who was of Turkish nationality, and they called him "Shahi Armen" which means "King of the Armenians." Then a certain emir came from Mesopotamia. He was also a Turk, named Artuk, and they were called Artukids.

THE CHRONICLE

Now the emperor of the Greeks, Michael,[234] was weak and a womanizer and had no interest in war. *He was afraid of the Turks.* He sat around eating and drinking. Then Nicephorus[235] rose against him, came to Constantinople with his troops, took the city, and began to destroy it. Then Michael took the crown in his hand, went before him, and said: "Take this crown which you are seeking and stop using your sword against the Christians." And Nicephorus took the crown. He ordered that Michael's hair be cut off and that he be taken to a monastery. And he took the emperor's wife as his own wife, and also castrated Michael's two sons. As a result, everyone loathed him. *This displeased the court and they hated him.* Consequently, one of the princes, named Alexius, took his many supporters and seized the empire. Alexius did to Nicephorus what the latter had done to Michael. Alexius[236] ruled over the Byzantines for 29 years.

At the start of his reign, Alp-Arslan took Damascus and killed Ak'sis. In that same year, some counts among the Romans assembled numerous troops and came to Constantinople and besieged it for seven years. The reason for their emergence was as follows. When the emir Artuk captured Jerusalem at the command of Malik-Shah, he placed the Church of the Sepulcher under taxation so that they would collect one red ducat from each person praying there. At that time one of the counts of the Franks named Raymond de Saint-Gilles had come to Jerusalem to worship at the places held by the infidels. When he entered the Sepulcher, they demanded from him more than the stipulated tax. *In this time, when the Turks ruled Jerusalem and the entire seacoast, a prince named Saint-Gilles came to Jerusalem to pray. They took a dahekan from him as they did from all pilgrims. But then they demanded more.* Now when he refused, the Muslims struck him such a strong blow that one of his eyes fell out. The prince took that eye and put it in his pocket, took it to Rome, and went around to all the counts

---

234 Michael VII, Parapinaces, 1071-1078.
235 Nicephorus III, Botaniates, 1080-1081.
236 Alexius I, Comnenus, 1081-1118.

and moved them to zeal for the Lord. They arose and first came to Constantinople. While they were besieging Constantinople, an earthquake occurred at Antioch.[237] The wall fell down and a tower completely collapsed down to its foundations. There they found many bronze statues which seemed to resemble images of Franks in their clothing, mounted on horses and bound with iron chains. The emir had the statues brought before him and then investigated what they might be. Some said that they were idols from ancient times, and he commanded that the statues be broken into small pieces, and this was done. An old and blind woman heard about it and said: "Those statues are talismans made by the Greeks *using magical means* to prevent the Franks from getting powerful, becoming kings, and crossing over the sea to us here. *You can tell from the iron chains which bind them.*" When the emir heard this, he was greatly saddened by the destruction of the statues. And at this same time the Franks took Constantinople, crossed over here, grew stronger, and came to Antioch by ship.

They had nine leaders. Two of them were from the line of kings, Bohemond and Tancred. Seven were counts: Roger, Bohemond, Baldwin, Joscelin, Valeran, Godfrey, and Salke'sn *and Dibaxt*. Now T'ĕodoros, whom the Armenian Philaretus had installed as ruler over Edessa, lived in those days. T'ĕodorus sent to the Franks at Antioch promising to give the city to Godfrey. And the Franks rejoiced greatly, saying: "Just as the city of Edessa believed in Christ before Jerusalem, and just as Abgar, king of the Armenians, who believed in Christ ruled first in Edessa, so shall we, by the grace of Christ, rule over Edessa first, before taking Jerusalem." Thus Godfrey sent his brother, Baldwin, and ruled over Edessa. Others besieged Antioch for nine months. Now the emirs of the city were Gisan and Aliwsan, *and they were in hiding.* Gisan arose and quit the city. Two *craftsmen*, men of Armenian nationality, encountered him. They killed him and brought his head to the Franks. There were in a tower two brothers, also Armenians, who took heart and killed the Turks with them in the tower and

---

237 ca. 1092.

then notified the Franks. The Franks came there, entered through that tower, took the city, and thereafter ruled over it. In this same period, Sulaiman, *who ruled over the land of the Byzantines*, was killed in Iconium and Kilij-Arslan[238] ruled as king.

When the sultan ruling in Khorasan heard about the Franks' assault on Antioch, he sent Kerbogha with 100,000 cavalry. Kerbogha came and besieged the Franks in Antioch. The Franks had so recently captured the city that as they were entering the city, the army of the Turks had already sacked Baghras. As a result, the Turks put them into great straits with hunger. Now the Franks took refuge in God with prayers and tears. But then they found the lance of Christ, *the patriarch discovered the lance of Christ preserved in the foundation of the church, and fortified by it*, the troops emerged and broke the Turks *in a noteworthy miracle*, killing for a day as they drove them along. And the Turks fled to Mesopotamia. Then the Franks went and took the seacoast and Joppa, and then went on to Jerusalem. Now before the Franks had come, the Egyptians had taken Jerusalem and were ruling it. *It was filled with Arabs who had come from Egypt and had taken it from the Turks.* The Franks took it from them and generally slaughtered them. Some fled to the Tachiks and went into the Temple. *Their notables fled and filled up the Temple.* The Franks brought them out and killed them. *The patriarch seized a street and proceeded to the Church of the Resurrection, killing as he went, where he washed his bloodstained hands, repeating the Psalm which says: "Let the righteous rejoice in the Lord and receive his reward and wash his hands of the blood of the sinners."*[239] And the Patriarch immediately offered the mass, exclaiming: "Never in my life have I offered such a joyous mass to God." Then Godfrey reigned as king over Jerusalem for two years,[240] followed by Baldwin who ruled for fifteen years.[241]

---

238 Kilij-Arslan I, 1092-1107.
239 *Psalm 57.11.*
240 Godrey of Boulogne, 1099-1100.
241 Baldwin I of Boulogne, 1100-1118.

In this period, Kilij-Arslan came against Melitene. Hearing about the strengthening of the Franks *and their capture of Jerusalem*, he turned back. At that point, Danishmend came against Melitene, burned its gates *and crops*, and turned back. He continued to do this for three years. Meanwhile, Gabriel the Greek, whom the Armenian Philaretus had appointed,[242] was in Melitene and harassed the people of the city worse than those outside were doing. In this period, there were among the chief princes of the Armenians Basil, who held Kesoun and Raban in the time of Philaretus. Other important princes were those called the sons of Ruben,[243] who were ruling in various places from Philaretus' time. They sent for and had brought to Cilicia the Catholicos of the Armenians. In this year the Greek Gabriel gave Melitene to Danishmend, thereby cheating the Franks to whom he had promised it. Danishmend brought ease and construction to Melitene and took care of them, bringing in bread, livestock, and freedom and they rebuilt it. This Danishmend took captive King Bohemond and ransomed him for 100,000 *dahekans*.

In this period, the kingdom of the Turks was wracked with rebellion in Khorasan. At this, the Tachiks raised their heads again. *There was dissension between the Tachiks and Turks and they fought each other.* The Tachik Molaghib arose in Hems and took Apamea and went on to Damascus. Dogas and Uraton, emirs in Aleppo, took Sanjar and Harran, and the Turks and Tachiks fell into contention. However, in Bithynia and Cappadocia there were not Tachiks. Instead, the Turks held them and contended with the Byzantine. The Tachiks held Egypt. There was enmity between Danishmend and Kilij-Arslan and they warred with each other. Danishmend died in these days—two years after taking Melitene. Then Kilij-Arslan went against Melitene, where *one of* Danishmend's sons, Aghusin was located. Kilij-Arslan took it with an oath.

---

242 or, *who was ruling from the time of Philaretus.*
243 i.e., the Rubenids.

THE CHRONICLE

In this period, they named as Sultan of Khorasan Ghiyath ad-Din who sent Chavli[244] with troops against the Franks. He arrived as Mosul. Emir Chkrmish, who was there, came out before Chavli and they battled. Chavli was defeated, seized, and led into the city in chains. But after a short while Chkrmish died and Chavli was freed. Now he went and assembled many other troops and again wanted to go against Mosul, for they had named Chkrmish's son as emir.

When the people of Mosul learned about Chavli's coming, they sent to Kilij-Arslan, brought him, and gave the city to him. Chavli went and took Xabur and Kilij-Arslan went against Xabur. But as Kilij-Arslan was crossing a river, he drowned. Then Chavli ruled over Mosul and Nisibis. He gathered up treasures and went back to Khorasan. In Melitene, they learned about Kilij-Arslan's death and they placed as king his son, Tughril-Arslan. Now the latter designated two men as military commanders, El-Arslan and Pizmish. Pizmish fell and died through a plot hatched by his mother, and Tughril took the mother as his wife. Now Kilij-Arslan had three other sons: Arab, Shahan Shah, and Masut. Danishmend's son, Amir ghazi, killed Arab, while Shahan Shah killed Masut.

Now in that period, when Baldwin was the second king of Jerusalem, there came from Rome to Jerusalem *on pilgrimage* a prince named Godfrey, along with thirty horsemen. He had vowed that he would never leave. After a year he became a monk and the thirty horsemen with him also changed their garb and lived in holiness and prayer. Now since the Turks were harassing the Christians, people begged them to go forth into battle against them [...][245] among the Christian forces, saying that *fighting the infidels to save Christians* was more pleasing to God and more beneficial to their souls. The king and the patriarch gave them land and properties, *fields and vineyards by the sea*, and the Temple as a residence. Others came and joined them and they established the rules of

244 Abu Mansur Djawali.
245 There is a lacuna in the text here.

their order. They became monastic brethren who lived in sanctity and celibacy and owned no individual private property. They fought against *the infidels and never against Christians, and called themselves soldiers of Christ.*[246] Word of this spread to Rome and everywhere else. The poor, the wealthy, and the princes allied with them and they received fortresses *and villages, ships, and income from taxes on the Christians*, and they grew rich, and became a separate force. This was the beginning of the Freres, *who are called Hospitallers, since they established hospitals for the poor and sick. Subsequently, others separated from the main body and formed a separate entity. And they said: "Give us in writing a share of all you have acquired in the past." The Freres did this. And the second group sold all of this and became wealthy. Then they requested and received as much land as a pack animal could traverse in one day and night. But then they realized that they could not survive as two separate communities, and so, they sent and bought back the lands at great expense with much gold, silver, and villages. Others also gave to their community, and called them Templars which means "house of the poor."* Such is what we heard about them.

In this period Paghak, who was of the Artukids, grew powerful and ruled over many districts. Kilij-Arslan's wife went to him and became his wife, leaving her children. There was no other Artukid who was Paghak's equal. In 1430 of the Syrian Era,[247] Emir Ghazi ruled and went against Antioch with 7,000 troops. Roger arose against him and was defeated by them. When Baldwin, the king of Jerusalem heard about this, he came and crushed them and put them to flight. In this year, the king of Melitene, Tughril-Arslan, took Ablstan and the Franks came and seized the Melitene land while the king of Melitene and Paghak went against Kamakh and captured it. The lord of Kamakh, Mangujak, fled to Trebizond, placing his hopes on the Byzantines. Taking troops from the Byzantines and, with Gabras at the head, he came against Paghak. The Byzantines were defeated and Mangujak and Gabras were

---

246 i.e., Knights Templar.
247 A.D. 1119.

captured. And they ransomed Gabras *and they ransomed them* for 30,000 *dahekan*s.

In these times, the offspring of Armenian royalty entered the Cilician country. They had earlier—during the days of Emperor Basil—come from Vaspurakan, dwelled in Sewast, Caesarea, and Xawatank', and had seized many places. *They had become reduced and weakened by harassment from the Byzantines. They entered Cilicia, seizing many districts with their fortresses and castles.* Some of them were known as Rubenians. This group consisted of two grandee families, descendants of Hayk and Senek'erim, who had mingled together through marriage ties and had ruled in Vaspurakan when the Bagratids reigned in Greater Armenia. Then they began to rule in the country of the Cilicians *and the Syrians*. Then there reigned with noteworthy bravery first Ruben, then Constantine, Lewon, T'oros, and others, one after the other.

Concerning the War of the Birds

In 1434 of the Syrian Era,[248] a great war of the birds took place. Cranes and storks assembled for many days in the country from Amida to Tellakum. Then they began sending emissaries back and forth *for three days*. After a good deal of this traffic, they commenced fighting from the third hour until the ninth hour, shrieking loudly the while. There was a great slaughter on both sides. The storks were defeated and fled, and the war ended. Only God knows the reason for this.

In the 500th year of the rule of the Tachiks, Ghiyath ad-Din, Sultan of Khorasan, heard that Satagha was ruling as king over Tikrit. The Sultan rose with all his forces and went against Satagha. They battled near the Tigris River. The Tachiks were defeated and Satagha was slain. With this, the kingdom of the Tachiks ended after lasting for 500 years. This event occurred in 1433 of the Syrian Era,[249] 70 years after the emergence of the Turks.

248 A.D. 1123.
249 A.D. 1122.

In this period Ghazi learned about the death of Paghak. He came against Melitene, but was unable to take it. Ghazi, who was Danishmend's son, turned back leaving his son in charge of the troops. It was he who put the besieged into great straits through hunger, and then took Melitene. He took pity on them and did not blame them, rather he brought in bread and lentils. *In this period Paghak died. When Danishmend's son, Amirxazi, heard about this, he went and took Melitene. He brought ease to them, since Paghak had greatly harassed them. The caliph sent a crown to him and styled him Melik Ghazi, King of the North.* He gave them an oath of peace, and departed. Emir Ghazi grew powerful and wiped out the Turks who were in the Cappadocia country.

Then he alone ruled. In these days, he heard that a Greek named Kasiae' held eight fortresses on the coast. Emir Ghazi went against them, and captured them. He subdued the Greek who gave up the fortresses. He came out before Emir Ghazi, and was in his hand. Emir Ghazi killed Masud the Artukid. When the Caliph and the Sultan of Khorasan heard about his valor, they sent him a crown and gifts and called him Melik-Ghazi and styled him king of the entire North.

In this period, John ruled over the Byzantines again.[250] He seized Castamon and two other fortresses. Melik-Ghazi heard about this, and went and retook Castamon. In this period, Zangi, the emir of Mosul came against Aleppo and the people willingly gave it over to him because of his reputation for justice. In this year, the Caliph and Ghiyath ad-Din sent to Melik-Ghazi four black standards, a golden chain for the neck and a gold staff which certified him and his descendants in the kingship. They also brought trumpets and drums. Now it happened that when they arrived, Melik-Ghazi had died and so they bestowed the honor to his son, Mahmud, declaring him king. *They put the golden chain around his neck and golden fetters on his feet, and struck him 12 times with the staff, signifying obedience.* This man was a great hater of Christians *and he harassed them*, and followed the Tachik's faith,

---

250   John II, Calojohannes, 1092-118 and 1118-1143.

not drinking wine and not committing shameful acts. He built the wall as Caesarea and pulled down many churches there. In this same period Zangi, the emir of Mosul, made war against the Artukids, and defeated them.

In this period the pope of Rome came to Jerusalem and then went on to Antioch. There were Chalcedonian Greeks there who slandered the Syriacs, *Jacobite Syrians*, saying: "These cheats hate the Council of Chalcedon and, moreover, they have *in a golden reliquary* the right hand of Barsama, who was anathematized by the Fourth Council. They claim that it works wonders and miracles. When we say 'open it so that we may see it' they reply: 'we do not dare to do that, lest there be downpours and hail.' They say this and then laugh." The Pope summoned the patriarch of the monastery of Mor Barsama *to bring the reliquary from the mountain to the church of Saint Peter*, and said:

"Bring forth that right hand so that I may see it." At that time locusts were polluting the country and so he said : "Bring it for help against the locusts so that, through it, God will take pity on the land." They replied: "We dare not remove it from its place." Then the Pope got angry at them and said with an oath: "If you do not bring it here, there will be no memory of you here in our city. Rather, I will remove you and all your people." Thus compelled, they went and brought it to the Church of Saint Peter. Then the Pope said: "Now open it so that I may have a look." They replied: "You should open it yourself, father." And so, taking the reliquary, he opened it. Suddenly, in the twinkling of an eye, the sky became covered with clouds and fierce rain began to pour down. There was thunder with lightning, and rain mixed with huge hailstones that threatened to wreck the city. Then the Pope and all the clerics fell on their faces, weeping and wailing prodigiously. When folk heard about this, the entire city—all the men and women—arose and came to the church. *They closed the reliquary and*, after much damage, the disaster ended.

In that year, locusts had come and were devouring everything in the confines of Antioch. The Pope asked the Syrians to hold a vigil about the plague of locusts through the intercession of the saint. The Pope also ordered that the ridiculers of the relic's efficacy should be seized. But no one could find them, since they had fled. Then the Orthodox Syrians and Armenians held a vigil among themselves, brought out the reliquary and protected the land. Immediately, by the mercy of God, the locusts went and filled up the sea. They glorified God and His servant, Mor Barsam, and the Chalcedonians gave him a place for a church, which they constructed and furnished. The Pope laid an injunction that no one should dare to anathematize those hating the Council of Chalcedon, for the Pope said "God, who penetrates secret things, resides in this relic and we must bow to His will. Let us only fight against the infidels and bring peace to the members of Christ."

The Lance of Christ

After this, the Pope wanted to know about the lance of Christ which had been found, and he held an investigation about it. Learned folk testified that the lance with which Christ had been pierced had been taken among the Armenians by the Apostle Thaddeus. This newly discovered lance is not that one. Rather, it is the one used by the Jews of Tiberius on Good Friday, *when the Lord was crucified*, when they stole a Christian *child*, took him to the desert, and crucified him using nails. Every insult and abuse which those impious and deranged Jews visited on Christ, they also visited on this other Christian, including a crown of thorns, the *purple and red* tunic, the beating of his head, the spitting and all the other insults endured by the Lord. They pierced the child's side with this second lance and blood and water flowed out. *The miracles associated with our Lord also took place here*: The sun darkened and the earth shook. The Christians learned about this and the Jews fled. Then the Jews sent a message saying that if the Christians let them alone, they would turn to Christ. They said: "For we believe that the true God, Christ, was crucified by the Jews." The Christians pardoned them and a multitude of the Jews turned to the Lord, confessing their sins. Now this is that lance which the Christians kept and revered which performed many miracles and wonders.

In that period, when the people who had come from Khorasan to Melik-Ghazi had returned, there was a severe earthquake in Khorasan on a Friday, which rent the ground and swallowed up a mosque with 8,000 men and women who had gathered to pray and to hear their sermon.

In 1455 of the Syrian Era,[251] Emperor John of the Byzantines died in Cilicia and his son—the younger son named Manuel, who was with him—ruled as emperor.[252] He went and took Constantinople and his senior brother did not oppose him. In the same year, Baldwin, king of Jerusalem, died and his son, Baldwin, became king, though since he was a boy, his mother looked after the kingdom. In the same year the Artukid Emir Davut, lord of Kharberd, died and his son, Qara-Arslan, took power. And Masud captured Ablastan.

In the year, 1456 of the Syrian Era,[253] *atabeg* Zangi[254] took Edessa from Joscelin, though we shall not describe how this occurred, since others have written extensively about it. A year after Zangi had taken Edessa, he was slain by Kilij and his principality was taken by his son, Nur ad-Din,[255] the lord of Mosul.

In this period, there appeared in Constantinople a heretic who was more wicked than Nestorius and other predecessors of ill renown. Furthermore, he had influence with the patriarch, many of his colleagues, clerics, and the laity. For they claimed that Christ had *worked His miracles and the Apostles had convinced* the world using demons and witchcraft. Many fell in with them and became devil worshippers. When the emperor learned about this, he killed many of them, but did not root out that heresy, which continues its wickedness in Constantinople to our own day.

When Joscelin learned about the death of Zangi, he mus-

251 A. D. 1144.
252 Manuel I, 1143-1180.
253 A. D. 1145.
254 Imad ad-Din.
255 Zangi.

MICHAEL THE GREAT

tered troops and came to Edessa, seized it in the night, and entered. When the Turks heard about this, they notified one another and massed against Edessa *and besieged it.* The Franks were terrified and, by their stupidity, caused the complete destruction of Edessa. They forcibly removed the multitude of *the Christian* people from the city and crossed them to the other side of the Euphrates River. The Turks immediately wiped them out. And they say that the number slain there reached 30,000 while 16,000 were taken captive. And thus was Edessa destroyed. You may read all about this *in detail* in the writings of other historians. However, here we shall mention how and by whom Edessa initially had been built and was named.

After the Flood, King Nimrod built and named it Ur'haw. "Ur'" *in our language* means village, and "haw" means Chaldean, hence "village of the Chaldeans." In the same way Melk'isedek, son of Ham, built a city in Palestine and called it Urishle'm, which translates "village of peace," *since according to our Syriac language, it was a village and could not be called a city.* We pronounce it "Jerusalem." Nimrod's construction endured for a long time. They say that Sennacherib,[256] king of the Assyrians, demolished it and it remained a ruin until the days of Alexander the Macedonian.[257] When Alexander was passing through the area, he was pleased by the charm of the place and remarked to *his friend* Seleucus: "Make this place into a city." After Alexander's death, Seleucus built a city there and called it Edessa, which translates from Macedonian: "I love this." It was so named because Alexander had said: "I love this. Build it into a city." Now the Greeks in their chronological writings call Edessa "*So'rtu Makedonios*" which means "Syrian Macedonia." The Syrian Era[258] began in this period.[259] After 70 years,[260] King Abgar, *Abgarios, king of the Armenians and Syrians,* son of Arjam *Arsham,* rennovated it, *since he found it lacking, and bethrothed it to Christ, as a holy queen.*

256 B.C. 704-681.
257 B.C. 356-323.
258 Calendrical system.
259 *i.e.*, the reign of Seleucus Nicator.
260 or, *300 years.*

After the time of Abgar and his sons, Edessa fell under the rule of the Romans with their idol-worship. They ruled it for 300 years. Martyred there were Shmona, Kori, Habib, Cosmas, Damiane', *the Gurians*, and many others with them. Under the rule of Constantine, monasteries *were built on the mountain* and Christians multiplied there. The impious Julian was unable to make it obedient, nor was the heretic Valens *able to degrade it with his heresy. Edessa bore much grief for the name of Christ.* The city remained in peace until Marcian,[261] who harassed it because of its Orthodoxy *but was unable to infect it with Chalcedonianism. Later, however, Edessa became weakened through senseless leadership.* Edessa came under the rule of the Tachiks for 400 years, from the time of Caliph 'Umar until the rise of the Turks. And in the days of the Tachiks the wall, which had been built by Seleucus, fell down. *For a short while the city came under the rule of the Franks. Disasters multiplied and they mourned the children of Zion. O, alas its destruction! May the Lord look upon it and visit it with glad tidings.*

In the year 1459 of the Syrian Era,[262] *Baron* T'oros came to the country of Cilicia from Constantinople *having escaped captivity* after the death of his father Lewon,[263] *whom the Byzantines, in their wickedness, had exiled from his homeland of Cilicia which he had taken by bow and sword.* T'oros came on foot to Lord At'anas, metropolitan of the *Jacobite* Syrians, who gave him his own horse and twelve men from among his students. At'anas sent him to Amutay which fell into his hands at night. The next morning the residents saw T'oros' standard and realized that the mercy of God had been bestowed upon the Christians, and they rejoiced greatly. After this, T'oros' holdings expanded greatly and he captured many other places. Fear of him spread among the Turks and Byzantines, and his renown spread through all lands. They say

---

261 A.D. 450-457.
262 A.D. 1148.
263 Lewon I, 1129-1138, d. 1141.

that when he went with 12 horsemen to Raban to marry Joscelin's daughter, he encountered many Turkish cavalry which had enslaved the land and were turning back. Strengthened by God, he struck and killed 3,000 of them. The surrounding areas and all his enemies trembled because of him—and he turned back, having won a name for valor. Then he took Anawarza and gradually the entire country fell under his sway.

Concerning the taking of Hr'omklay

In the same period, Joscelin went to the monastery of Mor Barsam. The clerics came out before him carrying crosses *and Gospels* and led him to the church. Joscelin made the place his fortress and placed troops there. Then he went on to Tell Bashar. Now in the same year he fell into the hands of the Turks and was reduced to naught. They say that he had gone hunting and his cavalry got separated from him. His horse threw him against a tree and he fell to the ground senseless. The Turks found him, took him to Aleppo, and sold him to a Jew, unaware of who he was. Later on, when they learned his identity, they took him to Nur ad-Din and put him in prison. Then Nur ad-Din took all his holdings: Azaz, Tell Bashar, Pir, Rabban, Marash, Behesne, Hisn Mansur, Samosata, Gargar, Kaght'ayn, and other places. *Joscelin was blinded and died.* All that remained was Hromklay where his wife and *two* daughters were located. Through the providence of God, Joscelin's wife had given this fortress to the Catholicos of the Armenians, Lord Grigor, and the place became the Catholicoi's eternal seat. *Joscelin's wife had sent to Lord Grigor, Catholicos of the Armenians, who was at Tsov, for him to come and reside in the fortress of Hromklay, since she wanted to cross the sea and return to her parents. Now she had a son and she resolved that if he lived and returned to Hromklay, the fortress would be given to him. "Otherwise," she said, "it is better that Hromklay belong to you than that the Turks take it." The Catholicos went there and remained until Joscelin's son arrived. With money, the Catholicos was able to persuade Joscelin's son to cede the fortress, and then Joscelin's son departed. For he was not sure that he could hold Hromklay in the midst of the Turks. Through the grace of God, Hromklay became their eternal See.*

In the same year, one day before the celebration of the Resurrection of the Lord, rain fell in Palestine mixed with drops of blood In Jerusalem, before the month of May, the morning dew had the color of blood. This was a sign of the blood of Christians which would flow in Jerusalem on its capture. Then, in the summer, *in the month of June*, red snow fell and covered the ground to a depth of two fingers.

In 1464 of the Syrian Era,[264] Baldwin, king of Jerusalem, having achieved his majority, wanted to removed his mother as regent of the kingdom. There were some in the army with the mother, and they went to the Tower of David, fortified themselves, and fought *for her* together with the Tower. The mother spoke *tender reproaches* to the king through the gates, *and the king wept*. He took pity and vowed that he would leave Jerusalem under his mother's care. Baldwin, taking his troops, went against Ascalon of the Palestinians, and *using siege machinery* destroyed part of its wall. Twenty thousand *armed and* outfitted Tachiks appeared at the breach and said to one another: "This city is the head of the Tachiks. Muhammad was strengthened by it *at the beginning of our faith*. Let us stand firm and die in it and not see the light of day anywhere but here." Four hundred Franks, *cavalrymen*, went against the 20,000 Muslims, and all were slain by them. The king and his troops were greatly saddened by this *and grieved bitterly*.

All night the Tachiks attempted to repair the section of the collapsed wall, but the king's great prince, Sir Renaud[265] labored mightily *at the risk of his life* and did not allow them to do so. Now at dawn, the king of Jerusalem took a cross in his hand, went close to the wall, and threw it into the city. And he said: "Behold, you who are Christians and believe, search for this symbol of Christ *which was dyed with the blood of God*." The Christians became in-

---

264 A. D. 1153.
265 Renaud de Chatillon.

flamed *with the love of Christ,* attacked from all sides *quicker than lightning,* and entered the city. *No one knows if these Franks were even armored.* Sixteen thousand people were killed there and many were taken captive.

A few others got into ships and fled to Egypt. Renaud, who had displayed great bravery against the Tachiks, was made prince of Antioch and head of the troops and they gave him in marriage the wife of Raymond de Boadi. In this period, the great prince of princes T'oros,[266] son of Lewon, son of Constantine, and great grandson of the royal Ruben *arose and* went to the Cappadocian country *against the Turks,* and returned home with the renown of a victor. Now Sultan Masud, who was one of the sons of the Qaqan, the king of the Turks, *was ruling as king in Konya.* He had given his daughter as a wife to Yakub-Arslan the Danishmendid. The two of them allied and *arrogantly* planned to go to Cilicia. But once they had approached the country, they discovered that it had been fortified with closed borders, *and ambuscades guarding the narrow passages,* and so they turned back in great disgrace. T'oros became even mightier and took from the Byzantines the remaining fortresses in Cilicia. When Manuel, the emperor of the Byzantines, learned about this, he became furious with *Baron* T'oros and sent the military commander Andronicus with a great mob of troops to Cilicia. *Baron* T'oros rose against him and they fought each other in the area around Tarsus. *God aided the Armenians, and the Byzantines were defeated before them.* The Byzantines were defeated and lost 3,000 of their noteworthy troops. The remainder fled by boat.

The great T'oros took their army and baggage and rejoiced, thanking the Lord *who let him take vengeance on his enemies.* And he *imprisoned and then* ransomed the Byzantine grandees for gold, *and he became very wealthy.*

In 1465 of the Syrian Era,[267] Zangi's sons in Mosul, Saif ad-Din and Qutb ad-Din Maudud who had pledged to support the Caliph, broke their oath and allied themselves with the emir

---

266 T'oros II, 1145-1169.
267 A. D. 1154.

THE CHRONICLE

of Tekrit in rebelling *from the caliph*. The caliph[268] was furious and came against Mosul, but was unable to take it. And so, he turned and went against Tekrit which he gave over to his troops for looting. They captured it, *took the booty*, and then pulled it apart, down to its foundation. Subsequently, they gave the fortress to Shems ad-Din who was a good, philo-Christian man. He quickly rebuilt the city and the churches and remained loyal to the Caliph.

In this period Nur ad-Din, lord of Aleppo, went against Damascus and took it with an oath, but then destroyed its princes and their patrimonies.[269] Then he demolished its brick wall and rebuilt it with one made of stronger stones. In the same year Tumurtash, lord of Mardin, died. He was an Artukid, a good and philo-Christian man who, as a result, rebuilt many churches. Now Timurtash grew ill with a fatal illness, so dangerous that the doctors abandoned hope and left off treating him *and departed*. Timurtash placed his hopes on the prayers of Christians and sent to the monastery of Mor Aba and they brought the relic of the saint's right hand. When they had entered Timurtash's home, they saw a fiery man who went and took Timurtash's hand. And Timurtash asked: "Who are you, lord?" The saint replied: "The Christians sent me here so that you would not die." The saint restored him and then Timurtash sat and glorified God, and was made well again. There was great comfort for the Christians *and the churches* throughout his reign, at Mardin, Nisibis, Mup'arkin, Rasala, Tara, and at many other places *under his sway*. Similarly, after his death, his sons displayed the same solicitousness for Christians *as he had bid them*. Timurtash gave Mardin and Mup'arkin to his senior son, Nejm ad-Din; the city of Xani *Harran* to Jemal ad-Din, another son; and Dara to his youngest son, Shems ad-Din.

In this period, the Byzantine emperor, Manuel, *learned that Sultan Masud was on the borders of Mesopotamia*. In accordance with the hatred Manuel had toward all Christians, he sent to Sultan Masud and beseeched him with great gifts to enter

---

268 Al-Muqtafi, 1136-1160.
269 in 1154.

and ruin the country of Cilicia. Masud gathered all the troops of Cappadocia and Mesopotamia and, with all preparation, went and entered the country of the Armenians. The Armenians, who had advance knowledge of Masud's movements, migrated to the mountains and secure places and fortified themselves there *while the Armenian troops took up positions in the mountains.* The sultan descended on Tell Hamdun. Then the Lord God of the Christians struck them—not with a fiery angel as He struck the troops of Sennacherib, and not through a woman, as happened to Holophernes. Rather, God afflicted them by means of tiny creatures: mosquitoes and flies. They say that God had also used insects to punish the ruthless Pharaoh. This was fatal to man and beast. *It was summertime and men and animals were dying from this, and so* the Muslim troops began to flee. Then the Armenian troops who were fortified in the mountains descended and killed many of them. And they took as booty the wealth of the infidels and filled up their homes with it, thanking and glorifying God. Then Baron T'oros swiftly arose, crossed through the mountains of Xawatane's and struck the Turks dwelling there. He returned with many captives and much booty, and with a reputation for glory from everyone. As for Sultan Masud, in great disgrace he escaped the sons of the Armenians by a hairsbreadth. He reached Konya where, in a second blow from the Lord, he died.[270]

In 1466 of the Syrian Era,[271] Masud's son, Kilij-Arslan, came to rule.[272] He had two brothers. One he had secretly strangled *he killed him using poison,* while the other fled to the seacoast and holed up in a fortress his father had given him prior to his death. His name was Shahanshah and was a son-in-law of the House of Danishmend. Because of this, they were united and his cousin[273] Yaqub-Arslan laid waste the country of Kilij-Arslan. When Nur ad-Din, lord of Aleppo and Damascus heard about this, he took

---

270 A. D. 1155.
271 A. D. 1155.
272 Kilij-Arslan II, 1155-1192.
273 Father's brother's son.

P'arzman and Ant'ap'. Then Yaqub-Arslan sent to Nur ad-Din and to Qara-Arslan, lord of Kharberd, so that they would take all of Kilij-Arslan's lands located on their borders in Mesopotamia and on the far side of the Euphrates River. However, in planning the seizure and division of the territory, they argued with one another and abandoned the idea.

Now the Arabs had held Egypt under their sway since the days of the Muslims' conquest, and the Turkish kings were unable to find an entrance. *The Turks were unable to rule there.* Their[274] Caliph descended from the line of 'Ali, just as the Caliph residing in Baghdad descended from the line of Muhammad.

The Almohads in the West: who they were and where they came from.

The Caliphs in Egypt were descended from the line of 'Ali until the period of Nur ad-Din, and then that line came to an end. They say that following them, *after the death of the Caliph of Egypt, his son, named Abas, wanted to take his father's place. But the prince of Egypt did not want this.* There was a certain Abdullah who had two sons named Abdlmin and Yaqub. These two had fallen into adultery with their father's wife. Now when the father found out about this, he wanted to kill them.

They learned about his intent and fled, taking from their father's house two books, named *K'emia* and *Semia*. *K'emia* taught alchemy by which it was possible to transform materials into gold, silver, precious stones, and pearls. The *Semia* taught about marvels and talismans with which to astound people. The brothers[275] took these books and went to the borders of western Africa and journeyed beyond that. They found a land of barbarians, speaking a foreign tongue somewhat resembling French. These people[276] were poor and lacked learning, literature, and laws. The brothers

---

274 i.e., the Egyptians'.
275 i.e., the Almohads.
276 i.e., the Portuguese.

MICHAEL THE GREAT

adhered to them and built very secure homes on cliffs that were difficult to access.

The brothers secretly practiced their craft and received wealth, which they liberally distributed. They had many servants who themselves received wealth and servants from the Almohads. Through their mildness and generosity, they attracted the natives to their side. They took wives from among them and had sons and they taught them writings and the study of astrology and magic. They built fortresses and cities, and expanded. Then they began to teach them their doctrine and creed and convinced them using sorcery and they also taught them their own language and writing.[277] They grew mighty. They created an army, became stronger, and captured many cities.

After this, the Almohads grew even more and went and took the island of Sicily. They ruled over many lands and placed the Romans in great straits. They say that it is for this reason that the Germans took the imperial honor from the French. This is because Rome, being harassed by the Arabs, sent to them the Germans so that the Germans would come and save them from the Arabs. The French similarly sent to the Germans beseeching them and saying that if the Lord gave them victory in combating the foreigners, they could take the imperial honor. They swore to this. The Germans, placing their faith in God, went against [...][278] destroyed them and made the survivors flee. Thus, the Germans took the imperial honor. Those Tachiks who now ruled over many lands and fortresses, established their own Sultan and Caliph. They exist to the present day.

In the year 1466 of the Syrian Era,[279] the Caliph of Egypt died and the prince of Egypt himself wanted to succeed the Caliph. But he was not from the line of Ali, and the land did not want him. Rather, they chose a certain Abas who was the son of the deceased Caliph. Now when Abas saw that the prince did not want to

---

277 i.e., Arabic.
278 There is a lacuna in the text here.
279 A.D. 1155.

establish him as caliph, he seized all the wealth of the House of the caliph. Then he brought out 3,000 servants of Armenian nationality, armed them, and rose in the night. Taking a Bedouin guide, he took the road leading to Nur ad-Din in Damascus. At dawn when the prince of Egypt learned about this development, he pursued them with troops. The army of the freed Armenian slaves turned and struck the Egyptian troops with severe blows. The remaining Egyptians fled. Now when they reached Palestine, one of the Bedouins went to Jerusalem to notify the Franks and also the city of Ascalon and they massed and went against them. When Abas saw this, he said to the Armenians: "My sons, strike them as you did the Egyptians and I will exalt you greatly." They organized themselves.

However, when the Armenians saw the symbol of the cross carried in advance of the Frankish troops, they started to weep. They dismounted from their horses and went before the cross, worshipping it as though they longed for it. The Franks easily took the inestimable wealth, seized Abas, and sold him to the prince of Egypt for a large amount of gold. The prince of Egypt took Abas and hanged him on a wooden pole. The Franks left the Armenians free to go wherever they wanted, but gave them nothing except the clothes they already wore. Thus, did they repay with ingratitude those Christians who had appealed to Christians, and through whom the Franks had acquired such a vast amount of wealth.

In this period, Renaud of Antioch, who was called Prince, disputed with Baron T'oros about the fortress in the confines of Sicily, which the Byzantines had taken from the Franks. Baron T'oros then had taken it from the Byzantines. Renaud said: "Turn it over to the *Freres* since they are fighting for the Christians, and this was the first fortress they captured." For this reason the Franks and the Armenians battled near Skandrun and many fell on both sides. Then they parted from each other *and Renaud returned home in disgrace.* Subsequently, Baron T'oros agreed and gave a fortress *in the vicinity of Antioch* to them of his own free will. The two conflicting sides vowed that they would assist the other to the point of death. *And the Franks pledged to help the Armenians in all their difficulties, even risking their lives.*

In 1468 of the Syrian Era,[280] Step'ane', who was the brother of Baron T'oros, rose and went to the Marash country. At night, he entered Marash and placed his troops in the homes of Christians, at the urging of a Christian cleric *from that city*. At daybreak Step'ane' took the city and slaughtered the Turks. Then the Christians waxed proud, *insulted the citadel guards*, and publicly disgraced the Turks' women. The Lord became angry and did not give the citadel into their hands. And so, Step'ane's troops burned the city, took the Armenians *the Christians* living there, and entered the country. However, the emir of Marash seized the cleric who had secretly brought those troops into the city, flayed him alive, and then burned his body with fire. In the same year, Renaud, lord of Antioch, after conferring with *Baron T'oros, with the assistance and aid of T'oros*, took his troops and went against the island of Cyprus. This resulted from two causes. First, it was due to a grudge held by the emperor of the Byzantines who was always inciting the foreigners to destroy the Armenians; and second, because the Greeks of Cyprus were killing Armenians and Franks. Thus Renaud went and captured the entire island *and looted it*. He led people and livestock to the shore, counted them, and fixed ransom amounts on all of them. Then he left them, taking along with him as hostages the bishop, *priests, and freemen* and numerous hostages and wealthy folk until they should receive their ransoms. Now Step'ane' seized a Turk from Pertous and demanded its fortress. And the Turk replied: "If you vow that you will let us live, we will surrender Pertous." And Step'ane' so vowed by the Cross and the Gospel that he would send them safely to Aleppo. They gave Pertous to him and he removed them to depart in peace. Now some of those taking them heard the Turks threaten thusly: "We will again arm, return, and ruin this land." This was related to *Baron Step'ane'.*

280 A.D. 1157.

Baron Step'ane' asked the clerics and they said: "If they are so threatening, then you are released from your oath." And so, he sent after the Turks and destroyed them. When all the foreigners heard about this, they were embittered against the Christians and consequently posed enormous danger.

In this year, the senior Sultan of Khorasan, Masud, died. He did not have a grown son, only a tiny child as a successor. As a result, a certain emir named Eltkuz acted as *locum tenens*. Eltkuz took the Sultan's wife, the baby's mother, for his own wife, and, after a few days, the child died. Thus, the Sultanate was Eltkuz's. Perhaps an heir would be born of the same woman. In any case, Eltkuz, who had been *atabeg* of the first child, became Sultan, even though he continued to be styled *atabeg*. Moreover, thereafter the kings of Khorasan, Nineveh, and Mesopotamia *to Mosul, and Aran* were called *atabeg*s and their clans, the house of the *atabeg*(s). Similarly, those who had been kings in Cappadocia, who were under Eltkuz's sway, were styled *atabeg*s, *they who had been called Qaqans and Saljukids. The Danishmends also were not full kings. Now since Kilij-Arslan and Qara-Arslan, lord of Sewast, were disputing with each other, Baron Step'ane' emerged and ruined both their countries.*

In 1469 of the Syrian Era,[281] Kilij-Arslan established friendship with Qara-Arslan, lord of Sewast. He came to the Mesopotamian country and took the places which his father previously had seized. He made friendship with *Baron* T'oros and Step'ane', and there was peace. In this year,[282] the king of Jerusalem went to Antioch, assembled troops *from the Armenians*, and then went and took Herim, enslaving *destroying* as far as Aleppo. Then he turned back. In this period discord arose between Kilij-Arslan and Qara-Arslan, and *Baron* Step'ane' endlessly ruined both their lands. Then some folk went to *Baron* T'oros and slandered his brother Step'ane', saying: "Your brother wants to kill you." T'oros believed them, seized his brother, and imprisoned

---

281 A.D. 1158.
282 Beaudon/Baldwin III.

him for ten months. Then, after the intercession of many people, he removed him from prison, and the two dwelled affectionately with each other. Kilij-Arslan took Tanum, the emir of Caesarea, a man who was dear to him, and removed him from allegiance to Qara-Arslan. This became the start of the collapse of the House of the Danishmendids.

In 1470 of the Syrian Era,[283] the Tachiks who are called Almohads advanced as far as Spain and began raiding. Arising against them were the troops of the Franks, and warfare was prolonged *for a year*. Now Manuel, Emperor of the Byzantines, finding the moment opportune, came to Cilicia issuing threats against *Baron* T'oros. T'oros and his troops evaded him and went into the mountains. Manuel subdued the plains, going as far as Antioch. But then he received the bad tidings that one of his military commanders wanted to reign in his place. Thus, he quickly turned around and departed, having made peace with Baron T'oros and Step'ane'. He sent to Kilij-Arslan requesting a transit route, and it was granted. Despite this, many of his troops were destroyed, openly and clandestinely. He reached Constantinople and was unsuccessful in carrying his stratagem. But when Manuel saw the diminution of his troops caused by the Turks, he dispatched other troops to wreck whichever districts of the Turks that they could. Thus, there were wars between the Byzantines and the Turks. When Nur ad-Din learned what was happening, he massed troops against Kilij-Arslan's districts and captured Behesne, Raban, and Marash, as well as monasteries and much else.

In 1471 of the Syrian Era,[284] Yacub-Arslan and Nur ad-Din made peace with Sultan Kilij-Arslan and returned the lands they had taken from him. In the same year the troops at Aleppo seized Joscelin's son, Joscelin, lord of Hermin, who died in captivity in Aleppo. There was great joy at Aleppo, for he had greatly harassed the Aleppo country because of his father's grudge. He was put into fetters and died there.

283 A.D. 1159.
284 A.D. 1160.

A year later they destroyed Parisha village in the Hermin country. Armenians lived there. They were killed or led into captivity.

In this year, Baldwin, king of Jerusalem, rose and took Damascus with its borders and Ptoyik' which had been under the sway of Nur ad-Din. They settled in Phoenicia. Then this area rebelled from Nur ad-Din and went under Frankish rule. Taking them, the Franks went into the Egyptian desert where they acquired an extremely large amount of booty and captives. They taxed them 160,000 *dahekans* and returned to Jerusalem in great glory. In this period, King Ge'orgi of Georgia attacked Emir Saltux *who resided at Karin city*. Ge'orgi seized and ransomed him. And he took the city of Ani. Again, a multitude of Turks assembled against Ge'orgi and they destroyed thousands and thousands and myriads upon myriads of them.

In 1472 of the Syrian Era,[285] a war took place between Kilij-Arslan and Yaqub-Arslan over Saltux's daughter. The Sultan had wanted to marry her. She was given in marriage to the lord of Melitene, with the approval of Yaqub-Arslan. Then the Sultan Kilij-Arslan massed troops against him. Yaqub-Arslan came out against him and waxed strong against the Sultan. He defeated him and caused him to flee and seized his dwelling place with its golden furniture and all its appointments. But he was magnanimous and returned all that he had taken and sought his friendship. They made peace and remained at peace with one another.

In the same period the king of Jerusalem was informed that Girard, lord of Sidon had organized ships full of pirates on the sea and was mercilessly killing Christians and Tachiks, *but he was harming Christians more than Turks*. Consequently, the king became angry with him, took Sidon, and chased him out. Girard then went to *Prince* the lord of Antioch, who gave Baghras to him. But he did not stop his evildoings on sea or on land, and he did very great harm. Now when they *the Prince* learned about this, they also took Baghras from him. And then Girard went to Nur ad-

---

285 A.D. 1161.

Din, who was delighted, since Girard had promised that he would make the entire coast his. Nur ad-Din gave him troops and Girard went and entered the Franks' territory where he began to loot and destroy the Christians *and to corrupt the shore*. The Franks massed troops and, invoking the name of Christ, went against Girard, arresting this source of evil and also killing Turkish troops. Girard, that vessel of Satan, was taken to Jerusalem and burned in the fire *and thus his evil ended.*

In these days Manuel, Emperor of the Byzantines, killed his wife with poison because of her barrenness. Then he took the daughter of *Prince* the lord of Antioch as a second wife, which was outside the law *for Christians.*

In 1473 of the Syrian Era,[286] Tugh-Arslan, emir of Melitene, died and his son, a ten-year-old boy, sat in his father's place. When Yaqub-Arslan heard about this, he came against Melitene and besieged it. However, he was unable to take it, and so he left troops there and departed. Now Qara-Arslan, the lord of Kharberd, did much to receive the fugitives from the district of Melitene. But afterwards Yaqub-Arslan turned from his anger toward the boy who had become emir—who was his brother's son—and made peace with him, and left the land of Melitene to him. Now in this period, Kilij- Arslan learned *from slanderers* that Yaqub-Arslan, united with many emirs, planned to depose him from his throne, *kill him*, and install his brother in his stead. He was frightened, *believed this*, and sent his chancellor Christopher to Emperor Manuel to seek aid and good will from him and approval that Kilij-Arslan be allowed to go to him in Constantinople. Manuel was delighted and swore an oath guaranteeing his safety. And so the Sultan, with 1,000 cavalry, went to Manuel in Constantinople, where he was received with great honor. He remained there for eighty days and was so honored that twice each day they sent him dishes and bowls of gold and silver all of which remained with the sultan and were not taken back. On the final day, they ate in a certain chamber, and all its appointments were given to the sultan.

---

286 A.D. 1162.

THE CHRONICLE

Whe he wanted to depart, he stood in the palace and was covered with gold to his height. Emperor Manuel also gave Kilij-Arslan his troops and he departed and hired many other troops from among the Turks. All the emirs of Mesopotamia with their troops assembled by Yaqub-Arslan and arose to make war against him. But when they approached each other, both were frightened at the multitude opposing them. They made peace and dispersed to their own places.

In that period, Prince Andronicus, who was Greek *and was in Cilicia at Manue's order,* summoned *Baron* Step'ane' to honor him *with a meal.* Now as Step'ane' departed and was returning home, he and those with him were treacherously slain. Some say that he was stewed in a copper pot. Then *Baron* T'oros, transported with rage, went against the Byzantines and killed more than 10,000 of them, it is said. Andronicus swore that he had not been the cause of his brother's slaying and he beseeched the king of Jerusalem to come and make peace, promising him much gold from Constantinople. The king[287] consented. He came and begged *Baron* T'oros about his brother Step'ane' and the Cilician Armenians stopped fighting with the Byzantines. After this *Paron* T'oros took Anawarza and T'il.

In this period, Ge'orgi, king of the Georgians, took Dvin and killed the Persians in it. And he pulled down the minaret which the Persians had built with the blood and bones of Christians.

In these days Reynald,[288] lord of Antioch, was seized by Nur ad-Din's troops, with 120 horsemen and 500 infantrymen in an ambush *as he was traveling in Aleppo.* He displayed many examples of valor there and, were it not for the fact that he was protecting his infantry, he could have fled easily. But his heart was inflamed and he halted. After many fights, he gave himself into the hands of the Turks. They took him to *Nur ad-Din* in Aleppo. And this occasioned great sorrow for the Christians *in the churches* and great joy for the Turks, for around the same time the Turks invaded the

---

287 Baldwin III, 1143-1163.
288 Of Chatillon, 1153-1160.

territory of Laodicea whence they led into slavery 7,000 Christians. Now when[289] the king of Jerusalem heard about this he went there *but was unable to do anything about the captives*. He made peace with Aleppo. Then he turned to go back to Jerusalem. However, when he reached Acre he died. His kingdom was given to his brother Amalric[290] in 1474 of the Syrian Era.[291] The latter took his brother's body back to Jerusalem and buried it there. And they mourned him for many days. He had ruled for 19 years.

Then Nur ad-Din entered Jerusalem, laid waste to it, took booty and captives, and departed. But then Amalric pursued Nur ad-Din's troops, caused them to flee, killed many of them, *retook the booty and captives*, and turned back.

In the same year, Yaqub-Arslan subdued Tanu, who was his brother's son, and who had rebelled in Armenian Caesarea. Then he went on to Kama, which is *Ani* Kamax, and killed the rebel emir who was there. That same year, Qara-Arslan went to Amida, but was unable to take it. He returned to Hasankef and summoned Yaqub-Arslan in friendship. However, the latter thought that Qara-Arslan was deceiving him, and so he angrily went against Yaqub-Arslan's territory *with many troops*. He seized Mshkatsak and enslaved 100,000[292] people from his lands as well as two bishops, Lord Ignatius and Lord Dionysius. Later they got free. Now after the capture of Renald, his wife ruled Antioch. Then *Baron* T'oros went there and established Renald's son, Bohemond, as prince of Antioch, against the mother's wishes.

In these times, Nur ad-Din massed troops and went and captured the Tripoli country. They encountered 300 Frankish cavalry and did not recognize them. Rather, the Turks thought that the king of Jerusalem had arrived. They abandoned what they had seized and fled. The Franks pursued and cut them down until they reached a certain open place. Then, when the Franks saw

---

289 Baldwin/Baudoin III.
290 Amalric I, 1163-1174.
291 A.D. 1163.
292 or, 10,000.

the multitude of Kurds, they realized that it was Nur ad-Din. Terrified, they ascended a hill, dismounted from their horses, kneeled down and prayed their final prayer, seeing death approaching them. Now when the Turks saw them praying, fear of the Lord came upon them and they fled *casting off their armor and* leaving their equipage behind. Taking heart, the Christ-loving troops pursued and cut down a great multitude of them *myriads and thousands of them [...]*[293] with the power of Christ. *The Christians loaded up with the enemies' furniture and belongings, delightedly praising Christ our God.* As for Nur ad-Din, he escaped by a hairsbreadth with a few troops.

In the same year, Yaqub-Arslan went to She'ran-shah, the sultan's brother, and was returning home happily. But he died when he reached Gangra on the Halys River. The troops hurried to enthrone Ismail, Sultan Yaqub's brother's son, and they forged unity with Tanu, the emir of Caesarea. However, the troops that were in Ablastan enthroned as Sultan Mahmud's son, Mahmud.[294] *And there was great disorder in the House of Danishmend.*

During the same year, the king of Jerusalem[295] went to Egypt *to collect taxes*. The Egyptians were divided into two groups—half were obedient to the king of Jerusalem, and half pridefully placed their hopes on Nur ad-Din. This latter group sent to Nur ad-Din *to help them*. Nur ad-Din sent troops under his military commander Shirkou to their aid. They went against the king of Jerusalem and were betrayed to destruction by the wrath of God, who put them to the sword of the king of Jerusalem. After this, Amalric descended on the city of Belbes and besieged it for five[296] months. When he heard that Nur ad-Din was besieging Herim with the entire multitude of the Turks, he abandoned Belbes and headed there. *The king*[297] *wrote to them with this*

---

293 There is a lacuna in the text here.
294 Mahdi.
295 Amalric.
296 or, *seven*.
297 Amalric.

advice: "Under no circumstances come forth from your city until I arrive." However, prior to his arrival, Nur ad-Din had already taken Herim because of the stupidity of the Frankish troops who did not heed his wise advice which he had written to them—that they should not come forth against the Turks until his arrival. Rather, the besieged ones massed, emerged, and drove the Turks away from the city. Then they remained out in the open, heedlessly. But the Turks came back against them *when they were unawares*, killed them, and took the city. They took into captivity the prince of Antioch[298] and many other notables.

In 1466 of the Syrian Era[299] Sultan Kilij-Arslan became strong and took Katuk, Ablastan, and Taranda which were in the hands of Tanu, and he chased out the sons of Danishmend.

Regarding Baron T'oros and Saladin; and about the questions of Lord Nerse's and the examination of the faith and about the expression of two natures of Christ.

In this year, *Baron* T'oros sent gold and silver to Aleppo to ransom those of his princes who were in captivity there. They took the gold but did not release the captives. T'oros *was furious and* issued threats against Nur ad-Din and he himself arose and went to Marash, *which he looted.* A multitude of Turks massed against him and he struck them with the strength of the Lord and captured *many of them, including* a notable and principal man. Nur ad-Din became frightened of him and sent him the captives he had sought. And he requested peace with him. Then the Franks spoke up and requested the Prince of Antioch. Nur ad-Din ransomed him to them for 100,000 *dahekans*. The prince arose and went to Constantinople to his sister and returned with an immense treasure. He brought along the Greek patriarch of Antioch who was named Athanasius[300] and established him at Antak. When

298 Bohemond III, 1163-1201.
299 A.D. 1155.
300 Athanasius VII, Bar Qutreh, 1138-1166.

the patriarch of the Franks, who was named Hermes, saw this he quit the city and went and sat in Xawsayr. And he excommunicated the city.

In 1477 of the Syrian Era,[301] Emperor Manuel went against the Bulghars, *was defeated by them, and* was seized by a man who wanted to take him to their king. Manuel made him a very grand promise of wealth if he would let him go and accompany him to Constantinople. The man consented, turned around, released the emperor, and then took him to Constantinople. And Manuel fulfilled his promise there.

Egypt then was under the sway of Nur ad-Din, and Shirk'aw ruled over them. In 1478 of the Syrian Era,[302] Amalric, the king of Jerusalem again went to Egypt where he defeated the troops of Nur ad-Din in Msr. Then he returned to Jerusalem. Hearing that the Tachiks had started to harass Christians *in Egypt*, he went a third time to Egypt. Sherak'aw, who was in Msr, arose against him and again was defeated and fled. *Amalric killed, captured, looted, and reduced their strength.* And then the king of Jerusalem took Msr and there was great joy among Christians. Then all of Egypt became tributary to Jerusalem.

In this year the emir of Kharberd, Qara-Arslan, died. His son, Nur ad-Din, ruled. In 1479 of the Syrian Era,[303] Andronicus the Greek, the slayer of *Baron* Step'anne', who was first cousin[304] of Emperor Manuel, fled from Cilicia and went to Acre, since his cousin, Theodora—widow of the deceased king of Jerusalem—was there. And he became trustee of her house. That impious man fell into incest with his own brother's daughter. She became pregnant and the evil was thus revealed. They fled to Harran where the wicked birth took place. The Turks loathed the Christians when they learned about this affair. Andronicus sent on to Mardin, but they did not receive him. Thence he went to the city of Karin and

---

301 A.D. 1166.
302 A.D. 1167.
303 A.D. 1168.
304 Father's brother's son.

got Turkish troops, with which he captured Christians and brought and sold them to the infidels.

In this same year, the great prince of princes *Baron* T'oros died,[305] having lived a life of venerable glory with great triumphs. Close to the end of his life he donned clerical garb and passed to Christ with great expectations. May his memory be blessed in Christ in the Orthodox churches. He gave the kingdom to his son who was an extremely young child, entrusting him to the princes. *Now Baron T'oros had a brother named Mleh, a perverse and cruel man, in whom he had no confidence.* T'oros gave nothing to him, knowing his wickedness, since prior to his death, Mleh had gone to Nur ad-Din and had given Cyrrhus to him. Moreover, Mleh had done many evil things to Christians with the assistance of the infidels. He had stolen Vanawer from the Armenians and mercilessly enslaved believers in Christ. I am unable to put in writing all the calamities he caused.

After these events, the Armenian princes and T'omas, the child's guardian, extracted an oath from him[306] that he would not deprive his brother's son and in exchange for which they gave him half the country if he would quit the place. Mleh so vowed, but he did not keep that vow. Instead, he grew stronger, doing very great evils, and came to rule over the entire country. *The baby's guardian fled with the child to Hromklay and nursed him there.*

In 1480 of the Syrian Era[307] the kingdom of the Arabs ended in Egypt. It had begun in the time of 'Umar in 949 of the Syrian Era[308] and ended as a result of a schism between two sectarian factions. One group, the Tachiks of Egypt, the R'ap'tik' who are the Shiites argued that there is only one God Who is not the author of evil, for God is one while evils are numerous. Satan to them is the source of evil. The other group, who were in Assyria and Mesopotamia said that evil and sins also derive from God.

305 d. 1169.
306 i.e., Mleh.
307 A.D. 1169.
308 A.D. 638.

They are called Sunnis. As a result of these doctrinal differences, the two groups hated each other. Both groups were in Egypt, the Sunnis were under the Franks, while the Shiites were under Nur ad-Din. Nur ad-Din sent a messenger to both sides *to the Sunnis* and promised freedom to all of them if they would support him and cease paying taxes to the Franks *and he would help their faith.* They heeded him *and went under the sway of the Turks* and cut off the taxes that went to the king of Jerusalem. They fortified Belbeis and stationed there 12,000 cavalry and 200,000 infantry. When the king of Jerusalem heard about this, he went and took Belbeis and generally killed everyone except the Christians.

Shawur, who was ruling over Msr, burned the city and went with the multitude of its inhabitants to the city of Cairo which he fortified. He sent *Sherak'aw* to Nur ad-Din to inform him of what had happened. Meanwhile, the king of Jerusalem returned home with much booty. Nur ad-Din sent the military commander Sherak'aw to Egypt with 100,000 cavalry. When he arrived, he killed the prince of the Tachiks named Shawer. Then he seized the Fatimid caliph and killed him, and exterminated his House, *and he himself ruled.* And thus was the rule and the caliphate of the Tachiks[309] eliminated in Egypt, while the race of the Turks ruled thereafter.

Sherak'aw died after three years and his principality was taken by Yusup', that is, Saladin, the brother's son of Sherak'aw. *As to who these people were, I will now relate.* They were of Kurdish nationality from the city of Dvin in Greater Armenia, sons of poor folk. Saladin's father was called Ayyub. This Ayyub, son of Sulaiman, and his brother, Sherak'aw, left Dvin because of poverty, and went to Tikrit in Mesopotamia. The people took them into the fortress as domestics. One night Ayyub saw in a dream that fire arose from his body and burned many lands. He related the dream to a Jew who interpreted it for him to mean that he would father a son who would rule *ruin* many lands. Then Ayyub wrote a statement that if his dream should be realized, then that son of his who

---

309 i.e., the Fatimids.

would rule would give the Jew and his sons yearly a thousand red ducats. *The Jew wrote down the time and year.* That same year, Yusup' was born. When he grew up, Sherak'aw, who was his uncle,[310] took him and went to Nur ad-Din.

Sherak'aw was a progressive and wise person *and successful in everything* and so Nur ad-Din made him a military commander and sent him to Egypt. *Although Sherak'aw was defeated by the king of Jerusalem twice, Nur ad-Din had him rule over Egypt.* As for Saladin, who was Yusup', he was skillful and found favor in Nur ad-Din's eyes. After the death of his uncle, Nur ad-Din sent Aladin in his place. As for that Jew, he came to Ayyub and asked for the gold. Ayyub said to him: "Come, let us go to the one who is reigning, and he will give it to you." And so, the two of them went to Egypt where they sought payment from Yusup'. Saladin asked the Jew: "How many years have passed since the dream you interpreted?" The Jew had the document with the date on it, which he took out and showed to him. And Saladin paid him a thousand red *dahekans* for each year which had passed. *The Jew delightedly returned to his home in Tigrit.* After a short while Saladin's father fell from a horse, was kicked in the head, and died. He was buried with honor. Then Yusup'[311] went and grew stronger, advancing day by day.

In the same year, Kilij-Arslan took Caesarea and Tsamndav from the sons of Danishmend. Meanwhile Yusup' issued an order in Egypt that Christians must always appear *in public* wearing a belt as a sign of servitude, and that they could not mount a horse or mule.

In the same year the Nestorian bishop *in Baghdad* seized a church of the Orthodox *Jacobites*, but the wrath of the Lord fell upon him and he immediately returned the church to its rightful owners. In these days the blessed Yakob, who had become bishop and was called Dionysius, distinguished himself by the splendor of divine grace and the glory of his teachings. He was the son of Salib,

---

310 Father's brother.
311 i.e, Saladin.

THE CHRONICLE

a righteous man. He produced many books of advice and religion and interpreted the entire Old and New Testaments. Miracles and wonders were effected by him to the glory of Christ our God.

In 1481 of the Syrian Era,[312] the Byzantine emperor Manuel sent to Lord Nerse's, Catholicos of the Armenians[313] and to me, Michael, Patriarch of the Syrians—who wrote this compilation—about unifying the religion and doctrine of our Churches. This was done first via *a certain* Christaphor, and then a second time via T'orian *a philosopher*. Lord Nerse's wrote to us that "they want us to proclaim two natures in Christ, to honor the Fourth Council of Chalcedon, to hold Christmas on December 25th, to mix yeast with the host, and to mix water with the wine in the chalice, and, in speaking of Holy God, not to say 'Who Was crucified.'[314] *In exchange for this, he would do many good things for us. What reply should I make?*" I wrote back to Nerse's:

> "*What they are asking for indeed is our faith, with the exception of accepting the two natures, the Fourth Council and their formulation of the Trisagion.* The faith which you hold is close to our own. I cannot alter the true faith of your Fathers either in great or small issues of doctrine. For that would indicate that until now your faith had been defective but now, with these changes, it had become correct. *We should not now, at the eleventh hour, change our faith to gain their adulation.* Rather, we see your faith as based on an Apostolic foundation, lacking nothing and without defects. *You yourselves know this.*"

We sent to Catholicos Nerse's one of our own students named *E"nt'er'ine'*, who was skilled in secular knowledge, to speak

---

312   A.D. 1170.
313   Nerses IV Klayets'i (Shnorhali), 1166-1173.
314   in the Trisagion.

on our behalf, *since they the Armenians lacked anyone so skilled in philosophy*. We had heard that the man who had come from the emperor was skilled in secular knowledge. Our student arrived there. The great Catholicos of the Armenians ordered him to discourse before him with T'oriane' about the natures of Christ. Our student asked the Byzantine: "How many parts is nature divided into?" He replied: "Two." The student asked: "What are they?" T'oriane' answered: "Personal and impersonal." Then the student asked him: "As for the two natures which you speak about *and demand that we recognize*, which are they, personal or impersonal?" *The Byzantine*, embarrassed, was silent for many hours and was confused *feeling that he had become entangled in an inextricable trap*. Finally he said: "Let us skip this matter, for what does our discourse have to do with the categories of secular philosophy?" The Catholicos lambasted him, saying: "Why do you evade the issue, you who have come here as a champion debater? Are you afraid to speak of two natures in secular philosophy but not in theological literature? *As for what you have advanced, it is nonsense and we will never accept it*." And so, after many days of discussion, the so-called philosopher T'o'riane' was embarassed.

Emperor Manuel also wrote to us requesting a statement of doctrine, which we wrote and sent. They expressed satisfaction with this and again wrote to us, praising our formulation. However, they beseeched us to go to them in Constantinople so that they might hear these words from our own mouth. We declined this invitation and instead wrote that "This is our profession of the faith: we glorify Christ—according to the Apostles, Prophets, and our Orthodox Fathers—as having one nature and one will and operation, *an operation indivisible in every act of His life*. We remain steadfast on this foundation. If someone is willing to make peace and friendship with us according to this doctrine, we too are ready for it. But if, instead, someone wishes to hate and fight *and persecute* us for the faith transmitted to us from our ancestors, then we will persist in our belief. We will offer our necks to the sword as martyrs to this faith as our ancestors did."

The great Catholicos of the Armenians also made answer according to his wisdom, although we did not see his response in full. *We do not know what response Lord Nerse's made, but he was a man well versed in Scripture, an honest and industrious man who followed the blessed Orthodox canons, resembling his ancestor, Saint Nerse's.* But we do know this, that the Lord obstructed the emperor's efforts to try to put the Chalcedonian issue before us, because Manuel became greatly occupied with the Turks. The great Nerse's, Catholicos of the Armenians, died at this time,[315] adorned with virtue after a life of modest behavior. And thus, the faith which we had received from our fathers remained steadfast on its foundations, *saved from the gates of Hell by the prayers, blood, and tears of our fathers.*

In the same year, 1481 of the Syrian Era,[316] the king of Jerusalem Amalric requested aid from the emperor of the Byzantines, who was his father-in-law. The emperor sent many troops, who went against Egypt by sea. But when the Byzantines reached Egypt, they betrayed the king of Jerusalem in accordance with their treacherous nature, and wanted to take Egypt for themselves. The Egyptians informed the king about what the Byzantines were planning, and they gave him gold and hostages to pay the tax, for Saladin was not yet ready to wage war against the king of Jerusalem. *The lord of Egypt, Saladin gave him the tax that was due and they promised to give hostages subsequently.* The king accepted this, and his forces took the gold and the hostages and turned back, leaving the Byzantines there.

The latter did not dare to remain in Egypt and so they boarded ships to go home. But winter came upon them and many were lost at sea.

---

315 A.D. 1173.
316 A.D. 1170.

MICHAEL THE GREAT

Regarding the earthquake which occurred on June 29th and about how snow fell to a depth of 25 t'iz[317] in the month of the Cross.

In the same year[318] a frightful earthquake occurred, during the summer, on June 29th, during the feast of the blessed Apostles Peter and Paul. This took place at the third hour during liturgy. The earth rocked at its foundations and it seemed that the ground rose and fell and roiled until the ninth hour. At the time of the earthquake, we were in the monastery of Mor Hana and we fell on our faces and then ordered that no one should leave the church until this wrath *of the Lord* had ceased. It is worth noting that, in truth, no one expected the earthquake to end, for everyone believed that the end of the world had come. But at the ninth hour of the day, God remembered concern for His creation and stabilized the ground. Then we took heart and came to our senses, and one could see tears in the eyes of everyone and hear every tongue *blessing and* praising God. Then news arrived from Aleppo that the wall and the fortress had collapsed and that rents in the ground had swallowed many people, that *the ground had torn asunder and* the city had become filled with black water, that countless multitudes had died in it, and that all buildings there had collapsed with the exception of a single church.

This was the righteous judgement of God seeking vengeance for the blood of Christians, since Christian people were being sold like animals there *and the blood of Christians was shed as though it were water. Moreover, the Christians there were being killed insatiably as though the slayers would find treasure. Through divine wrath the Christians and their opponents were killed in equal measure. Yet no one believed in the unquenchable fires that were awaiting them. Indeed, the doubters asked why no punishment had been visited upon them as had been the case with the deeds done at Sodom or the giants who had been drowned for*

---

317 Length of a palm (four inches); about 8.3 feet.
318 A.D. 1170.

their iniquity. And so, many shortsighted people doubted the judgement of God. Let us not mention the deeds of Sodom and the impiety of the giants who were destroyed by the Flood. There was such iniquity there that many despaired of a judgement from God, seeing their manifold evils.

The same occurred in Antioch also, for many buildings collapsed and the church of the Greeks collapsed on top of those offering liturgy. The Church of Saint Peter also collapsed. The Prince of Antioch *and the entire city* donned sackcloth and all the inhabitants of the city went and fell on their knees before their exiled patriarch so that he would re-enter the city, *since they thought that this disaster was the result of his banning.* But he replied: "Unless the false patriarch of the Greeks leaves, disgraced, I will not enter." Then the people went to evict the Greek patriarch and found him close to death in the collapsed church, pierced through, *for a stone had fallen on him.* And then the Latin Patriarch ordered that he be picked up, *placed on a litter,* and thrown out of the city which, in fact, was done. And he died outside the city, *dishonored,* and then the Patriarch of the Franks, Herim, entered.

Then we began to rebuild the devastated places. Throughout the land there were, likewise, many fortresses, churches, cities, and villages which had been ruined and destroyed by this strange and unheard-of earthquake. However, by the mercy of Christ, in Antioch and in all the coastal areas the churches of the Orthodox were spared—not because of our good deeds, but because of the prayers of our holy fathers and their martyrdom.

In 1482 of the Syrian Era,[319] Qutb-din, *atabeg* of Mosul and all Assyria, died. His brother, Nur ad-Din, heard about this and went to Nisibis and took the city without warfare. Similarly, he took Anjar *Sendjar.* Now the *fakirs* were *saddened*, since they loved *Qutb-din* as a man who kept the faith, did not drink wine, and never failed to say the designated prayers. Moreover, they claimed that he was a prophet. To the delight of the Turks and Tachiks, he loathed Christians and had their newly-built church-

---

319 A.D. 1171.

es demolished. Meanwhile Caliph Mustanjid[320] had died and his son, Mustadi,[321] held the honor. The latter banned the destruction of churches for the following reason. Nur ad-Din wrote to him when al-Mustadi had become the new Caliph, saying: "The decree of the Prophet Muhammad has expired, the one which says that for 500 years the Lord does not want the Christians destroyed. Now that the allotted years have expired, it is incumbent upon us to destroy Christianity." By the influence of God he wrote the following passage in that letter: "Order me to come to you so that we may confer on this matter." Now when the Caliph saw the letter and understood its contents, it occurred to him that Nur ad-Din might come to him treacherously to kill him and take for himself the office of caliph, just as he had eliminated the Caliphate in Egypt at his command *through Shirak'aw*. For this reason, Caliph al-Mustadi wrote to Nur ad-Din a very severe reply and reprimanded him. Then he sent all over his realm saying that Christians should build churches *and monasteries* and hold Christianity *and study it* fearlessly everywhere. He did this in opposition to Nur ad-Din *who did not allow the construction of churches and monasteries*, and he *summoned and* killed the Vezier who supported Nur ad-Din. He also freed from prison the sons of T'umay and returned to them their church which he had taken unjustly.

Then Nur ad-Din went and besieged Mosul where five *seven* of his brother's sons dwelled. Realizing that it would require a long time to take the city, he spoke to his nephews about peace and swore that he would leave the city and country to them if they would open the city gates and admit him peacefully. They heeded him and brought him into the city. Nur ad-Din went up to the citadel, took all the treasures it contained, *removed them from the city*, and placed his own men in the citadel, to hold it in his name. And he divided up the city and the land among his nephews. However, all the fortresses he put under his own control. Then he departed. Thereafter, he started to increase the tax on Christians and ordered

320 1160-1170.
321 1170-1180.

that Christians should not let their hair grow long[322] so that they be recognizable. He also ordered the Jews to sew a red patch on their turbans or right shoulders, so that they be recognizable. In this period, Amalric, the king of Jerusalem, went to Constantinople and returned to Jerusalem laden with great treasures.

In 1483 of the Syrian Era,[323] Kilij-Arslan came to Melitene but was unable to take it. He took captive 12,000 people and departed. Now Nur ad-Din assembled all the emirs, Ishmael the Danishmendid, and Shahnshah, Kilij-Arslan's brother, and went to Caesarea. The sultan did not want to come out against him and they sent to him demanding that he give up his brother's portion from his lands. Now it happened that five[324] of Shahnshah's sons were with him there. The ruler of Caesarea took and roasted one of those sons, and sent this to his father, saying: "If you do not quit this place, I will do the same to the remaining four." When the besiegers saw this, they *wept and* were frightened, made peace, and departed. Then Nur ad-Din was seized with a pain and grew ill. Great confusion came over them and many officers rose up against each other and destroyed one another, and there were great harms and deprivations visited upon Christians because of that chaotic state of affairs.

In 1484 of the Syrian Era,[325] in the month of the exaltation of the Cross,[326] there was such a severe cold and such snowfall—previously unheard of, and never before seen. For snow fell to a depth of 27 *t'iz*, and in India, which never has snow, they say that snow fell to a depth of 14 *t'iz*. Sources of water froze and fish died in the sea, birds *and reptiles* were wiped out as were wildlife in the valleys, while domesticated animals died from lack of food, and the seeds of all plants burned up.

When the next year came, there was very intense famine and want—to the point that the princes of Cappadocia killed *the*

---

322   or, *should cut their hair.*
323   A.D. 1172.
324   or, *seven.*
325   A.D. 1173.
326   September.

Danishmendid amir of Sebastia, Ishmael *Mslim*, seized his entire family, killed 500 people, took the grain which had been stored up and all his possessions and survived the severity of the famine. The deed of their killing was concealed for four months due to the winter season. But with the coming of spring, all the surrounding peoples learned about it. It seemed so wicked that many doubted the truth of it. Some of the inhabitants of the land sent to Damascus, to Danun the emir of Caesarea who was being persecuted by Kilij-Arslan with many relatives, and they called on him. *Danus had fled there with his relatives, escaping from the sultan.* He came and took the rule of Sebastia and exacted vengeance on many people for the merciless slaying of his relatives. Kilij-Arslan heard about this and came against Danun in Sebastia. Danun then placed his hopes on Nur ad-Din—who had arisen from his illness like one risen from the dead—*to save him from the sultan*. Once again fear of him came over the land. Nur ad-Din assembled a multitude of troops and went against Sebastia. The sultan was terrified, quit trying to take the city, and left. The Nur ad-Din turned and took Marash, Behesni, and K'esun. Now when Kilij-Arslan heard about this, he came against Nur ad-Din with an enormous multitude. Nur ad-Din went in advance of him and encamped by the Jihon River, while the sultan arrived and encamped on the other side of the river, close to him. Each feared the other and they did not fight for many days. Then famine beset both armies and many died from it. After many days, the sultan left Danun to remain in obedience to Nur ad-Din. And they established friendship and returned to their own places.

Let me discourse briefly about a heresy which appeared in our day, prior to the death of Catholicos Nerse's.[327] Here is what happened. There were two monks: one named Yusik and the other, Ge'org, and a presbyter named Karapet. They had gone to the blessed Nerse's in the Mesopotamian area and were upbraided by him because of their unseemly reputation. They rose from him sadly, rebelled, and went to Edessa.

327 d. 1173.

They began to slander and curse Lord Nerse's, claiming that he held the heresy of Simon the witch and was performing ordinations for money. They themselves became Chalcedonian and deceived 400 families in Edessa into following them. They were called Yusikeans *by that city, as an insult*. When the patriarch Nerse's heard about this, he wrote to the prince of the city so that he would expel them. And the prince of Edessa did expel them. The heretics went to Aleppo, to Nur ad-Din, where they took courage and returned *to Edessa*. Then I summoned them, blamed them, reestablished them in Orthodoxy, and sent them with my dignitaries to Lord Nerse's, begging him to reconcile with them. But when they had departed, Lord Nerse's died and went to Christ, in the year 1485 of the Syrian Era,[328] on Friday, the eighth of the month of the Mother of God. That impious Yusik turned around and went to Antioch where he was rebaptized and again became Chalcedonian.

Lord Nerse's had two bishops who were his brother's sons. *Their names were Grigor and Grigore's*. The senior nephew, Grigor, was not near his uncle at the time of his death. The younger one took Nerse's' ring and was declared Catholicos, *but was not ordained*. Now when the senior nephew learned about this, he came to the citadel where the Catholicosate was located, but they would not let him in.

And so he turned around and went to his brother-in-law, Baron Mleh. Mleh received him and took him to Nur ad-Din and, with his help, got him into Hr'omklay where he sat on the throne of his uncle's patriarchate. This man's name was Grigor. On the day of his ordination, he invited our Syriac bishops Lord Grigore's, bishop of Kesoun, and Lord Vasilios, bishop of R'aban. He honored them and put them by his side during his ordination. After the ordination he sent two bishops, *prominent men* to us in accordance with the old custom which exists between us, namely, that when a Syrian Orthodox patriarch is ordained, he sends a statement of his faith *and a declaration of friendship* to the Arme-

---

328 A.D. 1174.

nian patriarch, and when an Armenian Catholicos is ordained he sends a statement of his faith to the Syriac patriarch. I, Michael, was pleased and delighted at this for Grigor was a praiseworthy, *blessed*, and learned man.[329] However, I somewhat chided him since, according to canons, when a Patriarch is already named, the designation must remain as is. Moreover, I beseeched him to "eliminate the filthy reputation of simony from your venerable and renowned line which, except in this one instance, has remained pure and proper. *And do this so that the charges of simony made by the Yusikeans not be levelled against you, too.*" Grigor agreed to this and promised to implement it. In addition, I beseeched him regarding *his relative* Grigore's, the one already named as *Catholicos before him*, that he honorably install him somewhere "since the *large and populous* multitude of your people require *as many patriarchs as there are Evangelists*." Grigor agreed to this, too, and implemented it, sending Grigore's to Lambron, entrusting a large part of the diocese to him, *giving him the diocese of Tarsus and authority over the Cappadocian country*. This man's name was Grigore's *Apirat, and he occupied the Catholicosal throne after him*.

In the same year, in 1485 of the Syrian Era,[330] Nur ad-Din issued an order to assemble troops from all the lands of Yemen, Egypt, Syria, Cappadocia, Armenia, and Mesopotamia to eliminate the kingdom of the Franks in Jerusalem and the Sultanate of Kilij-Arslan. He himself had grown very prideful. For long hours, he would read and pray in silence and would not allow his troops to drink wine, nor could the sound of singing, gaming, or dancing be heard in his army. Through such virtuous behavior he expected that God would speak with him, for the deceitful Sheikhs *and Fakirs* had told him: "We have seen you rise into the sky" and "we have seen an angel talking to you." And he believed them.

And thus Nur ad-Din puffed up with pride in Damascus, where a countless multitude of cavalry assembled near him from all parts. And then, suddenly, he received a blow from the Lord

---

329 Grigor IV Tgha, Catholicos 173-1193.
330 A.D. 1174.

and died, having reigned for 28 years. His son, Melik Saleh, took power, while the troops dispersed to their own places. The king of Jerusalem[331] came against Damascus and captured the land. The Damascenes promised to pay him taxes, as before, *if he would leave*, but he did not want to turn back until he had taken the city. However, the sins of the Christians did not allow this to happen, for a fatal illness struck him. He took the taxes from Damascus and went to Acre where he died, after ruling for 12 years. This was 40 days after Nur ad-Din's death. And then there was sorrow among all Christians at his death. His fifteen-year-old son Baldwin became king in his place and sent to make friendship with Nur ad-Din's son. Now it happened that when Kilij-Arslan heard about Nur ad-Din's death, he came to Sebastia and took it along with Komana and Neocaesarea, and exterminated the remaining line of Danishmend. Thus was the rule of the House of Danishmend ended. Danishmendid rule had begun in 1366 of the Syrian Era[332] and continued for 122 years with six of their leaders ruling one after the other. Similarly, Nur ad-Din's brother, Sayf ad-Din Ghazi, emerged from Mosul and took Nisibis, Ragha, and Harran and his brother's sons in Aleppo submitted to him *His brother's son Melik Saleh submitted to him*. Sayf ad-Din returned to Mosul and removed the remaining edicts of Nur ad-Din which he had written on all the mosques saying that Muslims *Turks and Arabs* must not drink wine. Sayf ad-Din ordered that the inscriptions should be chiselled out and he allowed all areas to freely and openly drink, *including in the mosques should anyone want to*.

In that year, *Yusup,' who was* Saladin, who was ruling in Egypt, conquered and ruled the innermost areas of Arabia and part of the land of Nubia. In the same year, the fortresses which the Armenians had in the Sasun country, being harassed by the emir of Mup'arkin, were given to the Shah Armen, the emir of Xlat' which they[333] had held in olden times.

---

331 Amalric.
332 A.D. 1055.
333 The Danishmendids.

In 1486 of the Syrian Era[334] *Mleh*, the prince of Cilicia, was killed by the will of his own princes in the fortress. *Now since T'oros' son had died in Hr'omklay, they brought Ruben, son of Baron Step'ane', who was in Tarsus, and he ruled over the land.* Ruben III[335] tortured and killed the killers of his father's brother, since they say that when they killed Mleh, they threw his corpse to the dogs. For that insult, Ruben could not forgive them.

In the same year, Saladin rose from the land of Egypt and came to Damascus on the pretext of helping Melik Saleh. He took Damascus and went on to Aleppo. Melik was terrified of him. Saladin sent to him, saying: "I am your servant and have come to render assistance to my lord against his enemies." But Melik Saleh did not believe him and would not open the city gates to him. And so Saladin turned to Aleppo, took Hams and Hama in battle, removed the Frankish captives from Damascus and sold them cheaply. *And he made peace with the Franks.* Then he had a lot of gold brought from Egypt and assembled many troops. Sayf ad-Din heard about Saladin's muster and came against him with boasting *and insults*, calling him a mad dog that barks at his master. And they hurried to arrive so that Saladin would not flee from them. But Saladin sent to him *many times*, saying: "Let us not fight. We are one people and one faith and I am obedient to you." But Sayf ad-Din's forces did not heed him.

Rather, they went and attacked them and Saladin's forces began to destroy Sayf ad-Din's troops, which fled. When Saladin saw that the Mosulites had been defeated, he stopped his troops from killing them, saying: "Spare them, for we are one people." He went into the fray *angrily* and stopped his troops, *saying:* "Enough. God will be angered." He took the captives *who had survived* and freed them *and then buried the dead ones*. As a result, fear and dread of him gripped *all the Muslims*. Especially frightened were *the Turks* and Melik Saleh. He took the Frank captives and sold them cheaply: the Count of Tripoli for 80,000 *dahekans*; Joscelin's

334 A.D. 1175.
335 Ruben III, 1175-1186.

son, Joscelin, for 50,000; and Prince Renaud for 100,000. Then he established friendship with Antioch so that they would help him.

Sayf ad-Din again held a muster and took along with him the lord of Merdin and Hasankeyf and came against Saladin with 60,000 *cavalry*. Saladin had 12,000 troops. Saladin sent to Sayf ad-Din, saying: "Do not come against me and do not fight with me. *Who am I but your servant and what harm have I done to you?* It would not disgrace me to be conquered by my lord, but it would be a grave loss to you to be beaten by your own servant." But he was not heeded. Then Saladin secretly spoke with the emirs, promising that he would treat them well. And thus, when the battle was joined, Saladin again became stronger while Sayf ad-Din, *escaping by a hairsbreadth*, fled before him to Mosul, seated on a camel. Then Saladin took Manbij while the lords of Ant'ap' and Tell Bashar came to him in submission. Saladin went on to Azaz and fought against it. Suddenly, Assassins attacked and stabbed him, but he did not die. Rather, *he quickly recovered*, killed them, sent troops against the Assassins and captured their country. Saladin took Azaz in battle and then went and besieged Aleppo. At this, the people of Aleppo sent to the Franks and Renaud—the one who had been ransomed—came and his forces were destroyed by Saladin's forces. Renaud himself was put to flight. Saladin turned to Azaz and Aleppo and then he returned to Egypt. *Renaud destroyed a part of Saladin's forces, and put him to flight.*

In 1487 of the Syrian Era,[336] Nejm ad-Din, the lord of Merdin, died having ruled for 22 years. He was a good man and mild toward the Christians. His son Xutbdin then came to power. In the same year, a wild boar attacked the Byzantine emperor during a hunt, and it was noised about that he had died from this. Kilij-Arslan raided his land and captured many people *and looted many places*. However, the emperor recovered from his wounds and assembled many troops. With him were two of Danishmend's sons, who had fled to him and he made them military commanders, sending them in advance of himself. *He sent messengers to*

---

336 A.D. 1176.

Kilij-Arslan, saying: "Return the Danishmendid patrimony to its own lords who are here with me." He himself followed after the messengers and destroyed many Turks. Now the Turks of Uch secretly went north by their side and captured 100,000 women and children from the Byzantines, not to mention the men who were slain. When the emperor of the Byzantines heard about this, he was searching for the sultan who was in advance of them. *But the sultan did not want to fight them.* Then the Byzantine emperor gave 50,000 cavalry to a certain one of the Danishmendid sons and sent him against Neocaesarea. *They went and besieged it.* The Turks *ruling that city* practiced a ruse: they wrote a letter to the Christians who were besieging them and tossed it out from inside the city walls. The letter said: "That Danishmendid whom you have taken as your leader wants to betray you to the Turks. *They are making a trap to kill you.*" When the besiegers heard this, they believed it and started to flee. Then the besieged came out and gave chase, killing many, including the other military commander who was the emperor's sister's son. When they went to the emperor, he was deeply sorrowed. Then, in a rage, he went among the Turks near Konya, taking a position in a valley hemmed in by steep mountains. An enormous multitude of Turkmens from Bir encountered them and besieged them for five days, injuring the Byzantines by raining rocks and arrows down on them day and night. The Turks killed tens of thousands of men and animals, took hundreds of thousands, and *five hundred* horses with their supplies. The Byzantines were terrified and weakened and sent to the sultan, offering to give him three cities which they themselves had built, requesting friendship and pleading to be extricated from their position. The sultan *was delighted and* sent three emirs with cavalry to remove them from there and take them to Constantinople peacefully. The emirs came to them by night, chased away the Turkmens, removed the Byzantines thence, and took to the road. The Turkmens dispersed here and there and disrespected the sultan, who had established friendship with *their weakened enemies—* who had been besieged and were almost in their grasp.

However, the Turkmens followed them and unexpectedly struck at them *seizing clothing, weapons, and horses,* killing *many,* and looting, and from a distance also were shooting arrows *and slingshots,* and killing many of them. The Byzantines complained to the emirs, *blaming them and* saying: "This is your doing. *You are allowing this.* But the emirs swore to them that "it is not because of us, but because the Turkmens are unbelievers and savages and do not heed us *and no one can stop their depredations.*" By the time the Byzantines reached Constantinople there were 20,000 fewer of them. And thus, disgraced with a depleted army, Emperor Manuel reached his own country; Manuel, who attempted by noteworthy warfare to conquer the world and to conquer the Orthodox Church. *Thus, his two wars against the sultan and the Church ended in disgrace.* Following this, he sent much treasure to the sultan and purchased out of captivity those of his remaining troops who had survived. This occurred in 1488 of the Syrian Era.[337]

In this period, the Christians of Melitene were in great straits for two reasons: one, from continuing famine and two, from the stern behavior *debauchery* of its emir, who was a remnant of the Danishmendid line. The clerics told them that their misery was due to their sins, since "the word of the Lord has been fulfilled upon us, which says 'they mingled with the heathens and learned their ways and fell into scandal.' Come, let us turn from our evil ways and beg for God's mercy, for we are reduced and will be completely destroyed." The folk heeded this and began to fast and pray in tears, to hold vigils and implore God. And the Lord turned from His anger and entered the emir's heart, and made him repent of his deeds. The emir sent to the sultan, received treasure from him, and gave Melitene to him, while he himself rose and went to Kharberd. Then great ease came upon the Christians, an abundance of bread and goods, *and a reduction of taxes.*

In 1489 of the Syrian Era,[338] Saladin emerged from Egypt with 30,000 armored cavalry, not counting the ordinary soldiers

---

337 A.D. 1177.
338 A.D. 1178..

and infantry, and 52,000 pack animals following behind carrying weapons. Arriving in Palestine, he caught a Frank, sacrificed him, washed in his blood, and prayed. He prepared to go to war and to wreck the country. Now the king of Jerusalem, Baldwin,[339] gathered his troops, which were few in number, and fell on his knees before them facing East, as did his troops.

They wept and fervently prayed to the Lord. The troops swore before God and the king that they would not show the enemies their backs; rather, they would gladly die for the blessed Church. then they went against them. When the Franks saw the multitude [...][340] and their own small numbers, once again they dismounted their steeds and, with ash-covered faces, wept and beseeched the Lord. Strengthened by their faith, they went against Saladin's forces as an eagle pounces on a flock of partridges. Lord Jesus Christ, God of the Christians, stirred up a whirlwind in the face of the infidels, which threw them from their horses *without the Franks lifting a hand or using weapons*, and made them flee before them while the Franks killed them mercilessly, not letting anyone live. The infidels fled and scattered through the southern desert. From morning until sunset, the Franks did not stop their pursuit. Moreover, on the next day, from sunrise until the fifth hour, the Franks found them abandoned, hungry, and in hiding *and killed them*. The Franks took the immense weight of their provisions, *bows, arrows, spears, tents*, their furnishings and equipage, thereby loading up and getting rich. The Lord thus gladdens those who believe in Him and the renown of this never [...].[341] *The blessed Church resounded with this joyous news and gave thanks to God who broke the backs of the infidels and shattered their aspirations.* Now Saladin, *newly defeated and disgraced for the first time*, went to Egypt greatly reduced, donned black raiment, and remained locked in his home in the dark for many days *as a penance.*

---

339 Baldwin IV, 1174-1185.
340 There is a lacuna in the text here.
341 There is a lacuna in the text here.

THE CHRONICLE

Now because of this victory, in the same year,[342] the emir at Herim began to doubt his overseers and *turned from the Turks* in Aleppo, believing that the Aleppans wished him ill and wanted to kill him. And so, he consulted with the Prince of Antioch, requesting an oath that they would not remove him from his fortress, in exchange for his submission. They so vowed to him by the Cross and Gospel. Thus, the emir turned away from Aleppo in rebellion and went under the sovereignty of Antioch. However, the prince later regretted this and violated his oath. He brought there Ruben, the prince of Cilicia, through entreaty, *and, taking him along,* went against Herim. However, because *the prince* had broken his vow, the Lord did not give it into his hands. Rather, many of the Frank troops died while they turned Herim back to Aleppo's sovereignty, taking a pledge from them.

In 1490 of the Syrian Era,[343] the Franks of Palestine assembled and *the king of Jerusalem* went to encamp by the Jordan River where they began to build a city there, at a place called Jacob's Ford. Using this they would be able to cross over to Damascus. *They succeeded in this and Christians came and settled there.* Now Saladin heard about this *and was fearful for Damascus. Again, he assembled troops and went to that city.*

Now since the emir of Baalbek—which is called Sun City, Heliopolis—had rebelled, Saladin went against him. Through friendship, oaths, and promises, Saladin secured him and grew stronger. Then he went against the new city which the Franks had built. Meanwhile, the *glorious* Frank troops had learned about Saladin's arrival. They went against him *as though hunting deer* and put him to flight as far as Damascus. And the Frank troops followed up to the gates of Damascus, enslaving the country *and taking a lot of booty.* But then Saladin took heart and went behind them, seizing 100 *Freres*. Even more encouraged, Saladin *assembled Arabs from the desert and* went against the city they had built, and seized 100 *Freres* from them, too. *Now the king of Jerusalem was*

---

342 A.D. 1178.
343 A.D. 1179.

not there, rather only 500 Freres. Saladin's forces besieged the city and conquered it. They hurled fire into the city, which started to burn. *All the newly built structures burned down.* Now there were 500 Freres with their Master present.

When they saw that they had been defeated and were conquered, *some of them weakened and* they threw themselves into the fire or into the river, so that they not fall into the hands [...]³⁴⁴ the remainder of them were destroyed by Saladin. *Saladin's forces destroyed the other residents of the city, and then went to Damascus.*

In 1491 of the Syrian Era,³⁴⁵ *in 630 of the Armenian Era,*³⁴⁶ the Byzantine emperor Manuel died after a reign of 37 years.³⁴⁷ He was succeeded by his son Alex who was 12 years old.³⁴⁸ Twelve princes conducted the affairs of the empire. Alex's mother was a woman of faith, but she had the treasury under her control. Later she fell into adultery with one of the twelve princes. When the affair became known, the eleven other princes thought to kill the mother and her son and to crown Manuel's daughter, who had been born from the first legitimate wife. But they were unable to effect this. When mother and son heard about it, they tried to seize them. The eleven princes fled into the great church for sanctuary. *Executioners went to seize and kill them* while the rabble controlled the city *and held the door of the church* for seven days. They began to hit the church using a rock-hurling device. Now it happened that after seven days the Patriarch *went and beseeched the emperor and his mother* that the sanctuary-seekers be left in peace and safety. He got a pledge from the court. And so, he removed them from the church and took them to the imperial court. But the emperor and his mother broke their oath and blinded them, *a fate worse than death.* Then the Patriarch, who was named Theodorus, cursed the city, while he himself arose and quit the city. He thoughtlessly had

---

344 There is a lacuna in the text here.
345 A.D. 1180.
346 *A.D. 1180/1181.*
347 Manuel I, 1143-1180.
348 Alexius II, 1172-1180; 1180-1183.

cursed the city and the innocent folk there, who did not celebrate liturgy for eight months. Nor were those who were dying able to commune before death. *He foolishly cursed the innocent and not the emperor and his adulterous mother.*

In 1492 of the Syrian Era,[349] there was a war between the sultan and Nur ad-Din, who was the lord of Hasankeyf and Kessoun, since Nur ad-Din hated his wife, who was Sultan Kilij-Arslan's daughter. He put his hopes on Saladin. The sultan went and demolished Kessoun. Then Saladin arose and went against the sultan to avenge Nur ad-Din. Emir Hasan, speaking words of wisdom, made peace and they did not fight. Each returned in peace to his own place. In the same year, the emir of Edessa and Harran rebelled from the Mosulites and submitted to Saladin. This was the reason that Saladin now came to Mesopotamia. For the Mosulites massed but did not dare to fight with Saladin. They submitted to him. Then Saladin went and took Amida and gave it to Nur ad-din, since he had promised it to him.

In 1493 of the Syrian Era[350] *in 633 of the Armenian Era*[351] Melik Saleh, lord of Aleppo, died. Sayf ad-Din, lord of Mosul, also died and Aleppo and Mosul were given to the line of Sayf ad-Din. Izz ad-Din gave Aleppo to his brother and took Anjar from him. In 1494 of the Syrian Era,[352] *in 634 of the Armenian Era,*[353] the impious Andronicus, murderer of *Baron* Step'anne—*who had gone to Acre after an affair with his own relation and was then* circulating around, spreading his wickedness from place to place—now went deceitfully to Constantinople, as though going in obedience to, and concern for, the boy emperor. *He stayed some days in the palace.*

Then that evil-born one made manifest his wicked intentions. He harassed the Franks found in the city, drowned the regent

---

349 A.D. 1181.
350 A.D. 1182.
351 *A.D. 1184.*
352 A.D. 1183.
353 *A.D. 1185.*

mother and her son in the sea, killing 1,000 of the Byzantine princes, and ruining 14,000 villages and monasteries under Byzantine control. He took Alexius' wife as his own, chased out the Franks found in the city and district, and himself ruled.[354] He planned to kill the great prince P'sikos[355] who belonged to the line of the emperors. He sent and summoned him, but Isaac did not want to go, since he had been informed about the emperor's intentions. Then the emperor sent his military commander to go and fetch him, *telling the nuncio that he would kill him instead if he failed to bring Isaac back with him forcibly.* But Isaac pulled out a sword, and struck and killed the military commander. Then he went to the church and declaimed, with the bloody sword in hand: "Look and listen, every one of you. Andronicus wants to eliminate the empire of the Greeks." They listened and there assembled at the church the princes, soldiers, and the city mob, all of whom were wounded by Andronicus' deed and were furious with him. They said to Isaac: "You rule over us, and this storm will pass." They hastened to have the Patriarch anoint him emperor, and this was announced throughout the city. Now when Andronicus heard this news he got into a boat and fled. But they caught up with him and brought him back, and while doing this, they hacked him to pieces *throwing some of the parts into the sea.* Having brought the remainder of his body into the city, they burned it in fire. This occurred in 1497 of the Syrian Era.[356]

In 1493 of the Syrian Era,[357] Saladin, *who ruled Mesopotamia,* and all the emirs of Mesopotamia descended on K'arak *and besieged it and Shawpak.*[358] The Franks massed and went and put them to flight *through the grace of God,* and fortified the city *and the fortress on the coast.*

---

354 Andronicus I, 1182-1183; 1183-1185.
355 Isaac II Angelus.
356 A.D. 1186.
357 A.D. 1182.
358 Montreal Castle.

THE CHRONICLE

In the same year, Baldwin[359] became ill with leprosy *and doctors were unable to help him.* He made his sister's son *who was a very young boy,* also named Baldwin, his substitute. After a few days Baldwin died and the lad Baldwin reigned.

In the same period, Saladin went to Mup'arkin and took it. *Saladin went to Nisibis and took it.* Then he turned and went to Mosul. He was unable to capture it, but placed the city into very dire straits, until they swore to him that they would provide him with cavalry and stand in submission to him. *Then he went to Mup'arghin, took it, and returned to Damascus.*

In the same year, Nur ad-Din and Qutb-din died. They were lords of Amida and Merdin, who were related to each other and were of the Artukid clan there, *destroyers of churches, haters of Christians, and enemies of the truth.* Because Nur ad-Din had pulled down many churches in Amida, the anger of the Lord was roused and another Qutb-din who was his son from a concubine, took over his rule. Hasam ad-Din, Qutb-din's son, took Merdin. Upon Nur ad-Din's death, Umm ad-Din, lord of Palu, took Kharberd. In this period Emir Mihran, lord of Xlat' *the Shahi-Armen,* died. He was well-disposed and merciful to the poor and needy and effected many easements for the Christians and the churches. Following his death, his servant, Bek-Timur, took his position.

In the same period, the prince of Antioch[360] established friendship with Saladin and treacherously hunted Ruben, lord of Cilicia. He seized Ruben and put him in prison. Then Bohemond entered Cilicia and remained there the entire summer. However, he was unable to do anything *to harm the country,* since *Baron* Lewon, Ruben's brother, wisely *fought him* and managed the affairs of the country *keeping it flourishing and at ease.* Subsequently, *Lewon, for the love of his brother,* voluntarily gave him gold and T'il and Adana and got Ruben out of jail. But later on, they took back their places and scorned the Prince.

---

359 Baldwin IV, 1174-1185.
360 Bohemond III, 1163-1201.

In 636,[361] *there was warfare between the Medes, who are the Mark',*[362] *and the Turks, who are the Turkmens.* In this period there was warfare between Turks and Kurds and the disturbances lasted for eight consecutive years. Here are its causes: the Turkmens, who dwelled in tents and live out in the open, during winter came with their tents to the southern areas because of the mildness of the air. In summer, they arose and went north because of the *abundance of water and the* gentle and fresh air. In their coming and going the Kurds robbed them and became powerful. *Participating in this going and coming were the Mark' who, having lost their kingdom, roamed about here and there. Because of their poverty they seized the goods of others through clandestine ambushes. They went after the Turks especially, seizing their livestock.* In this year, the Turkmens found 200 Kurds hiding in ambush to do harm in the Shebeghtan country, and they killed them. As a result, 10,000 Kurds massed and twice that number of Turkmens, and there was a big battle in the Shebeghtan country.

The Kurds were defeated and completely wiped out. After this, the Kurds once more signaled to their people and assembled 30,000 in the areas of Nisibis and Turabdin. *When the nation of the Mark', who resided in the mountains of Chgheroy and in Tiwrewand, learned about this, they alerted each other and assembled 30,000 fighters and came to Nisibis and provoked the Turks.* The Turkmens assembled a countless number of fighters. They fought near Nisibis *between Dara and Nisibis* and again the Turkmens were stronger and hit the Kurds with very great blows and, *defeating them as before,* completely killed them. Then they went on and seized their camp ground. As a result, the nation of the Kurds was reduced in Mesopotamia. A few escaped and landed in the country of Cilicia *where they requested mercy from them,* and in secure places here and there.

---

361 *Of the Armenian Era, A. D. 1187.*
362 *Kurds.*

However, the Turkmens did not blame the Christians until they found some Kurds concealed in the Christians' homes. Thereafter, and with this as the reason, they began to harass Christians in different places. The Turkmens took Arabtil and Tellbasme where they killed or sold the Christians until all the emirs began to protect their territories.

In 1498 of the Syrian Era,[363] Saladin massed all those obedient to him—Egyptians, Assyrians, and Mesopotamians, *Egyptians, inner Libyans, Bedouins, Assyrians, and Mesopotamians—into a large and formidable army, having weapons and siege machines without number.* Then they went against the Franks near Tiberias *to avenge the defeat and losses Saladin had borne from them before when he had emerged from Egypt with 32,000 troops whose loss had weakened him. This second Jeroboam, Solomon's rival, came and encamped near Tiberias.* The Franks and the king of Jerusalem went against them. Then the sins of the Christians before the Lord were remembered, and their deviance from His just laws and the anger of the Lord hit the Franks. The Infidels grew strong and they put to the sword and destroyed the Christian-loving troops of the Franks. They seized the king of Jerusalem and all the Freres and there was great joy for the Turks.[364] But before the battle, the count of Tripoli fled and he, they say, was the cause of the defeat of the Christians since he had earlier made some agreement with [...][365] *the infidels. He made the troops thirsty, weakened them, and betrayed them to the enemy. Then he went over to the foreigners/infidels...they captured the young king of Jerusalem.* As for Saladin, he took Tiberias, wrecked and ruined it, and, killed with his own hands Renald, prince of Antioch[366] and 300 Freres and bathed in their blood. Then he went to Acre and the princes who were there fled by boat to Tyre. Saladin took Acre and took captive a very large number of people. The princes of Caesarea,

---

363 A.D. 1187.
364 *A lengthy lament for those fallen in battle appears here in the 1870 edition.*
365 There is a lacuna in the text here.
366 Reynald of Chatillon, 1153-1160; d. 1187.

Nazareth, and Jaffa abandoned these cities and Saladin easily ruled over them. No one can relate the insults suffered by the Christians, the spitting and trampling underfoot [...].[367,368]

Then Saladin went on to Ascalon and swore to the residents that he would leave them alive and free to go wherever they pleased. He gave them the king of Jerusalem and took the city. The residents took the king and went to Tyre. Then Saladin went against Jerusalem and besieged it for some days. Now since they had no expectation of help from any quarter, the residents thought to give him the city. Saladin set a price of 10 *dahekans* per head on the residents of the city which, if they gave it, they would be able to go wherever they wanted. And it was so arranged, and they gave over the city. Those unable to ransom themselves remained there in servitude. No one could restrain the tears shed by Christians quitting the city. Some 20,000 men and women remained there. Of these, Saladin freed 4,000 old men and women. He divided 7,000 boys and girls among his troops and sent 5,000 youths to Egypt to make bricks for walls, leaving 5,000 in Jerusalem to build up its walls. The Temple was washed with the blood of Christians and then washed again with rosewater. They established a *written* rule that Christians should not enter there, on pain of death *or else be converted*. Then he placed under taxation the Church of the Resurrection, such that everyone entering it paid a red *dahekan*. Then Saladin turned upon Tyre. However, a count named Margis,[369] a strong and wise man, appeared at this point *and entered the city before the siege began* and, by his efforts, saved Tyre. Then Saladin went and took Sidon, Beirut, Che'pe'l, and T'pni and ruled over them.

In 1500 of the Syrian Era,[370] Saladin took Shawpak' and Krak which overlook the sea. *In 640 of the Armenian Era*[371] *Saladin went against Krak and Shabak' and besieged them. After much*

367 There is a lacuna in the text here.
368 *Extended lament said to be covered in other sources.*
369 *Marquis* Conrad de Monferrat.
370 A.D. 1189.
371 *A.D. 1191.*

labor, his troops triumphed. They destroyed and ruined them and took captives. In Krak, they found an enormous cave full of unrefined silver which was just one smelting away from being completely processed. But they were unable to do what was needed to it, and were unable to find any craftsman who knew the details of such processing. *They left it thus and departed.* From there they turned and took Latik, Che'pe'l, Sehun, Baghras, and Darpasak. *After this Saladin went to the Sehon country, besieged Latik, and took it. He battled against Chepel, pulled it down, then left them and went on to Baghras, which he subdued. He demolished its wall.*

Then Saladin turned to Damascus and sacrificed his ur'kan. He brought joy to the Muslims, joy to his troops by giving them gifts and stipends, but mourning to Christ's faithful.

Now in this same year, Kilij-Arslan's son assembled troops to battle against his own father. The sultan's military commander, Hasan, had made the sultan furious with his son. When they wanted to engage in battle, the sultan's son-in-law, Varham, lord of Erznka, interceded and made peace. Many who were on the son's side were shamed by the sultan's old age, and war was avoided. However, subsequently, the sultan destroyed those of the Turks who had united with his son—some 4,000 troops, while the Turks killed the military commander, Hasan. In the same year one of the sultan's sons, who was named Xaysr-shah Azadin, ruled over Melitene *as his patrimony.*

In 1501 of the Syrian Era,[372] *in 641 of the Armenian Era*[373] the Franks stirred and crossed the sea in a very great *mixed multitude, without their king. Stirred in their souls because of the disasters endured by the Christians, and out of love for Jerusalem, they willingly crossed the sea.* They descended on Acre and battled with the city, but were unable to take it, since *Saladin had fortified the city and* there were 100,000 fighters present. Saladin did not dare to fight. The Franks built many homes and churches and 4,000

372 A.D. 1190.
373 *A.D. 1192.*

40,000 mills. Then the king of the Germans[374] came to Constantinople and fought against it. Subsequently, he made peace and came to these parts, but, through the *traditional treachery of the* Byzantines, they were led via waterless and difficult routes. Turkmens massed against them and killed many *and the Germans' numbers decreased day by day. But eventually the Germans reached the city of Iconium and killed many Turks. When the sultan learned about this, he received them and gave them passage and guides.* The sultan established friendship and gave them passage and they arrived at Seleucia. There their king Barbarossa drowned in a river. His body was taken to Antioch. Later on, two other European kings arrived, went to Acre, and seized many captives. Then they asked Saladin to swap the Frank captives in Damascus for these captives that they held. However, Saladin did not agree to this. Then the Franks brought out 25,000 captives, killed them, piled their bodies on top of one another, and then prayed, as Saladin had done. Then they established the sister's son of the king of England as count of Acre and made peace with Saladin. Some news had come from their country, and they turned around and departed. Then Saladin fortified the walls of Jerusalem, making them stronger than before.

In 1502 of the Syrian Era,[375] Kilij-Arslan began persecuting his sons. The people of Iconium took him to themselves. Kilij-Arslan's senior son raised up his head in Aghsarayn. The father, being impatient, gathered the troops he was able and went against his son. However, *en route* he sickened and died, and they brought his body back to Konya. He had with him a younger son, whom they put in the father's place. Kilij-Arslan died in 1504 of the Syrian Era,[376] having reigned for 38 years.[377] He left the kingdom to his 12 sons. *In 642 of the Armenian Era,[378] Kilij-Arslan died in Konya and was buried there.*

374 Frederick I Barbarossa, 1155-1190.
375 A.D. 1191.
376 A.D. 1193.
377 Kilij-Arslan II, 1155-1192.
378 *A.D. 1192/1193.*

Now in 1505 of the Syrian Era,[379] Saladin also died in Damascus, leaving 23 sons. Of these, the eldest son was established in Damascus, the second in Egypt, and the third in Aleppo. They were styled kings and sultans and had others under them. Saladin had a brother named Melik Edil, to whom he gave Edessa and Harran, Mup'arkin, *Merdin*, Samosata, Xlchpar, Krak, and Shawpak'. Saladin showed this concern for him close to the end of his life. *Melik Edil later also took Nisibis and Ragha.* Now the lord of Mosul forged unity with his brothers and with the lord of Chzira, the lord of Merdin, the lord of Ragha and Sinjar and came with them to take Harran. However, he became ill *en route*, returned to Mosul, and the others dispersed. Then Melik Edil went and took Nisibis, Ragha, Ghapur and the other emirs submitted to him as they had done to his brother, Saladin. Then Melik Edil went to the Armenian areas, to Xlat', but was unable to take it, and turned back. In the same year the lord of Mosul, Izz ad-Din died and his son, Nur ad-Din, took his place.

In this year Lewon, the brave and renowned prince of the Armenians, seized Bohemond, prince of Antioch, and subjected him to torture in return for the tortures Lewon's brother, Ruben, had endured from him. Then Sir Henri, count of Acre *Antioch, who was a peace-loving and good man*, arrived and, through his entreaties, freed the Prince and sent him to Antioch. The most valiant Lewon himself ruled over 72 fortresses, some of which his ancestors had held, others of which he himself had seized from the Byzantines and Turks. *Both the Byzantines and the Franks hastened to send him crowns, praising him. Thereafter he was a rich and renowned king.* Awe and fear of him came over all the peoples in the lands bordering his. Moreover, Sultan Kilij-Arslan's sons took refuge with him, *since they had grown weak after the division of the sultan's authority. They were divided into many parts: one, the younger, was king in Konya; one was in Ablastan; one was in Neocaesarea; while others held other portions of the land. And there was discord among them.* Melik Saleh of Ablastan, who

---

[379] A.D. 1194.

ruled the upper lands, came to him in submission. *Melik Saleh, who sat in Ablastan, especially placed his hopes on him. He arose and enlarged his portion with more fortresses and districts.*

Now it happened that the king of Egypt, Melik Aziz, came to Damascus against his brother Afdal. Melik Edil, the father's brother, went to make peace between them. But he performed a great treachery, for he drugged Melik Aziz, who died when he reached Egypt. Melik Edil then took Egypt for himself *and ruled it* and deceived Melik Saleh, telling him: "Go, dwell in peace in the most tranquil places *in my own country*, such as Samosata *and I will give you* Harran and Ragha while I *will stay in Damascus and* resist the Franks and others *and all our enemies.*" Melik Saleh was convinced of the truth of this proposal and said: "I will take my father's treasure and depart. You hold Damascus." Melik Edil replied: "*Could it be that you don't trust me?* Go, and I will gather everything up and send it to you." So he arose and departed for Ragha, but they, *knowing Edil's wishes*, did not accept him there *did not let him inside or respect him*, nor *did they accept the simple-minded man* at Edessa, nor elsewhere. Then he *turned around, enraged, and* went to Samosata, which they gave over to him, since they secretly had been told to do so. Then Melik Edil circulated about and, seeing Saladin's treasury, *was astounded at its wealth and value.* He became greedy and did not give it to *his nephew.* Rather, *he played a joke on him:* he went into one treasury building *which was* filled with astragal[380] *which is popularly called Marux and, and which was being stored there for some purposes.* He took twenty loads worth, secretly sealed it with his signet ring, and sent this to him in place of his inheritance. When Melik Saleh saw this deceit, he was inconsolably hurt and deeply embarrassed, but he was in no condition to do anything. He left the judgement to God who requites everything appropriately.

---

380 *matutak*; liquorice, milk-vetch.

www.sophenebooks.com

www.ingramcontent.com/pod-product-compliance
Lightning Source LLC
Chambersburg PA
CBHW030254100526
44590CB00012B/396